Christopher Wyvill

Report on the scientific results of the voyage of H.M.S.

Challenger during the years 1873-76

Christopher Wyvill

Report on the scientific results of the voyage of H.M.S.
Challenger during the years 1873-76

ISBN/EAN: 9783742828590

Manufactured in Europe, USA, Canada, Australia, Japa

Cover: Foto ©Andreas Hilbeck / pixelio.de

Manufactured and distributed by brebook publishing software (www.brebook.com)

Christopher Wyvill

Report on the scientific results of the voyage of H.M.S.

THE VOYAGE OF H.M.S. CHALLENGER.

ZOOLOGY.

REPORT on the HUMAN CRANIA AND OTHER BONES OF THE SKELETONS collected during the Voyage of H.M.S. Challenger, in the Years 1873-76. By Sir WILLIAM TURNER, Knt., M.B., LL.D., F.R.SS. L. & E., Professor of Anatomy in the University of Edinburgh, Foreign Member of the Anthropological Society of Paris.

PART II.—THE BONES OF THE SKELETON.

THE Crania having been described in the First Part of this Report (Zool. Chall. Exp., part xxix., 1884), I shall now proceed to the consideration of the characters of the other bones of the skeleton. In my inquiries into this division of the subject, as in the study of the crania, I have not restricted myself to the examination of the bones brought home by the Challenger. I have also studied a valuable series of human skeletons of various races, some of which have been for a long period in the Anatomical Museum of the University of Edinburgh, having been collected by my predecessors in the Chair of Anatomy, Professors Alexander Monro *tertius* and John Goodsir, whilst others have been obtained by myself during the last twenty years.

In the course of this inquiry I have also consulted the previous literature on the same subject, so far as I have had access to it, and have endeavoured, as far as the material at my command would admit, to make this part of the Report an essay on the Comparative Osteology of those Races of Men whose bones are described in this Report.

CONTENTS.

PART II.—THE BONES OF THE SKELETON.

	PAGE
Pelvis—	
Introduction,	3
External Dimensions of Pelvis,	6
Dimensions of Cavity of True Pelvis,	7
Dimensions of the Individual Bones,	8
Of Australians,	9
Of Pacific Islanders,	12
Of African Negros,	14
Of Andaman Islanders,	16
Of Asiatics,	18
Of Guanches and Bush,	20
Of Esquimaux and Laplanders,	22
General Remarks on the Pelves,	24
1. Sexual Characters,	24
2. Race Characters,	26
a. Relations of Breadth and Height,	27
b. Pelvic Brim,	31
c. Sacrum,	46
3. Minor Peculiarities in the Pelves,	54
4. Age Characters of Pelvis,	56
Spinal Column,	59
Peculiarities of Individual Vertebræ,	59
The Lumbar Curve of the Spinal Column,	65
Sternum,	78
Clavicle,	79
Measurements of the Clavicle,	79
Scapula,	81
Measurements of the Scapula,	82
Shaft of the Superior Extremity,	89
Measurements of the Bones,	90
Shaft of the Inferior Extremity,	97
Measurements of the Bones,	99
General Summary,	115
Appendix to Part I. on Human Crania,	121
Index,	129

BONES OF THE HUMAN SKELETON.

PELVIS.

Introduction.

Anatomists have long recognised that marked sexual differences exist in the male and female pelvis, and obstetricians have carefully studied this part of the skeleton in women in its relations to the mechanism of parturition. Numerous measurements, more especially of the cavity of the pelvis, with its brim and outlet, in the principal European races, have been recorded by observers in their respective countries, so that the normal form, size, and proportions of the pelvis in these races have been satisfactorily ascertained. Some isolated observations on the form and dimensions of the pelvis in non-European races were also made at the end of the last century and the beginning of the present. P. Camper pointed out [1] in 1785 some differences which existed between the subpubic angle of a woman from Celebes and a Negro as compared with the European. Von Sömmerring in the same year [2] published some remarks on the characters of the pelvis in the Negro. In 1797 M. Rollin [3] observed that the pelvis of the Indian women near the Baie des Français, north-west America, was characterised by its large diameters. In 1817 Cuvier described [4] the pelvis of the so-called Hottentot Venus.

The publication by Vrolik in 1826 of an important memoir on the diversities of the pelvis in the different races of men gave a new impetus to the study of this branch of anatomy, and since that time numerous valuable memoirs on the race characters of the pelvis have appeared, the most important of which are named in the following list :—

Vrolik, G., Considérations sur la Diversité des Bassins de différentes races humaines, 1826. Beschouwing van het verschil. der bekkens in onderscheidene volkstammen, Amsterdam, 1826. Also Musée Vrolik; Catalogue par J. L. Dusseau, Amsterdam, 1865.
Weber, M. J., Die Lehre von den Ur- und Rassen-formen der Schädel und Becken des Menschen, Düsseldorf, 1830; and previously in v. Gräfe u. v. Walther's Journ. der Chirurgie, 1823.

[1] *Verhandlingen der Batnafsch Genootschap te Rotterdam*, Bd. i.
[2] *Körperliche Verschiedenheit des Negers vom Europäer*, Frankfurt und Mainz, 1785.
[3] *Voyage de la Pérouse autour du Monde*, publié by Milet Mureau, t. iv., 1797.
[4] *Mémoires du Muséum d'Histoire naturelle*, t. iii., 1817.

not in all cases measure between the same points of the pelvis, are in my judgment too few, and do not sufficiently bring out all the characters which require attention.

I have employed, therefore, a larger number than these last-named observers, though not so many as M. Verneau, and have arranged them under the three following heads :— A. External Dimensions; B. Dimensions of the Cavity; C. Dimensions of the Individual Bones. The measurements are recorded in millimètres. All the dimensions of the non-European pelves and of the Laplanders have been taken on macerated and dried specimens, the majority of which were articulated under my direction by my museum assistant, Mr. James Simpson. Into each sacro-iliac joint a thin piece of wash-leather was introduced to represent the substance of the sacro-iliac cartilages, and the pubic symphysis was filled in by folds of leather approximating in thickness to the corresponding cartilage.[1]

A. *External Dimensions of Pelvis.*

1. Breadth of pelvis is the greatest diameter between the outer lips of the iliac crests.

2. Height of pelvis, *i.e.*, height of innominate bone, or ischio-iliac diameter, is from the summit of the iliac crest to the most depending part of the tuber ischii.

3. *Breadth-height index* is the relation of the maximum breadth and height of the entire pelvis to each other, and is computed by the formula [2] $\frac{\text{height} \times 100}{\text{breadth}}$

4. Breadth between anterior superior iliac spines is, as is customary with obstetricians, the greatest breadth between the outer lips of these spines.

5. Breadth between posterior superior iliac spines. The postero-superior spine varies in arrangement in different pelves. Sometimes it is fused with the roughened posterior part of the crest, which gives attachment to the gluteus maximus, and forms the free posterior end of that surface; in others this spine is separated from that surface by a depression, and forms a distinct tubercle to its inner and posterior part. The callipers are placed in either case on the spine close to its inner border.

6. Breadth between ischial tubera is the greatest distance between their outer borders.

7. Breadth between ischial spines is between their tips, but as these were frequently broken this measurement could only sometimes be made.

8. Greatest diameter of cotyloid is between opposite points of the margin of this cavity. As a rule there is not more than from 1 to 2 mm. difference between the

---

[1] It is possible that in a few specimens the transverse diameter may have been increased a little beyond the normal by the interposed leather being somewhat thicker than the natural cartilage.

[2] In calculating this and the other indices, when the fraction was below 0·5 I have not taken it into account. When 0·5 or above 0·5 I have either stated it or given the benefit of the fraction to the preceding whole number.

vertical and transverse diameters of the cotyloid at its brim, and more usually the vertical is a little greater than the transverse; the letters v. and t. in the tables express the diameter which prevailed in each pelvis. In this and in the measurements of the obturator foramen the right innominate bone was selected.

9 and 10 are the greatest diameters of the obturator foramen in the vertical and transverse directions.

11. *Obturator index* expresses the relative height and width of this foramen, and is obtained by the formula $\frac{\text{transverse d.} \times 100}{\text{vertical d.}}$

12. Subpubic angle is taken with the useful goniometer devised and figured by Dr. Garson.[1]

B. *Dimensions of Cavity of True Pelvis.*

These dimensions are to be taken at the brim, at the outlet, and in the cavity itself.

13. Transverse diameter is the greatest transverse width between the ilio-pectineal lines.

14. Conjugate or antero-posterior diameter would in a fresh pelvis be taken from the mid-point on the promontory of the sacrum to the back of the upper end of the symphysial cartilage, but in the dried pelvis the posterior surface of the body of the os pubis immediately adjacent to the upper part of the region of the symphysis has been selected. In some pelves the body of the os pubis curves backward a little below the brim, but this projecting part has not been taken as the point on which to place the callipers.

15. *Pelvic* or *Brim index* is the relation of the conjugate diameter to the transverse. It is computed by the formula employed by Professor Zaaijer,[2] $\frac{\text{conj. d.} \times 100}{\text{transverse d.}}$, in which the transverse diameter is regarded as $= 100$.

16. Oblique diameter is the distance between the sacro-iliac joint on the one side, and the ilio-pectineal line on the opposite side of the brim internal to the pectineal eminence. As there is sometimes a want of symmetry in the pelvis, it is necessary that both the right and left oblique diameters should be taken.

17. Inferior sagittal diameter is measured from the middle of the antero-inferior border of the body of the fifth sacral vertebra to the lower border of the pubic symphysis.

18. Coccygeo-pubic diameter from the tip of the coccyx to the lower border of the

---

[1] Pelvimetry, Journ. Anat. und Phys., vol. xvi. p. 106, pl. v., October 1881.
[2] Untersuchungen ueber die Form des Beckens Javanischer Frauen, Holländischen Gesellschaft der Wissensch. zu Haarlem, Deel xxiv., 1866.

pubic symphysis. As the coccyx was so often broken or absent this measurement could frequently not be taken.

19. Intertuberal diameter between the inner borders of the ischial tuberosities immediately below the small sciatic notch.

20. Depth of pubic symphysis is the distance between its upper and lower borders.

21. Depth of pelvic cavity is the distance between the brim near the pectineal eminence and the most depending part of the ischial tuber.

C. *Dimensions of the Individual Bones.*

In addition to determining the length and breadth of the sacrum and of the coccyx when present, I have taken the length of each of the three elements of the os innominatum. The ilium, ischium, and os pubis, both in man and other mammals, may each be regarded as having the fundamental form of an elongated rod-like bone possessing three surfaces, three borders, and two extremities.[1] The central end of each bone terminates in the acetabulum, where the three bones become, as is well known, fused together. The peripheral end of the ilium is the highest point of the crest, the peripheral end of the os pubis is at the pubic symphysis, the peripheral end of the ischium is the most depending part of the tuber. The actual line of junction of these bones with each other in the acetabulum disappears when the ossification of the os innominatum is completed, but there are certain marks at the bottom of the acetabulum in the adult which indicate with a fair amount of precision the lines where they have become fused together. The junction of the ilium and ischium corresponds almost exactly to the upper border of the non-cartilaginous covered surface, where it forms an angle with the posterior border of the same surface. The junction of the os pubis with the ischium and ilium corresponds with the upper border of this surface opposite the pectineal eminence; a slight notch in this border, or in the margin of the cotyloid, often marks the junction, and I have sometimes seen a shallow furrow extending across the smooth cartilaginous-covered surface immediately above the rough area.

22. Height-length of ilium is measured from the angle formed by the junction of the upper and posterior borders of the rough area at the bottom of the acetabulum to the highest point of the iliac crest.

23. Breadth of ilium is the distance between the antero-superior and postero-superior iliac spines.

---

[1] See the description of these bones in man in my article Anatomy in the *Encyclopædia Britannica*, ninth edition, 1874, and in my Introduction to Human Anatomy. In the discussion which followed the reading of Dr. Garson's paper on pelvic measurements before the Anatomical Section of the International Medical Congress in 1881, I referred to the importance of the rod-like form of these bones and of expressing their length in tables of pelvic measurements (see *Transactions of Congress*, vol. i. p. 190).

24. *Iliac index* is the relation of the height-length to the breadth of the ilium obtained by the formula $\frac{\text{breadth} \times 100}{\text{height-length}}$.

25. Breadth of innominate bone is from the postero-superior iliac spine to the top of the pubic symphysis.

26. Length of os pubis is from a point at the bottom of the acetabulum, at the upper border of the rough surface opposite the pectineal eminence, to the pubic symphysis.

27. *Pubo-innominate index* is the relation of the length of the os pubis to the breadth of the innominate bone, and is computed by the formula $\frac{\text{pubic length} \times 100}{\text{innominate breadth}}$.

28. Length of ischium is from the angle formed by the junction of the upper and posterior border of the rough area at the bottom of the acetabulum to the most depending part of the tuber ischii.

29. *Innominate index.*—The height-length of the innominate bone being the same as the height of the pelvis (2), the relation of the breadth of the bone to its height is computed by the formula $\frac{\text{breadth} \times 100}{\text{height-length}}$.

30. *Ischio-innominate index* is the relation of the length of the ischium to the height-length of the innominate bone or pelvic height (2), and is computed by the formula $\frac{\text{ischial length} \times 100}{\text{pelvic height}}$.

31. Length of sacrum is from the middle of the promontory to the middle of the antero-inferior border of the *fifth* sacral vertebra.

32. Breadth of sacrum is the greatest breadth of the base of the sacrum.

33. *Sacral index* is computed by the formula $\frac{\text{breadth} \times 100}{\text{length}}$, length = 100.

34. Length of coccyx is the length from the base of the first coccygeal vertebra to the tip of the coccyx.

35. Breadth of coccyx is the greatest breadth of the first coccygeal vertebra. Owing to the coccyx being frequently either imperfect or broken in the macerated pelvis, the dimensions of this bone could only seldom be taken. A coccygeal index might be computed by a formula similar to that used in estimating the sacral index.

AUSTRALIANS.—TABLE I. Plate I.

I have examined and measured eight Australian pelves, of which six were adult males, one an adult female, and one a young male. They, with one exception, were portions of the skeletons to which the skulls described in the First Part of this Report from Queensland, Riverina, Swan Hill b, Table III.; from Eucla, Perth, Table IV.; from West Victoria, Table V.; and from near the Murray River, Table VI., belonged. The additional skeleton, a male from Manly Cove, New South Wales, I have received from Professor Anderson

Stuart of the University of Sydney since the publication of the First Part of this Report. As the number of adult male pelves afforded a fair amount of material for comparison, I shall especially describe their characters.

In three males the bone was very thin in the iliac fossa, in three it was not so. As a rule the bones were heavy and the iliac fossae looked inwards. The maximum breadth was 278 mm. in the Queensland skeleton, in which the wings of the ilia were more expanded than in the other specimens; the minimum breadth was 232 mm. in the Eucla male, and the mean breadth of the six males was 252 mm. The maximum height was 205 mm., the minimum 180 mm., and the mean 194 mm. The mean breadth-height index was 77. The breadth between the antero-superior iliac spines in each pelvis was more than three times as great as that between the postero-superior iliac spines, and in the Manly Cove and Queensland specimens was four times as great. The greatest diameter of the cotyloid ranged from 50 to 55 mm. The mean vertical diameter of the

TABLE I.—AUSTRALIANS.

	Collection,	Swan Hill. E.U. A.M.	Perth. E.U. A.M.	Eucla. E.U. A.M.	Queensland. Chal.	Riverina. E.U. A.M.	Manly Cove. N.S.W. E.U. A.M.	W. Vict. Chal.	Murray River. E.U. A.M
	Sex,	M.	M.	M.	M.	M.	M.	F.	Young M.
A. External dimensions.	1. Breadth of pelvis,	260	237	232	278	265	240	212	...
	2. Height of pelvis,	198	180	191	205	205	183	161	...
	3. Breadth-Height Index,	76	76	82	74	77	76	76	...
	4. Between ant. sup. iliac spines,	227	207	205	244	220	210	189	...
	5. Between post. sup. iliac spines,	71	58	64	60	71	54	79	63
	6. Between ischial tubera,	128	116	145	131	141	121	129	111
	7. Between ischial spines,	...	66	...	67	81	65	94	...
	8. Greatest diameter of cotyloid,	54v	50v	54v	55v	55d	55vt	44v	52v
	9. Vertical diameter of obturator foramen,	51	47	52	53	49	51	39	46
	10. Transverse diameter of obturator foramen,	32	33	33	39	31	28	33	28
	11. Obturator Index,	63	70	63	75	63	55	85	61
	12. Subpubic angle,	64°	56°	69°	47°	70°	63°	89°	58°
B. Dimensions of cavity of true pelvis.	13. Transverse diameter of brim,	113	102	105	123	122	98	109	97
	14. Conjugate diameter of brim,	110	101	96	109	105	114	105	91
	15. Pelvic or Brim Index,	97	99	91	89	88	116	96	94
	16. Oblique diameter of brim { Right, Left,	122 122	103 103	109 105	121 125	110 124	105 105	104 115	99 99
	17. Inferior sagittal diameter,	113	90	102	111	102	101	87	83
	18. Coccygeo-pubic diameter,	...	...	...	...	...	94	...	...
	19. Intertuberal diameter,	90	81	97	80	91	74	100	67
	20. Depth of pubic symphysis,	36	37	42	41	38	40	35	34
	21. Depth of pelvic cavity,	97	89	91	100	100	92	71	...
C. Dimensions of individual bones.	22. Height-length of ilium,	122	110	113	116	124	111	100	...
	23. Breadth of ilium,	150	140	147	159	156	145	126	...
	24. Iliac Index,	123	127	130	137	126	131	126	...
	25. Breadth of innominate bone,	164	140	147	160	156	157	141	135
	26. Length of os pubis,	74	64	64	77	74	65	62	...
	27. Pubo-innominate Index,	45	46	43·5	48	47	40	44	...
	28. Length of ischium,	88	77	81	95	83	80	64	...
	29. Innominate Index,	87	78	77	78	79	86	88	...
	30. Ischio-innominate Index,	44	43	42	46	40	44	40	...
	31. Length of sacrum,	110	104	96	111	105	108	88	88
	32. Breadth of sacrum,	110	97	92	104	111	108	89	89
	33. Sacral Index,	100	93	96	94	106	100	101	101
	34. Length of coccyx,	...	...	...	...	...	35	...	...
	35. Breadth of coccyx,	...	...	...	...	...	40	...	...

obturator foramen in the males was 50·5, the mean transverse 33 mm., and in all these the vertical diameter very considerably exceeded the transverse; the mean obturator index was 65. In the female pelvis these diameters were more nearly equal, and the obturator index was as high as 85. The subpubic angle showed a considerable range of variation in the males, viz., from 47° to 70°, with a mean of 61°·5, and it is somewhat remarkable that the pelvis from Queensland, which was the broadest both in its external dimensions and at the brim, should have had so small a pubic angle as 47°. In the female the subpubic angle of 89° was considerably greater than in the male with the widest angle.

The greatest transverse diameter of the brim was nearly 3 cm. in front of the sacro-iliac joint, from which point the brim sloped downwards, forwards, and inwards to the pubic symphysis so as to give a cuneiform outline to the brim. In the Manly Cove specimen the transverse diameter of the brim was considerably less than the conjugate, so that the pelvic index was as much as 116; in the other pelves the transverse diameter exceeded the conjugate, though to a very slight extent in two of the adult males. The transverse diameter of the brim in these males ranged from 98 to 123 mm., and the mean was 110·5. The conjugate diameter ranged from 96 to 114 mm., and the mean was 106. The mean pelvic or brim index was 97. In each male pelvis the intertuberal diameter was markedly below the transverse diameter of the brim, but in the only female the intertuberal approximated more to that of the transverse. The mean inferior sagittal diameter in the adult males was 103 mm., which was slightly below the mean conjugate.

The pubic symphysis in the adult males ranged in depth from 36 to 42 mm. The pelvic cavity ranged in depth in the males from 89 to 100 mm., and its mean was 95 mm., which was considerably higher than that of the only female Australian measured. The pubo-innominate index, which expresses the proportion contributed by the os pubis to the breadth of the innominate bone, had a mean in the adult males of 45; in the only female this index was 44. A comparison of the lengths of the ilium and ischium shows the ilium to bear a much larger proportion to the height of the innominate bone than the ischium. The maximum length of the male ilium was 124 mm., the minimum 110 mm. The mean iliac index was 129. The maximum length of the ischium was 95 mm., the minimum 77 mm. In the Riverina pelvis the ischium is two-thirds the length of the ilium, but in the other males the ischium was more than two-thirds, and in the Queensland specimen it was about four-fifths the length of the ilium. In the female, again, the ischium was not quite two-thirds the length of the ilium. The ischio-innominate index, which expresses the proportion contributed by the ischium to the height of the pelvis, had a mean in the adult males of 43; in the only female this index was 40. In three of the adult males the length of the sacrum exceeded the breadth, and the sacral index was consequently less than 100; in two specimens the length and breadth were equal; in the sixth the breadth appreciably exceeded the length. The mean sacral index was 98. In the only female the sacral index was 101.

Pacific Islanders.—Table II. Plate I.

These specimens consisted of three entire pelves and of two others, each with only the right innominate bone, collected by the Challenger at Oahu in the Sandwich Islands. The crania of A., B., and L. are amongst the dolichocephali in Table XI. of the First Part of this Report; I. is amongst the brachycephali in Table X., and M. amongst the mesaticephali in Table XII. I have also examined the sacrum of a Tonga Islander collected by the Challenger, and the pelves of two New Zealanders from skeletons in the Anatomical Museum of the University of Edinburgh.

The pelves from Oahu were all from adult women, and in them the delicacy and

Table II.—Pacific Islanders.

		Oahu, Sandwich Islands.					Tongan.	New Zealand.	
	Collection,	A. Chal.	B. Chal.	L. Chal.	I. Chal.	M. Chal.	Chal.	Otago E.U. A.M.	Auckland E.U. A.M.
	Sex,	F.	F.	F.	F.	F.	...	M.	M.
1.	Breadth of pelvis,	229	275	...	252	...	...	238	255ap
2.	Height of pelvis,	174	195	189	176	176	...	188	221
3.	Breadth-Height Index,	76	71	...	70	...	...	79	87
4.	Between ant. sup. iliac spines,	207	...	...	213	...	...	206	...
5.	Between post. sup. iliac spines,	78	91	...	91ap	...	...	50	69
6.	Between ischial tubera,	152	167	...	163	...	...	129	155
7.	Between ischial spines,	...	...	...	...	...	...	77	...
8.	Greatest diameter of cotyloid,	43sf	50sf	52u	47sf	43sf	...	52sf	58sf
9.	Vertical diameter of obturator foramen,	41	50	46	47	48	...	55	58
10.	Transverse diameter of obturator foramen,	28	35	31	36	39	...	36	40
11.	Obturator Index,	68	70	67	77	81	...	65	69
12.	Subpubic angle,	93°	84°	...	102°	...	...	65°	...
13.	Transverse diameter of brim,	121	134	...	129	...	...	109	122
14.	Conjugate diameter of brim,	100	121	...	99	...	...	104	118ap
15.	Pelvic or Brim Index,	83	90	...	77	...	...	95	97
16.	Oblique diameter of brim {Right, Left,	117 / 121	140 / 134	...	125 / 126	...	...	107 / 111	125 / 122
17.	Inferior sagittal diameter,	103	121	...	104	109	...	99	104
19.	Intertuberal diameter,	130	134	...	134	...	...	86	121
20.	Depth of pubic symphysis,	34	37	36	36	37	...	41	43
21.	Depth of pelvic cavity,	85	95	96	84	88	...	92	106
22.	Height-length of ilium,	101	118	105	101	101	...	106	135ep
23.	Breadth of ilium,	138	164	165	149	142	...	149	...
24.	Iliac Index,	137	139	157	147·5	141	...	140·5	...
25.	Breadth of innominate bone,	145	177	176	152	158	...	149	...
26.	Length of os pubis,	68	77	76	72	70	...	67	...
27.	Pubo-innominate Index,	47	43·5	43	47	45	...	45	...
28.	Length of ischium,	75	82	90	78	81	...	83	91
29.	Innominate Index,	83	91	93	86	87	...	79	...
30.	Ischio-innominate Index,	51	46	48	44	46	...	44	...
31.	Length of sacrum,	98	100	94	105	101	101	101	120
32.	Breadth of sacrum,	108	122	114	114	105	116	97	115
33.	Sacral Index,	110	122	121	108·5	104	115	96	96

smoothness of the bones were well marked. They had evidently been buried in sand; with one exception they were light and friable and semitranslucent in the iliac fossa. The wings of the ilia were expanded, especially in L. The maximum breadth was 275 mm., the minimum 229, and the mean of three pelves was 252 mm. The maximum height was 195 mm., the minimum 174, and the mean of five pelves was 182 mm. The mean breadth-height index was 72. The breadth between the antero-superior iliac spines was more than twice as great as that between the postero-superior spines. The greatest diameter of the cotyloid ranged from 43 to 52 mm. The mean vertical diameter of the obturator foramen was 46 mm., and the mean transverse was 34 mm., whilst the mean obturator index was 73. The subpubic angle ranged from $84°$ to $102°$.

The pelvic brim did not possess a cuneiform but an oval shape, the long axis of the oval being transverse. The mean transverse diameter was 128 mm., the mean conjugate 107 mm. Owing to the transverse diameter in each pelvis being so much in excess of the conjugate, the mean pelvic or brim index was 83. The intertuberal diameter was either equal to or in excess of the transverse diameter of the brim. The mean inferior sagittal diameter was 109 mm., which was slightly above the mean conjugate.

The pubic symphysis ranged in depth from 34 to 37 mm.; the pelvic cavity from 84 to 96 mm., the mean depth being 90 mm. The pubo-innominate index had a mean of 45. The maximum length of the ilium was 118 mm., the minimum 101, and the mean iliac index was 144. The maximum length of the ischium was 90 mm., the minimum 75 mm. In all these pelves the ilium was longer than the ischium; in A. the ischium was three-fourths the length of the ilium, in I. and M. something more than three-fourths, in B. something less than three-fourths, and in L. the ischium was six-sevenths the length of the ilium. The mean ischio-innominate index was 44·6. In each pelvis the breadth of the sacrum exceeded the length and contributed materially to the great transverse diameter of the pelvic brim which one finds in these female pelves. The sacral index was therefore high, and had a mean of 113. In the sacrum of the Tonga Islander the sacral breadth was considerably in excess of the length, and the sacral index was 115.

The two New Zealand pelves were males, the one from Otago, the other was found in a cave at Te Aroha,[1] Auckland. The wings of the ilia were moderately expanded; the Otago pelvis was thin in the iliac fossæ. The Auckland pelvis exceeded that from Otago in its dimensions, but the latter had not reached its full magnitude, as the epiphyses were only partially ankylosed. The ilia and ossa pubis had unfortunately been broken in the Auckland pelvis. The measurements, so far as they could be made, are given in

[1] Mr. A. C. Purchas, M.B., by whom the imperfect skeleton of this Maori was presented to the Museum, told me that the bones were found by his brother in 1883, in a recess in the cave, which was the usual mode of burial in former times amongst the natives.

Table II., but the specimens are too few on which to frame a race average. In the Auckland pelvis the height of the pelvis was great in relation to the breadth, and the breadth-height index was as high as 87. In the Otago pelvis the distance between the postero-superior spines was one-fourth of that between the antero-superior spines. The mean obturator index was 67. In both, the transverse diameter of the pelvic brim only slightly exceeded the conjugate, and the mean pelvic index was 96; the outline of the brim approached the cuneiform. The intertuberal diameter was, in the Otago pelvis, much below the transverse diameter of the brim, but in the Auckland specimen they were about equal. The mean inferior sagittal diameter was 101 mm., which was distinctly below the mean conjugate diameter, 111 mm. The mean depth of the pelvic cavity was 96 mm. In the Auckland pelvis the ischium was two-thirds the length of the ilium, in that from Otago the ischium was more nearly three-fourths the length of the ilium. In each specimen the length of the sacrum exceeded the breadth, and the index in both specimens was 96.

African Negros.—Table III. Plate II.

I have examined and measured the pelvis in four adult male skeletons marked Negro, three of which are in the Anatomical Museum of the University, and one in the Barclay collection in the Museum of the Royal College of Surgeons, Edinburgh. Also the pelves of two Negresses and that of a male skeleton marked Creole in the University Museum.

The bones of the Negros, both male and female, were substantial in texture. The iliac fossæ looked forwards, upwards, and inwards, and the breadth of the alæ was small. The maximum breadth of the male pelvis was 260 mm., the minimum 230 mm., the mean 244 mm.; the mean breadth of the females was 241 mm. The maximum height of the males was 210 mm., the minimum 177 mm., the mean 196 mm.; the mean height of the females was 176·5 mm. The mean breadth-height index of the males was 80, that of the females was 73. In the males the breadth between the antero-superior iliac spines was between three and four times greater than that between the postero-superior spines, whilst in the females it was not three times as great. The greatest diameter of the cotyloid in the two sexes ranged from 47 to 56. The mean vertical diameter of the obturator foramen in the males was 52·5 mm., and in the females 44·5. The mean transverse diameter of this foramen in the males was 32, and in the females 30·5 mm. The mean obturator index in the males was 60, and in the females 68·5. The subpubic angle ranged in the males from 52° to 68°, and in the females from 71° to 76°.

In the male the pelvic brim approximated somewhat in outline to the cuneiform, but the female was more rounded; in both sexes the transverse diameter of the brim always exceeded the conjugate. In the males the transverse diameter ranged from 97 to 119 mm., and the mean was 110; in the females it was from 115 to 126 mm., and the mean was 120·5. The conjugate in the males ranged from 85 to 109 mm., and the mean was 95; in the females from 102 to 109 mm., and the mean was 105·5. The mean pelvic or brim index was 87 in the males, 88 in the females. In both the males and females the intertuberal diameter was considerably less than the transverse diameter of the brim of the pelvis. The mean inferior sagittal diameter in the males was 107, in the females 133; in each sex it was considerably above the mean conjugate of that sex.

The pubic symphysis varied in depth in the males from 36 to 42 mm., and in the females it was 33 and 34 mm. respectively; the depth of the pelvic cavity was less in the females (mean 89 mm.) than in the shallowest (92 mm.) of the males. The mean pubo-innominate index in the males was 41, and in the females it was also 41. The maximum length of the ilium was 125 mm., the minimum 96; the mean iliac index was 130 in the males and 146 in the females. The maximum length of the ischium (a male) was 88 mm., the minimum (a female) 76. The ischium was usually about two-thirds or three-fourths the length of the ilium, but in one male it was as much as seven-eighths

TABLE III.—NEGRO.

	Collection,	E.U.A.M.	E.U.A.M.	E.U.A.M.	Barclay Mus.	E.U.A.M.	E.U.A.M.	Creole. E.U.A.M.
	Sex,	M.	M.	M.	M.	F.	F.	M.
A. External dimensions.	1. Breadth of pelvis,	243	245	246	250	237	245	276
	2. Height of pelvis,	194	210	205	177	170	188	211
	3. Breadth-Height Index,	80	81	83·5	77	72	74	76
	4. Between ant. sup. iliac spines,	211	223	223	214	219	234	258
	5. Between post. sup. iliac spines,	58	64	66	56	76	80	58
	6. Between ischial tubera,	120	148	140	124	137	152	141
	7. Between ischial spines,	67	93	87	71	91	112	73
	8. Greatest diameter of cotyloid,	54v	56v	52v	47v	48v	53rt	58r
	9. Vertical diameter of obturator foramen,	57	55	49	49	41	48	50
	10. Transverse diameter of obturator foramen,	38	37	30	25	27	34	34
	11. Obturator Index,	67	67	61	51	66	71	68
	12. Subpubic angle,	52°	68°	59°	54°	76°	71°	61°
B. Dimensions of cavity of true pelvis.	13. Transverse diameter of brim,	115	119	108	97	115	126	127
	14. Conjugate diameter of brim,	109	94	93	85	109	102	115
	15. Pelvic or Brim Index,	95	79	86	88	95	81	90·5
	16. Oblique diameter of brim Right.	120	119	107	95	121	123	132
	Left.	119	118	116	95	119	120	129
	17. Inferior sagittal diameter,	105	124	102	97	117	150	110
	18. Coccygeo-pubic diameter,	...	119	...	...	...	...	89
	19. Intertuberal diameter,	83	93	85	77	98	101	95
	20. Depth of pubic symphysis,	38	42	37	36	34	33	42
	21. Depth of pelvic cavity,	92	98	99	97	87	91	94
C. Dimensions of individual bones.	22. Height-length of ilium,	115	125	118	96	96	101	131
	23. Breadth of ilium,	152	147	151	135	138	149	155
	24. Iliac Index,	132	118	128	141	144	147·5	118
	25. Breadth of innominate bone,	167	163	158	...	172	156	...
	26. Length of os pubis,	67	70	65	64	68	75	77
	27. Pubo-innominate Index,	40	45	41	...	39·5	45	...
	28. Length of ischium,	81	85	86	84	76	83	94
	29. Innominate Index,	86	78	78	...	101	96	...
	30. Ischio-innominate Index,	42	42	44	47	45	45	44·5
	31. Length of sacrum,	96	97	96	90	93	111	110
	32. Breadth of sacrum,	104	116	111	101	101	90	120
	33. Sacral Index,	108	119	116	112	103	80	105
	34. Length of coccyx,	...	22	...	...	...	...	33
	35. Breadth of coccyx.	...	32	...	...	...	...	46

of the iliac length. The mean ischio-innominate index in the males was 44, in the females 45. In each pelvis the breadth of the sacrum exceeded the length, with the exception of one of the females. The mean sacral index of the four males was 114, of the two females 99.

ANDAMAN ISLANDERS.—TABLE IV. Plate II.

The specimens under examination consisted of one adult male, two adult females, a young male and a young female, all in the University Anatomical Museum, and presented by Drs. Joseph Dougal, J. S. Forrester, and D. D. Cunningham, and an adult female in the Museum of the Royal College of Surgeons, Edinburgh, presented by Dr. E. S. Brander.

The following description is drawn up from the adult pelves, the general dimensions of which were small, and in relation to the short stature and generally small proportions of the race, but the pelvic bones were substantial, not translucent in the iliac fossæ, and the alæ were expanded. In the three females the breadth of the pelvis varied from 196 to 235 mm., with a mean of 214 mm.; in height they ranged from 157 to 166, with a mean of 162 mm. The mean breadth-height index was 76. In the adult male the proportion of height to breadth was somewhat smaller, and the mean index was 75. In both the females and the adult male the breadth between the antero-superior iliac spines was between two and three times greater than between the postero-superior iliac spines. The greatest diameter of the cotyloid in the two sexes ranged from 42 to 47 mm. The mean vertical diameter of the obturator foramen in the females was 42 mm.; the mean transverse diameter was 30 mm.; the mean obturator index of the females was 72, the index of the only adult male was 70. The subpubic angle ranged in the female from 81° to 88°, in the male it was only 68°.

In both the adult male and females the pelvic brim inclined to the cuneiform shape, though in the females, owing to the greater transverse diameter of the brim, the form was more rounded than in the male. In the females the transverse diameter ranged from 106 to 117 mm., with a mean of 111; in the male the transverse diameter was 102 mm. In the females the conjugate diameter ranged from 92 to 100 mm., and the mean was 97; in the male this diameter was 99 mm. The mean pelvic or brim index in the adult females was 87, the same index in the male was 97, and in both the young male and young female the transverse and conjugate diameters were so nearly equal that their mean pelvic index was 100. In the male the intertuberal diameter was much less than the transverse diameter of the brim, but in the females and young specimens it closely approached it in the same pelvis. The mean inferior sagittal diameter in the females was 109 mm., which was considerably above the mean conjugate, but in the male the inferior sagittal diameter was less than the conjugate.

The pubic symphysis ranged in depth from 27 to 39 mm. In the adult females the

REPORT ON THE BONES OF THE HUMAN SKELETON. 17

pelvic cavity had a mean depth of 79 mm., in the male it was also 79 mm. The mean pubo-innominate index of the adult females was 45·5, that of the male was 45. The maximum length of the ilium in the adult females was 105 mm., the minimum 93, the mean was 100 mm.; in the male the length was 99 mm. The maximum length of the ischium in the adult females was 71 mm., the minimum 68, the mean was 70 mm. In the adult females the ischium ranged from about two-thirds to three-fourths the length of the ilium; in the male the ischium was nearly two-thirds the length of the ilium. The mean ischio-innominate index in the adult females was 43, and this index was also 43 in the single adult male. In each adult pelvis the breadth of the sacrum exceeded the length; the mean sacral index in the adult females was 111, and the same index in the adult male was 114. In the young female the index was only 96·5.

TABLE IV.—ANDAMAN ISLANDERS.

	Collection,	E.U.A.M	E.U.A.M.	E.U.A.M.	R.C.S. Ed.	E.U.A.M.	E.U.A.M.
	Sex,	M.	F.	F.	F.	Y. M.	Y. F.
A. External dimensions.	1. Breadth of pelvis,	211	210	235	196	194	...
	2. Height of pelvis,	159	166	164	157	152	...
	3. Breadth-Height Index,	75	79	70	89	78	...
	4. Between ant. sup. iliac spines,	189	...	218	180	176	...
	5. Between post. sup. iliac spines,	68	76	81	67	70	59
	6. Between ischial tubers,	113	129	139	135	120	117
	7. Between ischial spines,	66	...	94	...	69	75
	8. Greatest diameter of cotyloid,	44e	42e	46t	47e	45e	44e
	9. Vertical diameter of obturator foramen,	43	37	42	46	40	42
	10. Transverse diameter of obturator foramen,	30	29	30	31	26	25
	11. Obturator Index,	70	78	71	67	·65	59·5
	12. Subpubic angle,	68°	84°	88°	81°	78°	81°
	13. Transverse diameter of brim,	102	106	117	109	90	94
	14. Conjugate diameter of brim,	99	90	100	92	92	92
	15. Pelvic or Brim Index,	97	84	85	84	102	98
B. Dimensions of cavity of true pelvis.	16. Oblique diameter of brim { Right,	108	109	114	111	95	97
	{ Left,	108	111	120	111	93	97
	17. Inferior sagittal diameter,	90	103	111	112	84	82
	19. Intertuberal diameter,	77	104	105	104	85	89
	20. Depth of pubic symphysis,	35	27	39	34	33	31
	21. Depth of pelvic cavity,	79	76	79	82	74	75
C. Dimensions of individual bones.	22. Height-length of ilium,	99	101	105	93	90	...
	23. Breadth of ilium,	124	123	130	125	113	...
	24. Iliac Index,	125	122	124	134	125	...
	25. Breadth of innominate bone,	143	147	154	...	134	...
	26. Length of os pubis,	64	70	67	62	59	58
	27. Pubo-innominate Index,	45	48	43	...	44	...
	28. Length of ischium,	69	71	68	71	68	66
	29. Innominate Index,	90	89	91	...	88	...
	30. Ischio-innominate Index,	44	44	44	43	43	...
	31. Length of sacrum,	84	87	102	87	87	87
	32. Breadth of sacrum,	96	100	114	93	92	84
	33. Sacral Index,	114	115	112	107	106	96·5

(ZOOL. CHALL. EXP.—PART XLVII.—1886.) Aaa 3

ASIATICS.—TABLE V   Plate II.

In Table V. I have given the measurements of the pelves of five Asiatics, all in the Anatomical Museum of the University. With the exception of two Hindoos, the rest are single specimens of their respective races—Sikh, Chinese, and Malay.[1] They can only be taken therefore as individual specimens, and in themselves do not give us the mean of their respective races.

TABLE V.—ASIATICS.

	Collection,	Hindoo.	Hindoo.	Sikh.	Chinese.	Malay.
		E.U.A.M.	E.U.A.M.	E.U.A.M.	E.U.A.M.	E.U.A.M.
	Sex,	M.	F.	M.	M.	M.
A. External dimensions.	1. Breadth of pelvis,	241	245	278	265	235
	2. Height of pelvis,	187	172	220	193	200
	3. Breadth-Height Index,	78	70	79	73	85
	4. Between ant. sup. iliac spines,	211	239	266	251	193
	5. Between post. sup. iliac spines,	57	75	76	75	69
	6. Between ischial tubera,	120	140	148	147	151
	7. Between ischial spines,	70	...	82	89	85
	8. Greatest diameter of cotyloid,	57v	45vd	62ct	58v	54v
	9. Vertical diameter of obturator foramen,	47	45	56	45	55
	10. Transverse diameter of obturator foramen,	31	32	38	25	34
	11. Obturator Index,	66	71	68	55·5	62
	12. Subpubic angle,	57°	78°	62°	76°	76°
B. Dimensions of cavity of true pelvis.	13. Transverse diameter of brim,	108	120	125	114	110
	14. Conjugate diameter of brim,	96	112	113	97	116
	15. Pelvic or Brim Index,	89	93	90	85	105
	16. Oblique diameter of brim { Right,	113	125	130	113	116
	{ Left,	113	122	127	117	115
	17. Inferior sagittal diameter,	108	106	114	100	106
	18. Coccygeo-pubic diameter,	91	85	...	...	...
	19. Intertuberal diameter,	78	109	94	105	109
	20. Depth of pubic symphysis,	39	34	51	35	42
	21. Depth of pelvic cavity,	91	84	102	94	100
C. Dimensions of individual bones.	22. Height-length of ilium,	108	100	130	109	113
	23. Breadth of ilium,	143	130	163	152	150
	24. Iliac Index,	132	130	125	139	133
	25. Breadth of innominate bone,	154	156	181	160	171
	26. Length of os pubis,	64	68	79	62	69
	27. Pubo-innominate Index,	42	44	44	39	40
	28. Length of ischium,	83	75	95	84	90
	29. Innominate Index,	82	91	80	83	85·5
	30. Ischio-innominate Index,	44	44	43	43·5	45
	31. Length of sacrum,	99	81	97	108	112
	32. Breadth of sacrum,	108	103	121	106	106
	33. Sacral Index,	109	127	124·5	98	95
	34. Length of coccyx,	27	30	...	...	...
	35. Breadth of coccyx,	28	26	...	...	...

[1] The Hindoo pelves and skeletons were presented by Sir Joseph Fayrer; the Sikh and Malay, by Dr. D. D. Cunningham.

The Hindoo pelves were a male and a female. In them, as in the male Sikh, the alæ of the ilium were expanded. In the Sikh and female Hindoo the iliac fossæ were semi-translucent, but this was not the case in the male Hindoo. The Sikh dominated largely in its dimensions over the Hindoos, indeed it is one of the largest pelves that I have measured in the course of this inquiry. But notwithstanding this difference in absolute size, there was in many particulars a great similarity in the relative proportions of the Sikh and the male Hindoo. The breadth-height index of the male Hindoo, 78, closely approached that of the Sikh, 79. The obturator indices in these males also closely approximated, in the Hindoo being 66, in the Sikh 68, whilst the female Hindoo again had a higher index, 71. Although in both the Hindoo and the Sikh the transverse diameter of the pelvic brim was greater than the conjugate, yet in these males the inlet narrowed towards the symphysis so that the outline of the brim approximated to the cuneiform. In the female Hindoo this narrowing was not so rapid, and the outline of the brim was more rounded. The pelvic index in the male Hindoo was 89, in the Sikh 90, in the female Hindoo 93. In both these males the intertuberal diameter was about 30 mm. below the transverse diameter of the brim. The inferior sagittal diameter in the male Hindoo and in the Sikh somewhat exceeded the conjugate; in the female Hindoo it was somewhat below the conjugate. The pelvic cavity both in the male Hindoo and in the Sikh was deeper than in the female Hindoo. They differed in the relative value of the iliac index, for in the Hindoo it was 132, in the Sikh 125. The pubo-innominate index in the male Hindoo was 42, in the Sikh 44; the ischio-innominate index, again, in the male Hindoo was 44, in the Sikh 43. They differed also in the sacral index, which in the Sikh was as high as 124·5, and in the male Hindoo only 109, whilst in the female Hindoo it was 127; the breadth of the sacrum, 121 mm., in the Sikh, was indeed quite remarkable for a male pelvis, but as the subpubic angle was only 62°, this great sacral breadth, though associated with a correspondingly wide brim, had not occasioned an opening out of the subpubic angle.

The Chinese pelvis in its external dimensions was in most of its measurements larger than the Malay. In both the iliac fossæ were somewhat thinned, but the alæ were expanded, flattened, and thrown outwards in the Chinese, and more nearly vertical and looking inwards in the Malay. In the Chinese the anterior border of the ilium sloped upwards and outwards, and the anterior inferior spines were 173 mm. from each other, being 78 mm. less than the diameter between the anterior superior spines; in the Malay the anterior border of the ilium was nearly vertical, and the anterior inferior spines were 183 mm. asunder, being only 10 mm. below the distance between the anterior superior spines. The proportions of breadth and height were very different, the index in the Chinese being 73, in the Malay 85. The dimensions of the obturator foramen were larger in the Malay pelvis, in which the obturator index was 62, whilst in the Chinese it was 55·5. They differed materially from each other in the shape and diameters of the pelvic brim, for the Malay was ovoid in the conjugate diameter and had a pelvic index of 105; the Chinese was ovoid from side to side, and had a pelvic index of 85. Whilst the Chinese was 4 mm. greater in the transverse diameter of its brim, the conjugate diameter of the Malay was 19 mm. in excess of the Chinese, but the subpubic angle was in each 76°. The intertuberal and the transverse diameters of the brim were almost equal in the Malay, but in the Chinese the transverse diameter was 9 mm. in excess of the intertuberal. The iliac index was in the Chinese 139, in the Malay 133. The pubo-innominate and ischio-innominate indices were in the Chinese respectively 39 and 43·5, in the Malay 40 and 45. In both pelves the sacrum was distinctly longer than broad, but in the Chinese, whilst the sacral index was 98, in the Malay it was only 95.

Guanche and Bush.—Table VI. Plate III.

The specimens of Guanche pelves were an entire male, the sacrum and right innominate of another male, and the left innominate of a third pelvis. They were collected by Dr. W. H. Miller of Las Palmas, in caves in the Grand Canary Island, and were presented to the Anatomical Museum, along with four Guanche skulls, through Professor Alexander Simpson.

The bones in these specimens were substantial in texture and were not translucent in the iliac fossæ. The only entire specimen was well formed and symmetrical, and with well-expanded ilia, not semitranslucent in the iliac fossæ. Its breadth-height index was 77. The subpubic angle was 62°, and the pelvic or brim index 85. Although the transverse diameter of the brim was considerably in excess of the conjugate, yet the outline of the pelvic inlet could not be described as oval but rather as something intermediate between round and oval. The intertuberal diameter was much below the transverse diameter of the brim. In all three the greatest diameter of the cotyloid was vertical. The obturator index ranged from 68 to 78, with a mean of 74. The inferior sagittal diameter slightly exceeded the conjugate. The pelvic cavity varied in depth from 86 to 101 mm. The mean pubo-innominate index of the two males was 41, and the mean ischio-innominate was 43. The length of the ischium in these specimens was about three-fourths that of the ilium. The maximum length of the ilium was 129 mm., the maximum length of the ischium in the same pelvis was 93 mm. There was but little variation in the innominate index, the range being only 3. In both the specimens with a sacrum, the breadth of that bone exceeded the length by several millimètres, and the mean sacral index was 108·5.

The Bush pelvis belonged to the male skeleton from Umzimkulu, the measurements of the skull of which are given in Table I. in the First Part of this Report. The dimensions of this pelvis were small in accordance with the small stature and proportions of the race; the bones also were light, but substantial and not translucent in the iliac fossæ; these fossæ looked almost directly inwards, the wings and the anterior border of each ilium approached the vertical in direction, and the crest was short. The distance between the anterior inferior spines was 161 mm., only 13 mm. less than that between the anterior superior spines. The breadth of the pelvis was restricted in relation to the height, so that the breadth-height index was as much as 91. The obturator index was 75·5, which expresses a relatively wide obturator foramen. The transverse diameter of the pelvic brim was markedly below the conjugate, and the shape of the inlet was oval in the antero-posterior direction; the pelvic index was 109. The intertuberal diameter corre-

TABLE VI.—GUANCHE AND BUSH.

Collection.		Guanche.			Bush.
S-x,		E.U.A.M. M.	E.U.A.M. M.	E.U.A.M.	E.U.A.M. M.
A. External dimensions. {	1. Breadth of pelvis,	265	...	...	202
	2. Height of pelvis,	205	213	207	183
	3. *Breadth-Height Index*,	77	...	...	91
	4. Between ant. sup. iliac spines,	...	...	...	174
	5. Between post. sup. iliac spines,	75	...	...	57
	6. Between ischial tubera,	143	...	...	122
	7. Between ischial spines,	...	...	...	74
	8. Greatest diameter of cotyloid,	55c	55c	55c	49c
	9. Vertical diameter of obturator foramen,	50	56	46	45
	10. Transverse diameter of obturator foramen,	38	38	36	34
	11. *Obturator Index*,	76	68	78	75·5
	12. Subpubic angle,	62°	...	...	72°
B. Dimensions of cavity of true pelvis. {	13. Transverse diameter of brim,	122	...	...	93
	14. Conjugate diameter of brim,	104	104	...	104
	15. *Pelvic or Brim Index*,	85	...	...	109
	16. Oblique diameter of brim { Right,	118	...	...	100
	{ Left,	120	...	...	100
	17. Inferior sagittal diameter,	106	109	...	92
	18. Coccygeo-pubic diameter,	...	...	...	79
	19. Intertuberal diameter,	96	...	...	93
	20. Depth of pubic symphysis,	38	49	43	39
	21. Depth of pelvic cavity,	92	101	86	88
C. Dimensions of individual bones. {	22. Height-length of ilium,	117	129	118	108
	23. Breadth of ilium,	160	157	160	131
	24. *Iliac Index*,	137	122	135	121
	25. Breadth of innominate bone,	169	192	175	150
	26. Length of os pubis,	70	74	83	63
	27. *Pubo-innominate Index*,	41	41	47	42
	28. Length of ischium,	87	93	84	81
	29. *Innominate Index*,	82	85	84·5	82
	30. *Ischio-innominate Index*,	42	44	40·5	44
	31. Length of sacrum,	104	116	...	98
	32. Breadth of sacrum,	118	121	...	96
	33. *Sacral Index*,	113	104	...	98
	34. Length of coccyx,	...	...	...	28
	35. Breadth of coccyx,	...	...	...	29

sponded with the transverse diameter of the brim. The inferior sagittal diameter was below the conjugate. The subpubic angle was 72°. The ischium was something more than four-fifths the length of the ilium; the iliac index was only 121. The innominate index was 82. The pubo-innominate index was 42, and the ischio-innominate index was 44. The sacrum was a little longer than broad, and the sacral index was 98.

ESQUIMAUX AND LAPLANDERS.—TABLE VII. Plate III.

The Esquimaux pelves belonged to two skeletons, a male and a female, which the University Museum acquired from the collection formed by Dr. Alexander Monro *tertius*.

TABLE VII.—ESQUIMAUX AND LAPLANDERS.

		Esquimaux.		Laplanders.	
	Collection,	E.U.A.M.	E.U.A.M.	E.U.A.M.	E.U.A.M.
	Sex,	M.	F.	M.	F.
A. External dimensions.	1. Breadth of pelvis,	274	253	236	228
	2. Height of pelvis,	211	196	190	171
	3. *Breadth-Height Index*,	77	77	80·5	75
	4. Between ant. sup. iliac spines,	226	227	210	196
	5. Between post. sup. iliac spines,	78	80	54	67
	6. Between ischial tubers,	143	160	128	160
	7. Between ischial spines,	...	107	74	117
	8. Greatest diameter of cotyloid,	57v	55v	51v	48v
	9. Vertical diameter of obturator foramen,	57	51	50	37
	10. Transverse diameter of obturator foramen,	43	36	33	27
	11. *Obturator Index*,	75	70·5	66	73
	12. Subpubic angle,	69°	74°	70°	104°
B. Dimensions of cavity of true pelvis.	13. Transverse diameter of brim,	126	132	105	120
	14. Conjugate diameter of brim,	111	111	98	87
	15. *Pelvic or Brim Index*,	88	84	93	72·5
	16. Oblique diameter of brim { Right,	126	131	107	114
	{ Left,	125	129	109	122
	17. Inferior sagittal diameter,	117	134	96	113
	19. Intertuberal diameter,	88	118	95	123
	20. Depth of pubic symphysis,	42	36	40	33
	21. Depth of pelvic cavity,	102	94	92	80
C. Dimensions of individual bones.	22. Height-length of ilium,	122	115	111	93
	23. Breadth of ilium,	163	151	142	143
	24. *Iliac Index*,	134	131	128	154
	25. Breadth of innominate bone,	188	171	167	161
	26. Length of os pubis,	80	75	66	70
	27. *Pubo-innominate Index*,	42·5	44	39·5	43
	28. Length of ischium,	92	83	81	77
	29. *Innominate Index*,	89	87	88	94
	30. *Ischio-innominate Index*,	44	42	43	45
	31. Length of sacrum,	80	109	86	93
	32. Breadth of sacrum,	111	116	91	104
	33. *Sacral Index*,	139	106	106	112

REPORT ON THE BONES OF THE HUMAN SKELETON. 23

Both pelves were well developed, and, in the external dimensions of breadth and height, were amongst the largest measured in their respective sexes. The alæ of the ilium were moderately expanded, the male only was semitranslucent in the iliac fossæ. The breadth-height index was 77 in each pelvis. The distance between the antero-superior spines was not quite three times more than that between the postero-superior spines. The obturator index in the male was 75, in the female 70·5. The subpubic angle in the male was 69°, in the female 74°. In both, the conjugate diameter of the brim was less than the transverse. In the female the pelvic inlet was oval from side to side, and the index was 84; in the male the transverse elongation was not marked, and the pelvic or brim index was 88. In both, the intertuberal diameter was considerably below the transverse diameter of the brim, though the difference was not nearly so marked in the female as in the male. The inferior sagittal diameter in both exceeded the conjugate, and markedly so in the female. The pelvic cavity was 8 mm. deeper in the male than in the female. The pubo-innominate index was less in the female than in the male, but the ischio-innominate index was greater. In each, the ischium was about three-fourths the length of the ilium, and there was but little difference in their iliac index. The innominate index showed only a slight variation in the two sexes. In both, the breadth of the sacrum exceeded the length, and this was especially the case in the male pelvis, in which the sacrum with its five vertebræ was the shortest that has been recorded in these tables, and the sacral index reached 139.

The Laplanders, a male and a female skeleton, were purchased from a dealer, Mr. Nordvi. The texture of the bones was firm, the alæ of the ilia were moderately expanded, and they were not translucent in the iliac fossæ. In their general dimensions these pelves were larger than either the Bush or Andamanese specimens, but not so large as the Esquimaux. The height of the pelvis was greater in proportion to the breadth in the male than in the female, and the breadth-height indices were respectively 80·5 and 75. The distance between the postero-superior spines was, both absolutely and relatively to that between the antero-superior spines, much greater in the female than in the male. In the male the obturator index was 66, in the female 73. The subpubic angle was 70° in the male and 104° in the female. In both, the transverse diameter of the brim exceeded the conjugate, but this was especially so in the female pelvis, in which the pelvic index was only 72·5, whilst in the male it was 93. These differences very materially affected the form of the pelvic inlet, which was oval transversely in the female, but, in the male, owing to the rapid inward slope of the pubic bones, approximated to the cuneiform. In the male the intertuberal diameter was 10 mm. less than the transverse diameter of the brim, in the female it was 3 mm. more than the transverse diameter. The inferior sagittal diameter was almost equal to the conjugate in the male, but considerably above it in the female. The pelvic cavity was 8 mm. deeper in the male than in the female. Both the pubo-innominate and ischio-innominate indices in the male were below the corresponding indices in the female. In the male the ilium was much longer than in the female, but the breadth of this bone was almost equal in the two specimens, so that there was a great difference in their respective iliac indices. The difference between the lengths of the ilium and ischium was much greater in the man than in the woman. The innominate index was distinctly greater in the male than in the female. In both, the breadth of the sacrum exceeded the length, the index in the male being 106, in the female 112.

General Remarks on the Pelves.

The pelves, the measurements of which are recorded in the foregoing tables, are from a number of races living for the most part a savage and primitive life, and in several instances, as the Andaman Islanders, Bush, and Laplanders, are people of diminutive stature. They consist, including both pelves and separate innominate bones, of twenty-four adult males and fourteen adult females.

1. Sexual Characters.

As sex influences in a very important manner the form and proportions of the pelvis, I shall, in the first place, make some observations on their sexual characters.

The female pelvis in its construction and proportions is modified so as to give space for the enlargement of the uterus during gestation, and for the expulsion of the child during parturition; and, in relation to these two functions, its inlet and outlet require to be more open, and its cavity more capacious and shallower than in the male. In accordance with the shorter stature and generally smaller bulk of a woman than of a man, the external dimensions of the entire pelvis are on a smaller scale in the female than in the male. The mean height in the series of adult males now before me was 197, and in the adult females 175; the mean breadth in the males was 248, and in the females 235. It will be seen therefore that the height diminished in a greater ratio than the breadth, and this difference is expressed by the mean breadth-height index, which was only 74 for the adult females, but 80 for the adult males. The pelvic cavity was as a rule shallower in the women than in the men; the mean depth in the females was 85 mm., in the males 95 mm.

The proportions of the obturator foramen also differed in the two sexes, for whilst there was not, as a rule, any very marked difference in its transverse diameter in the two sexes, the vertical diameter, in accordance with the greater depth of the pelvic cavity, was considerably more in the males than in the females. The females therefore had a much higher obturator index than the males; the mean of the series for the females was 73, for the males 67. The greater relative capacity of the female than of the male pelvis, and the relatively larger areas of the inlet and outlet, are also shown in the tables. In the series of female pelves the mean sacral breadth was 106 mm., and the broadest sacrum measured, that of a woman from Oahu, was 122 mm. In the series of males, notwithstanding the greater general dimensions of the pelvis and the unusually broad sacrum in the Sikh (121 mm.), the Creole (120 mm.), and a Guanche (121 mm.), the mean sacral breadth was not more than 107 mm. The mean sacral index in the males was 106, in the females 110, so that the sacrum was broader in proportion to its length in the women than in the men. The diameter between the postero-superior spines was, in relation to that between the antero-superior spines, greater in the females than in the males. Thus whilst in twenty males the mean diameter between the antero-superior spines was 218 mm. and that between the postero-superior spines only 64 mm., in ten females with a mean antero-superior diameter of only 211 mm., the mean postero-superior was as high as 78 mm. The subpubic angle was much wider in the females than in the males; the range in the males was from 47° in an Australian to 76° in both a Chinese and a Malay, the mean of the series being 64°; the range in the females was from 71° in a Negress to 102° in an Oahuan and 104° in a Laplander, the mean of the series reaching 85°.

The mean transverse diameter of the brim in the males was 109 mm., in the females 120 mm. The mean conjugate diameter of the brim in the males was 104 mm., in the females 103 mm. Whilst the mean antero-posterior diameter of the pelvic inlet was almost equal therefore in the two sexes, the mean transverse diameter was considerably greater in the women than in the men, and consequently the brim more usually assumed in the women an oval outline with the long axis transverse. These differences are expressed in the brim or pelvic index, which had a mean in the whole series of males of 93, in the females of 86. The mean intertuberal diameter, which expresses the transverse diameter of the pelvic outlet, was 113 mm. in the females and only 90 mm. in the males; in the females the intertuberal diameter approximated to the transverse diameter of the brim in the same sex, whilst in the male pelvis the intertuberal diameter fell much below the transverse; the side wall of the pelvic cavity inclined therefore downwards and inwards in the male, whilst it was more nearly in the vertical plane in the female. The mean inferior sagittal diameter, which expresses the antero-posterior diameter of the immovable part of the pelvic outlet, was in the males 104 mm.—precisely the same as the mean conjugate diameter of the brim in the same sex, whilst the mean sacro-pubic diameter in the females was 113 mm., which was considerably in excess of the mean conjugate diameter in that sex; the antero-posterior diameter of the pelvic cavity therefore increases in women very materially from brim to outlet. As the pubo-innominate index was in the males 42·7 and in the females 44, the os pubis contributed a larger proportion to the breadth of the innominate bone in the women than in the men. In the series of adult males the mean ischio-innominate index was 43·5, and in the adult females 43·7, so that the proportion which the ischium contributed to the height of the pelvis was practically alike in the two sexes. The mean innominate index in the males was 82·2, in the females 90·7, so that the innominate bone in relation to the height of the pelvis was considerably broader in the women than in the men. The mean iliac index in the males was 130, in the females 138, so that in the women the ilium was broader in relation to its length than in the men.

The sexual characters of the female pelvis, as deduced from the examination of this series of pelves belonging to different races, may be summarised as follows :—The height was proportionally less than the breadth, the pelvic cavity was shallower, the difference between the vertical and transverse diameters of the obturator foramen was not so great, the sacrum was relatively broader, the distance between the postero-superior iliac spines was greater, the subpubic angle was much wider, the transverse diameter of the brim was greater, the pelvic inlet was more usually oval transversely, the intertuberal diameter was greater, the side wall of the pelvic cavity was more nearly in the vertical plane, the inferior sagittal diameter was greater, the os pubis formed a larger proportion of the breadth of the innominate bone, and both the innominate bone itself and its iliac portion were relatively broader in the women than in the men. To the above characters, obtained by pelvimetrical methods, should be added the greater delicacy and smoothness of the bones, owing to the muscular ridges and processes being less strongly marked in the women than in the men. The constancy of these characters, with occasional individual exceptions in some one feature or other, in the female pelves necessarily mask in them such differences as may be due to race, so that the male pelvis is more suitable for the study of racial differences than is the female.

2. Race Characters.

We may, in the next place, proceed to the consideration of the race characters of these pelves, though, unfortunately, the number of pelves belonging to some of the races is so small that it is impossible to say whether the special features which they exhibit are racial or only individual characters. Still, the measurements record the several diameters which have been taken, and they may be useful to future observers, who may be more fortunate in obtaining a greater number of specimens, as furnishing them with additional material for comparison.

The points which will more especially require attention are the breadth and height of the entire pelvis, the shape of the pelvic brim, the relations of its transverse and conjugate diameters, and the relative length and breadth of the sacrum. But reference will be also made to some other questions which have arisen in the course of this enquiry.

a. *Relations of Breadth and Height.*

In the first instance I shall consider the relations of the breadth and height of the entire pelvis, and may premise by stating that when the breadth-height index is high the height of the pelvis is great in relation to the breadth, whilst conversely a low breadth-height index expresses a broad pelvis in relation to the height. I shall begin by referring to some observations on the breadth and height of the pelvis of Europeans. Several anatomists and obstetricians have recorded the mean height and breadth of the entire pelvis in both the men and women of some of the nations of Europe. M. Verneau gives the mean height of sixty-three male pelves, presumably French, as 220 mm., and of thirty-five female pelves as 197 mm. John Wood's height-dimensions of pelves, presumably British, are for fourteen men 221 mm. (8 inches 7 lines), and for eighteen women 190 mm. (7 inches 5 lines). J. G. Garson's measurement of the pelvic height in fourteen European women, without specification of the particular race, is 202 mm., somewhat higher therefore than those of M. Verneau and J. Wood for the same sex. The maximum breadth of the pelvis between the iliac crests is stated by Meckel to be 211 mm. in men and 239 in women, by Burns to be 280 mm. (11 inches) in women, by Verneau to be 279 mm. in men and 266 in women, and by Garson to be 271 in women. From measurements which I have made on pelves in the dissecting room, and therefore presumably Scotch, the mean maximum breadth in six men was 300 mm., and in eleven women 293 mm. Verneau places the breadth-height index in European males at 79, and in females at 74; whilst the same index, calculated from Garson's measurements of European women, is 75. C. Martin states that in the European female pelvis the alæ of the ilium are for the most part translucent, and that the distance between the opposite iliac crests and spines is the largest amongst all the races that have been measured.

Although there is a certain amount of variation in the breadth and height dimensions as recorded by the above observers, yet it will be seen, from an examination of the preceding tables, that the Sikh was the only pelvis which in its height, 220 mm., and in its breadth, 278 mm., equalled the European male standard, and its index 79 corresponded with the index of Europeans obtained by Verneau; the male Esquimaux with a height of 211 mm., a breadth of 274 mm., and an index 77 closely approached it. These deficiencies in breadth and height, as compared with Europeans, are without doubt correlated with the shorter stature of the races comprised in the tables, and these defects in stature will appear more strongly in the chapter on the bones of the shaft of the lower limbs.

When compared with each other, the pelves measured in this Report exhibited differences in the relative proportions of breadth and height, which differences were expressed by variations in the breadth-height index. Amongst the female pelves these differences were not very great, and ranged from an index of 70 in the single Hindoo and

72 in the series of Sandwich Islanders to 77 in the single Esquimaux. Amongst the males the variations were much more strongly marked, and ranged from an index of 73 in the single Chinese and 75 in the single adult Andamanese to 91 in the single Bush pelvis.

This Bush pelvis is distinguished therefore from all the other pelves by its height in proportion to its breadth, and by the vertical direction of the ilium, and we may now enquire how far these relations, so strongly marked in this male pelvis, are a characteristic of the race. Pelves of Bushmen or Bushwomen have now been examined and described by Vrolik, Johannes Müller, Pruner-Bey, C. Martin, Görtz, Gustaf Fritsch, Verneau,[1] and myself. Unfortunately, some of these observers, although recording the maximum breadth between the iliac crests, have not given in numbers the height of the pelvis. Vrolik had, however, remarked on the great height of his female pelvis in relation to its breadth and on the vertical direction of the ilium. Johannes Müller stated that his female specimen resembled in an extraordinary manner the one figured by Vrolik, and he especially referred to the vertical direction of the ilium, so that the antero-superior and inferior iliac spines were almost in the same vertical plane. In his male pelvis, however, the ilia were much more oblique, and from the measurements of this pelvis given by Gustaf Fritsch the breadth-height index was apparently only 79. Görtz's female pelvis, again, was not so high as Vrolik's and Müller's specimens of the same sex, neither was the ilium so vertical. In Fritsch's adult female the breadth-height index was 84, whilst in the male it was only 81. Verneau stated that in his two female Bush pelves the direction of the ilium and of its anterior border was but a little inclined, I presume, therefore, almost vertical; on the other hand, it would appear that the height was not in them disproportional to the breadth, as he placed the breadth-height index at 77. Although therefore there is not an absolute uniformity in these characters in the several Bush pelves which have been examined, still it is clear that there is a strong tendency in this race for the ilium and its anterior border to approach the vertical in direction, so that the diameter between the antero-superior spines only slightly exceeds that between the antero-inferior spines. It is evident also that the pelvic height is large in proportion to the breadth, and although the variation is considerable from an index of 77 to one of 91, in the five pelves the measurements of which in these diameters have been recorded, yet the mean breadth-height index of the five, both males and females, is 82, considerably above the European mean, and the lowest index in the Bush women 77, is above the mean of European women as given both by Verneau and by Garson. There is no information of the proportion which the ischium contributes to the pelvic height except in the specimen which I have measured, in which it will be seen that the ratio is 81, the length of the ischium, to 183 the height of the pelvis.

[1] It is unnecessary for me either here or subsequently to repeat the references to the papers of the writers referred to in the text, as the titles of their respective memoirs are given in the Bibliographical list on pp. 3, 4, 5.

In one of the male Australians the breadth-height index was 82, but the mean index in the six males was 77, a little below the European male standard. Verneau gives the breadth-height index of one man as 79, and the mean of two women as 74. From Garson's measurements of five Australian women the corresponding index is 76·6, which is also the index of my single female specimen. The Australians therefore, both men and women, correspond closely in the proportions of pelvic height and breadth to Europeans.

In the Sandwich Island women the mean breadth-height index was 72. Of these A. and B., with a breadth-height index of 76 and 71 respectively, belonged to skeletons of dolichocephalic people, whilst I., with a corresponding index of 70, belonged to a brachycephalic person. The range of variation, therefore, of this index in these female pelves was not very great. M. Verneau, who has described five male pelves from Tongatabu, Mangareva, Noukahiva, and Hawaii, has pointed out that in them a wide range of variation existed both in this and some other features of the pelvis, so that he recognised two types of pelvis—the one, represented by the specimens from Tongatabu and Mangareva, he regarded as pure Polynesian, whilst the other bore traces of a Papuan element. The Tongan and Mangarevan were distinguished by the high breadth-height index, which in the former was 85, in the latter 93, whilst in the Noukahivan and Hawaian pelves this index was 79 and 77 respectively. The actual height of the pelvis in the Tongan was 220 mm., in the Mangarevan 228 mm., whilst in the Noukahivan and Hawaian it was only 194 and 200 mm. The Tongan and Mangarevan are, I presume, the pelves of a brachycephalic race, but in the relations of pelvic breadth and height they differed most materially from my brachycephalic Sandwich Islander; still it must be remembered that my pelvis was that of a woman, in which, therefore, for sexual reasons, the breadth dominates over the height much more than in the male. In the two male New Zealanders the breadth-height index of the pelvis was 79 and 87 respectively. I do not possess the cranium belonging to the skeleton from Te Aroha, and I have been unable to identify the skull which belonged to the Otago pelvis.[1]

The Negro pelves in their breadth-height index presented in the males a mean of 80 and in the females one of 73, both of which approximate to the European average in the two sexes. M. Verneau gives the relations of breadth to height in a Negress from Mozambique as 74, exactly the same as in the European female, whilst in other Negresses the same index varied from 73 to 79. In his male pelves, on the other hand, the corresponding index was considerably higher, for in a Negro from Mozambique it reached 85, and in a Nubian it was 84.

In my only adult male Andamanese the breadth-height index was 75, and the mean

[1] Although in the pelvis of the Otago skeleton the epiphyses of the iliac crests and ischial tubera were not in their entire extent fully ankylosed to their respective bones, yet in all probability the pelvic cavity with its inlet and outlet had attained its normal form and proportions.

of the three adult females was 76, two of these pelves being respectively 79 and 80. From the data which are furnished by Professor Flower in his table of pelvic measurements of this race the mean breadth of eight males was 212·1 mm., and the mean height was 175·5 mm., whilst the mean breadth of nine females was 203·8, and the mean height was 165·4. The breadth-height index for the men was therefore 82·7, and for the women 81, so that this index is, when a larger average is taken, higher in both sexes than would appear from my more limited series of measurements.

The specimen which is of most interest in the table of Asiatic pelves is the Malay, which, though on a considerably larger scale, approximated in the form of its ilium to that of the Bushman, and its breadth-height index was 85. C. Martin and H. Fritsch have both described pelves of Malays, and remark on the translucent character of the bone in the iliac fossa. Martin speaks of the Malay pelvis as narrow, and that the iliac spines and crest, in comparison with the antero-posterior diameter of the entire pelvis, are not far separated from each other, a character with which my specimen also corresponds.

The only entire male Guanche pelvis in my series had a breadth-height index of 77, and approximated therefore closely to the European standard. M. Verneau, who has examined both a male and female Guanche pelvis, stated that whilst the female differed very little, except in the pelvic inlet, from that of a European woman, the male on the other hand had strongly marked differences. Amongst these he says that the ilia were feebly developed and with not much of an incline, and that the greatest transverse diameter of the pelvis was considerable in relation to the vertical and antero-posterior diameters. He gives 81 as the breadth-height index of the male, and 75 as that of the female Guanche pelvis.

In both the male and female Esquimaux the breadth-height index was 77, and the pelves were large, well formed, and with moderately expanded iliac wings. Dr. Struthers, who many years ago described a female Esquimaux, stated that the diameter between the iliac crests was (11 inches) 280 mm., and between the anterior superior iliac spines (10 inches) 254 mm., so that its dimensions in these diameters were larger than either the male or female in my table. He does not, however, give the pelvic height, so that I am unable to compute a breadth-height index. M. Verneau has also examined an imperfect male pelvis of this race. The maximum breadth in it was only 245 mm., and the height 205, whilst the breadth-height index was 84. Verneau directs attention to the diminution in breadth of this pelvis from the iliac crests to the ischial tubera, whilst the antero-posterior and vertical diameters are, he says, but little modified. Whilst the iliac fossæ are very concave, the ilia are less developed, especially in the vertical direction. From the difference in the relation of breadth and height in Verneau's Esquimaux and in mine it is evident that we are not yet in a position to state what the general form of the pelvis is in this race.

The pelvis of the male Laplander had a breadth-height index of 80·5, and the female of 75, numbers which closely approximate to the ordinary European average. Pruner-Bey was the first to describe a male Lapp pelvis, and the same specimen, together with another male, was redescribed by Verneau, who gave 76 as the breadth-height index of his two males. The pelvis was distinctly smaller in this race than in Europeans generally, though in the proportion of its two great dimensions it does not seem to differ very materially from the European average.

b. *Pelvic Brim.*

That the inlet to the true pelvis presented variations in outline and in the relative proportions of its conjugate and transverse diameters has been recognised by anatomists since the form of the pelvis in the different races of men began to be studied.[1] Thus Vrolik pointed out that in the Negro the conjugate diameter of the brim was very great, in proportion to the transverse diameter, when compared with the European. But the first to put these variations into systematic shape was Professor M. J. Weber of Bonn, who described four prime forms of pelvis, which he designated oval, round, four-sided, and wedge-shaped. In the oval pelvis the transverse diameter of the brim distinctly exceeded the conjugate, and the pelvic inlet was transversely ovoid; in the round pelvis the transverse and conjugate diameters were almost equal, and the pelvic inlet was circular ; in the four-sided pelvis the transverse diameter exceeded the conjugate, and the sides and anterior and posterior boundaries of the pelvic brim were flattened so as to give it a quadrangular shape ; in the wedge-shaped pelvis the inlet was laterally compressed, and the transverse diameter greatly reduced near the symphysis, so that the pubic bones joined at an acute angle, the conjugate diameter was therefore greater than the transverse, and the outline of the inlet was cuneiform. Although he recognised that differences existed in the dimensions of the conjugate and transverse diameters in the same pelvis, yet Weber did not give such a numerical expression to these differences as to enable them to be referred to a common standard. A few years afterwards von Stein divided the form of the pelvic inlet into four classes—truncated-cordate (abgestumpfte Kartenherzform); elliptical, where the transverse diameter is the larger ; round ; and elliptical, where the conjugate diameter is the larger. He stated also that one would be justified in speaking of a difference of breadth-index in the pelvis as in the skull. Like Weber he does not appear, however, to refer these differences to a common standard. This was, however, subsequently done by Professor Zaaijer of Leyden, who, in his important memoir on the form of the pelvis in the women of Java (1866), suggested that in order to give a fixed standard of comparison between the conjugate and transverse diameters, the transverse

---

[1] This section on the Index of the Pelvic Brim as a basis for the Classification of the Races of men, as well as that on the Sacrum, have had several additions and modifications made to them since the publication of my papers on these subjects in the *Journ. of Anat. and Phys.*, vol. xx., October 1885, and January 1886.

diameter should be regarded as equal to 100. Then by multiplying the conjugate diameter by 100 and dividing by the transverse diameter, the proportion which the conjugate diameter bore to 100, or in other words the pelvic or brim index was obtained. When these diameters bore to each other the relation of 100 to 90 or under, then he regarded the pelvic inlet as round. But when the conjugate was greater in relation to the transverse, he called it longish oval. About the same time Carl Martin published an account of his measurements of the female pelvis in Europeans, Negresses, Mulattos, Bushwomen, Malays, Melanesians, and one Australian woman. As a result of his measurements he grouped these female pelves into a, those with a round inlet, in which the conjugate was almost as large as the transverse diameter, or at the most one-tenth smaller; and in this group he placed the aboriginal Americans, Australians, Malays, and Pacific Islanders: and b, those with a transversely oval inlet, in which the conjugate was more than one-tenth smaller than the transverse diameter, and in this group he placed the pelves of European and African women, though the Europeans had the widest pelvic inlet.

The mode of estimating the brim or pelvic index after the formula of Professor Zaaijer has been adopted by the majority of anthropologists, though some would have preferred to have reversed his formula and to have taken the conjugate diameter as equal to 100.[1] This, indeed, was at one time the opinion of M. Topinard, though subsequently in his *Eléments d' Anthropologie générale*, he has conformed to the usual practice.

The attempts which were made by Zaaijer and Martin to frame a classification of the pelvis, either in the same or in different races, on modifications in the relative proportions of the conjugate and transverse diameters of the brim, were not successful and did not find much favour amongst anthropologists, so that one meets with but little reference to them in current literature. This failure is, I think, in a great measure to be accounted for partly by the paucity of the observations, but mainly because they based their calculations largely if not exclusively on the study of female pelves, in which, for sexual reasons, there is to a considerable extent an approximation in form in different races, so that one does not meet in them with such striking variations in shape as when one compares the male pelves in different races with each other. In the males, therefore, the form characteristic of the race is more fixed, and from their study it is, I think, possible to frame a classification of the pelvis.

There are two groups of measurements which, from their importance, might serve as a basis for such a classification, viz., a, the breadth and height of the entire pelvis, from which a breadth-height index, such as has been discussed in an earlier part of this chapter, can be computed; and b, the conjugate and transverse diameters of the pelvic brim, from which the pelvic or brim index can be calculated. There can, I think, be little doubt

[1] See for example Carl Martin's paper in *Corresp. Blatt. der deutsch. Gesellsch. f. Anthrop. Ethn. u. Urgesch.*, März, 1881.

that, if sufficiently reliable data are obtainable, a classification of the pelvis into readily recognisable groups would be extremely convenient, and would save much time and trouble in description. Craniologists must be for ever grateful to Anders Retzius for grouping the skulls of the races of men into the two great divisions of dolichocephalic and brachycephalic, whilst the separation from the more extreme forms of these groups of an intermediate or mesaticephalic division by Paul Broca has been of material service.

Owing to the paucity of pelves in our museums as compared with the number of crania of the best known races, we are not in a position to speak with so much certainty of the characteristic pelvic form as we are of the head form in so many races, but there is now I think, sufficient material belonging to a number of races to enable me to offer for the consideration of anthropologists a classification which may, I trust, be regarded as satisfactory.

The dimensions which I shall take as presenting, in my judgment, the most reliable data for comparison, are the conjugate and transverse diameters of the pelvic brim, and the classification will be based on the modifications in the range of the brim index —the so-called pelvic index. I shall not, however, as was done by Zaaijer and Martin, limit myself to a division into two groups, but shall make three divisions, two of which will represent extreme forms in opposite directions, whilst the third will be intermediate. I shall express these divisions in terms derived from the Greek, so that the nomenclature in pelvic classification may be as far as possible on the same lines as the well-known divisions of crania. Neither the ancient Greek nor Roman physicians appear to have recognised the pelvis as a chief division of the skeleton,[1] for they associated the sacrum and coccyx with the spine, and the innominate bones with the lower limbs. No word, therefore, was employed in ancient Greek to designate this part of the skeleton. But the term πέλλα or πέλλις, a bowl or pail, may be regarded as equivalent to the Latin pelvis.[2] The modern Greeks, however, designate the anatomical pelvis by the word λεκάνη, a dish;[3] if one were therefore to conjoin either with πέλλα, or λεκάνη, the prefix δολιχός, long, to express one extreme form, πλατύς, wide, to express the opposite form, and μεσαίτατος, middlemost, to express the intermediate condition, one would obtain descriptive terms to suit our purpose. By *dolichopellic* (*dolicholekanic*) is to be understood a pelvis in which the conjugate diameter of the brim is either longer than the transverse or approaches closely to it ; by *platypellic*[4] (*platylekanic*), a pelvis in which the transverse diameter of the brim greatly exceeds the conjugate ; by *mesatipellic* (*mesatilekanic*) a pelvis in which the transverse diameter is not so greatly in excess of the conjugate. It may not be possible in the present state of our know-

[1] Onomatologia anatomica, von Professor Joseph Hyrtl. Wien, 1880.
[2] Liddell and Scott's Greek English Lexicon. Killian in his essay entitled "Das Stachelbecken" (Schilderung neuer Beckenform, Mannheim, 1854) employs the term πέλλις in combination with ἄκανθος, akantho-pelys, pelvis spinosa, to express a pelvis with a sharp pectineal line or a process projecting from it.
[3] ΑΝΘΡΩΠΟΛΟΓΙΑ, ὑπὸ Π. ΔΙΑΜΑΝΤΟΠΟΥΛΟΥ ἐν ΣΜΥΡΝΗ. 1880, p. 36.
[4] I have not used the word "brachypellic" ("brachylekanic") as I wished to bring out by the employment of the prefix πλατύς that relatively great width was the characteristic feature of this form of pelvic brim.

ledge to fix definitely the numerical limits of each group, as it may need a wider range of material for comparison, both as regards the races and the number of pelves in each race, than we at present possess. In any case, indeed, just as in the classification of crania, the numerical limits would be arbitrary; still it will be advisable to give to each division such a range as will in all probability include within it those pelves in a given race that present the characteristic form. For the present then, we will assume that pelves with a brim index above 95 are dolichopellic (dolicholekanic), that those with a brim index below 90 are platypellic (platylekanic), whilst those whose brim index ranges from 90 to 95, both inclusive, are mesatipellic (mesatilekanic). But it is quite possible that these limits may subsequently need some modification.

First, we will enquire into the value of the brim index in Europeans, and about them we are fortunate to possess a good deal of information, as the dimensions of the brim have been measured in numerous pelves in most of the principal nations. Thus if we take British pelves and reduce the measurements from inches to millimètres we find that of those measured by J. J. Watt, the males had a transverse diameter of 116 mm. (4 in. 6 lines.), and a conjugate of 102 mm. (4 in.) which gives a brim index 87·9; the females, again, had a transverse diameter 142 mm. (5 in. 6 lines) and a conjugate 124 mm. (4 in. 9 lines), giving a brim index 87·3. The pelves measured by John Wood gave for the males—transverse 120 mm., conjugate 103, the brim index being 85; and for the females—transverse 132 mm., conjugate 114, the brim index being 86. My own measurements of six males presumably Scotch,[1] gave a mean transverse diameter 127 mm. and a mean conjugate 98 mm., with a brim index 77; and of eleven females a mean transverse of 137 mm. and a mean conjugate of 109 mm., with a brim index 79. M. Verneau, in his table of the measurements of Europeans, presumably French, states that this index is 80 in the men and 78 in the women. Gegenbaur gives the mean dimensions of the brim in pelves presumably German as follows :[2]—for the males—transverse diameter 128, conjugate 108, the brim index being 84; for the females—transverse diameter 135, conjugate 116, the brim index being 85·9. W. H. Flower states that his measurements of eleven European males—the nationality not being specified—gave a pelvic index 81, and of fourteen females an index of about 78. In the measurements made by John Wood, Gegenbaur, and myself, the brim index in the male pelvis is a little below the brim index in the female, but in those measured by J. J. Watt, Verneau and Flower the brim index of the males somewhat exceeded the females. Additional observations on the pelvic brim in European women have been made by Garson, whose measurements give 80 as the brim index; by Navas, whose measurements of Spanish women furnish a brim index 81, and by C. Martin, whose measurements give 69 as the brim index of Irish women.

[1] The pelvis of J. Howieson, figured in Plate I., had the following dimensions: breadth 231 mm., height 217 mm., conjugate of brim 89 mm., transverse diameter of brim 129 mm., pelvic index 69.
[2] Lehrbuch der Anatomie des Menschen, p. 265, 1883.

REPORT ON THE BONES OF THE HUMAN SKELETON.   35

Through the investigations of A. Weisbach we possess considerable information on the form and dimensions of the pelvis in ten of the races in the Austrian empire. His measurements were made on the unmacerated pelves of men between twenty and thirty years of age. The mean brim index in these races is as follows. The mean of eight South Slavs 81·5, of twelve Germans 82·5, of six Slowaks 84·1, of eight Czechs 84·3, of twenty Magyars 88·3, of twenty Italians 89·1, of thirteen Ruthenians 89·2, of five Gipsies 90·4, of eleven Poles 91·2, and of nine Roumanians 91·6.

The lowest mean brim index recorded in any European race or nation is 77 for the males in the Scottish pelvis, and 69 for the females in the Irish pelvis; and almost without exception this index amongst European races, both males and females, is below 90. The highest mean of these races is met with in the male Magyars with a brim index 88·3 in the male Italians with a brim index 89·1, and in the Ruthenians with a brim index 89·2, so that the European pelvis is platypellic (platylekanic). In three however of the races in the Austrian empire the mean brim index, as Weisbach's measurements show, rises above 90, viz., the Gipsies, Roumanians, and Poles. The Gipsies however are not a European race, and the Roumanians have in all probability a strong Oriental admixture. It may be, I think, a question whether the eleven pelves described by Weisbach as Polish, and to which he gives a mean brim index 91·2, were either altogether or in great part of a pure Sclavonic race, for the mean index of his eight South Slav pelves was only 81·5, and that of his eight Bohemian Czechs was 84·3. I do not consider therefore that the higher mean index of these so-called Polish pelves should interfere with the general statement already made that the European pelvis is platypellic (platylekanic).

In placing the European pelvis, both male and female, so far as it is represented by these nations, in the platypellic division, it is not of course to be understood that no individual European pelvis ever attains a brim index of 90 or upwards, but that the mean in both sexes is below 90, and as a rule is markedly below that number.

In the next place I shall speak of another type of pelvis, and shall begin by considering the brim index in the Australian pelvis. All the anatomists who have written on the characters of the male pelvis in this race agree in stating that the pelvic brim is narrow in its transverse diameter as compared with the conjugate. Professor Huxley, who was one of the first, if not the first, to give a numerical expression to these diameters in this race, gives the mean pelvic index of five males which he had measured as 101, and of one female as 87. In only one of these males was the transverse diameter in excess of the conjugate. In Ecker's Australian male the index was 100, in Keferstein's 95, and the mean index of the five Australian males in the Blumenbach collection, as measured by Spengel, was 92. In the single male Australian measured by M. Verneau the brim index was 98, and the mean of this index in two females was 80. Professor Flower, in his account of the osteology of the Andaman Islanders, incidentally stated that ten male

Australian pelves which he had measured, and which probably included the five pelves previously measured by Professor Huxley, and that measured by Dr. Barnard Davis, gave an average pelvic index of 98. From Dr. Garson's measurements of five Australian female pelves an index of 91 has been computed. In my series of six adult males, recorded in Table I., the mean brim index was 97, and in the only female 96; of the six males three exceeded 95, one of them very considerably so, and three were below that number.

There is now, I think, sufficient material before us to pronounce a definite opinion on the relative size of the transverse and conjugate diameters of the pelvic brim in both sexes of Australians. It is clear that in the women the transverse diameter is larger, and not unfrequently considerably larger, than the conjugate, so that the pelvic index is for the race relatively low. If we include M. Verneau's two female pelves, which, from their low index of 80, one might be disposed to doubt if they belonged to genuine Australians, the mean index of the nine females measured was 88·5, and, if we exclude these, it was 91·3; in either case being considerably above the European mean for the same sex, and placing the Australian female pelvis on the verge between the mesatipellic and platypellic groups. In the males, on the other hand, the conjugate diameter very often exceeds the transverse, and seldom falls much below it, and as the transverse diameter rapidly diminishes in the pubic region, a cuneiform pelvic brim is produced. The mean brim index of the twenty-four males measured by Ecker, Keferstein, Huxley, Spengel,[1] Verneau, Flower, and myself is 96·6, so that they distinctly belong to the dolichopellic (dolicholekanic) group.

Data for enabling one to obtain a knowledge of the brim index in the Bush race have been furnished by several anatomists. The brim measurements of five males have been recorded by Johannes Müller, Huxley, G. Fritsch, and myself, and of eight females by Vrolik, Müller, Huxley, Görtz, Verneau, and Fritsch.[2] In the females the transverse diameter in some specimens considerably exceeded the conjugate, thus in Verneau's table the mean of his two pelves, one of which was the well-known Hottentot Venus described by Cuvier, gave 87 mm. for the conjugate and 122 mm. for the transverse diameters, with a brim index therefore of 71; whilst in the woman Afandy, described by Görtz, the conjugate was 111 mm. and the transverse 110 mm., which give an index of 100·9. The mean brim index in the eight women was 89, which places the female pelvis in the highest term of the platypellic group, though individual specimens belonged to each of the three divisions. The male Bush pelves, again, showed a much smaller range of variation in the brim index, and the conjugate and transverse diameters were more nearly equal. The lowest index, 93, was in Fritsch's specimen, in which the conjugate diameter was 96 and the transverse 103 mm., and the highest index, 109, was

---

[1] Spengel's measurements of pelves in the Blumenbach collection at Göttingen, are given by Barnard Davis in the Supplement to his Thesaurus Craniorum in a Table opposite page 96.

[2] Professor Humphry gives in his treatise on the Human Skeleton, p. 106, the transverse and conjugate diameters of the pelvic brim in three Bush skeletons, but he does not state the sex.

in the pelvis recorded in my Table VI. The mean of the five males was 99·5, so that they have a well-marked dolichopellic character. Notwithstanding the high proportion of the conjugate to the transverse diameter, the shape of the brim, if I may judge of its form from my specimen, and from the two pelves figured by G. Fritsch, is not cuneiform, for the two pubic bones do not rapidly approximate to each other as in the Australian pelvis; in my pelvis the term antero-posteriorly oval properly expresses the form of the brim.[1]

The pelvic index of a male Hottentot measured by Jeffries Wyman was 94·4; but the fullest information that we possess on the pelvis of the Hottentots is contained in the valuable treatise on the aborigines of South Africa by Gustaf Fritsch. He puts the dimensions of the pelvic brim of a Hottentot woman at 96 mm. for the transverse diameter and 101 mm. for the conjugate, giving a brim index 105, which is remarkably high for the female pelvis. The transverse diameter of two male Korana Hottentots is respectively 105 and 91 mm., whilst the conjugate of the same is 96 and 108 mm., from which a brim index of 91·4 for the one and 118 for the other can be computed, giving a mean for the two of 104·7. So far then as we can judge from these few specimens, the Hottentot pelvis is dolichopellic. Fritsch also gives the measurements of six male and one female Kaffir pelvis, and from these measurements I have calculated their indices. The female, with a transverse diameter of 107 mm. and a conjugate of 96, had an index of 89·7, whilst the males varied in the brim index from 95 to 108, and had a mean of 100·6. Weber had also previously figured the pelvis of a male Kaffir, in which the transverse diameter of the brim was 3 in. 9 lines, the conjugate 4 inches, the brim index therefore was 102·6. He placed it in his wedge-shaped group. There can be no doubt, therefore, that the pelvis in the male Kaffirs is dolichopellic (dolicholekanic).

A considerable number of Negro pelves have now been measured. As a rule nothing definite has been stated, or, in all probability indeed, known of the exact districts or tribes from which most of these pelves were obtained, but Verneau in his essay especially mentions Nubia, Mozambique, and Guadeloupe as the localities from which certain of his specimens were derived. The measurements of the Negresses which have been described by Vrolik, Weber, J. Wood, Fritsch, Verneau, Martin, and myself amount to thirty-one, though it is possible that the same specimen may have been measured by more than one of these observers. The lowest brim index, 75·7, was that recorded by Fritsch, and the highest, 106, was the pelvis measured by John Wood; the mean of the series was 88·3. The measurements of the Negros described by von Sömmerring, Vrolik, John Wood, Huxley, Barnard Davis, Spengel, Verneau, and myself amounted to thirty-five, though with them it is also possible that the same pelvis may have had its

---

[1] Zuckerkandl states in his account of the skulls of the Novara Expedition (Wien, 1875), that the pelvis of a Bushman about fourteen years old had a transverse diameter 9 cm. and a conjugate 8 cm. The brim index of this youth was 88·8.

measurements recorded by more than one observer.[1] The lowest brim index was 72, measured by Spengel, and the highest a male described by John Wood, with an index of 105, whilst the mean of the series was 92·7. In the male Negro, therefore, there was a greater difference as a rule between the transverse and conjugate diameters than in the Australians, Bush race, and Kaffirs, and the transverse diameter was proportionally wider. The males were mesatipellic, and the females were in the higher term of the platypellic division. The brim, therefore, as a rule, was not cuneiform, but had a more rounded outline.

The most extensive series of measurements of the pelvis of the Andaman Islanders has been given by Professor Flower in his memoir on their Osteology and in his Additional Observations thereon. His measurements of the pelvic brim gave a mean index in thirteen females of 96·4 and in twelve males of 98·8. Dr. Garson's measurements of apparently the same thirteen female pelves furnish the same mean index, 96·4. These numbers are higher than I got in my much more limited series, Table IV., where the three adult females had a mean brim index of 87 and the single adult male an index of 97. Notwithstanding these differences, it is, however, quite clear that, as the brim index was about 98 in the males, the pelvis in this sex was distinctly in the dolichopellic division. In the females, again, the index was lower, and, if the mean of Flower's and my observations be taken, it was 91·7, which places their pelvis in the mesatipellic (mesatilekanic) group.

In the Dresden Museum is the skeleton of a female Negrito from Palauan, Luzon, measured by Meyer and Tüngel, in which the pelvic brim has a transverse diameter 112 mm. and a conjugate 100 mm., the index being 89; in the same museum another Negrito female skeleton, from Bontoc, Luzon, called an Igorrote, has a transverse diameter of the brim of 122 mm., and a conjugate of 97 mm., the index being 79·5. M. Hamy, in his description of the skeleton of a female Negrito of the tribe of Aëta, from the neighbourhood of Binangonan, Luzon,[2] found the transverse diameter to be 112 mm., the conjugate 88 mm., and the brim index was only 78·5. In each of these three female Negritos the brim index was below 90, and the pelvis was platypellic. Von Franque described a female pelvis from Luzon, in the Semper collection in Würzburg, as that of a Papuan, but from the place where it was obtained it may have been a Negrito. Hennig, who has recently measured it, gives[3] the transverse diameter 115 mm., conjugate 105 mm., the brim index being 91, i.e., it was mesatipellic. Another female pelvis often said to be that of a Negrito, in the museum at Halle, has been described both by H. Fritsch (Nonnulla de pelvibus), and by Hennig;[4] and the latter states that the transverse

---

[1] Professor Humphry in his treatise on the Human Skeleton (p. 106) states that the mean transverse diameter of twenty-five Negro pelves is 4·6 inches, the mean antero-posterior 4·1 inches; the calculated index therefore is 89. The sex of these skeletons is not stated, but probably both male and female.

[2] *Archives du Muséum*, ser. 2, t. ii., 1879.   [3] *Sitzungsb. der Naturf. Ges. zu Leipzig*, May 11, 1880.

[4] *Op. cit.*

diameter is 117 mm., and the conjugate 100 mm., the brim index therefore is 85. A. B. Meyer, however doubts if this pelvis is that of a Negrito, and considers it to be a Negress.[1] It will be observed that all these pelves are those of women, and so far as I know no male Negrito pelvis from the Philippines has yet been described, although apparently a number of specimens are in German museums, so that the mean brim index of the male pelvis cannot at present be stated.

The measurements of a single male Nikobar Islander in the Berlin Museum have been given by Gustaf Fritsch in his Table II. The transverse diameter of the brim was 102 mm., the conjugate 91 mm., and the pelvic index was 89. It was therefore in the higher term of the platypellic division, but in all probability the mean index in this race will be found to be higher when a large average has been obtained.

Dr. Barnard Davis has given the dimensions of the pelvis in three male and one female Tasmanian skeleton. The pelvic index in the female was 83, and the mean index of the three males was 93·3. M. Verneau has recorded the measurements of a single male Tasmanian pelvis; its transverse diameter was 108 mm., its conjugate 95 mm., and its brim index 88. The mean of the four male pelves was 92, and not one exceeded 95, so that in all probability the Tasmanian pelvis is mesatipellic (mesatilekanic).

In the series of Papuan bones in the Dresden Museum collected by Dr. A. B. Meyer, near Rubi, Geelvinks Bay, New Guinea, are several sacra and innominate bones, and from these a male and a female pelvis have been artificially articulated. The dimensions of the brim of the male pelvis have been given both by Meyer and Tüngel and by Winckel as transverse diameter, 111 mm., conjugate, 107 mm., the pelvic index was therefore 96·4; those of the female pelvis as given by Winckel are transverse, 114 mm., conjugate, 106 mm., pelvic index 107·5. M. Verneau has stated the brim measurements in a female from New Guinea (erroneously marked male in his Synoptic Table), to be, transverse diameter, 136 mm., conjugate, 113 mm., with a brim index therefore of 83.

Of the smaller islands of the Pacific, M. Verneau has measured a fine series of pelves from New Caledonia, three of which were females and twelve males. The mean transverse diameter of the brim in three females was 123 mm., the mean conjugate 110 mm., and the brim index was 89. The mean transverse diameter in twelve males was 114, the mean conjugate 104 mm., and the brim index was 91. The same observer has recorded the transverse diameter of the brim in a male Loyalty Islander, from Lifu, as 116 mm. and the conjugate diameter as 124 mm., with a brim index 107. His two male Sandwich Islanders had a mean transverse diameter of the brim of 114 mm. and a mean conjugate of 92 mm. which yielded a brim index of 81, and the mean brim index in my three female Sandwich Islanders was 83. M. Verneau's male pelvis from Tonga had a transverse diameter of 126 mm. and a conjugate of 121 mm., with a brim index of 96; his male pelvis from Mangareva had a

[1] *Sitzungsb. der Naturf. Ges. zu Leipzig*, November 9, 1880.

transverse diameter of 119 mm. and a conjugate of 118 mm., with a brim index of 99; his male pelvis from Noukahiva had a transverse diameter of 108 mm. and a conjugate of 94 mm., with a brim index of 89. Dr. Barnard Davis has given the transverse diameter of the brim of a male dolichocephalic Loyalty Islander from Lifu (Awita) as 114 mm. and the conjugate as 106 mm., the index of which is 92; also the transverse diameter of a male brachycephalic Tannese[1] as 121 mm. and the conjugate as 110 mm., index 81. In my two New Zealand pelves the mean brim index was 96, and in a young Maori measured by Meyer and Tüngel it was 90·9.

There is therefore a wide range of variation in the relative transverse and conjugate diameters of the brim in the pelves of the Pacific Islanders, so that the index ranged, amongst the pelves measured, from 81 in a male Tannese and in a male Sandwich Islander to 107 in a male Loyalty Islander. This is in all probability to be accounted for in part at least from the fact that the series consisted of pelves, some of which were obtained from islands populated chiefly by the Melanesian race, others chiefly by the Polynesian or Mahori race, others again by a mixture of the two races.[2] The specimens which have been measured are too few and too doubtful as to the race to which they belonged to enable one to state with any certainty what is the characteristic form of the pelvic brim in each of these two great races, or the modifications which may arise in its form when the two races are intermingled. If one, however, may regard the pelves from New Caledonia as derived from the Melanesian race inhabiting that group of islands, then it would seem as if in the females the mean brim index did not reach 90, so that they belonged to the platypellic group, whilst in the males the same index was at or about 91, so that they were mesatipellic. On the other hand, however, in one of the male Loyalty Islanders, also in all probability of the Melanesian stock, the pelvic index was, as just stated, as high as 107, and therefore very strongly dolichopellic, and in both the male and female Papuan pelves in the Dresden Museum this index was also dolichopellic (dolicholekanic). Again, if one may regard the male pelves from Tonga, Mangareva, Noukahiva, and New Zealand as from people of the Polynesian or Mahori race, then it would seem as if this race had a higher brim index than the Melanesians of New Caledonia, and was either dolichopellic or approaching that group. On the other hand, it should be remembered that the brim index in Verneau's two male Sandwich Islanders and in Barnard Davis's brachycephalic Tannese was as low as 81, i.e., platypellic.

One must still leave in doubt, therefore, the exact position of both Polynesians and Melanesians, but should the opinion which I have just expressed, that the male Melanesians are mesatipellic, be confirmed by a more extended series of observations,

[1] The length-breadth index of the skull of the Lifu Islander, Awita, is said by Dr. Barnard Davis to be 74, and that of the Tannese 85.
[2] For a résumé of the facts on which this statement of the distribution of the two great races of the Pacific is made, I may refer to the chapter on the Races of the Pacific Ocean in the First or Craniological Part of this Report.

then they would correspond in the form and proportions of the pelvic brim with the Negros rather than with the Australians, Bush race, Hottentots, Kaffirs, and Andaman Islanders, all of whom are distinctly dolichopellic. We may, however, look for much additional light on this matter when the observations which I understand Dr. Prochownick of Hamburg is making on the large series of pelves from the Pacific Islands in the Godeffroy Museum have been published.

In addition to the specimens of the pelves of the Guanche people recorded in my Table VI., M. Verneau has described the characters of a male and a female pelvis. Of the female he says that the inlet was very sensibly elongated antero-posteriorly, but on the contrary its transverse diameter was slightly diminished. With the exception of the inlet it differed very little from a European woman. The transverse diameter of the brim was 132 mm., the conjugate 120 mm., and the brim index was 91. In his male as in the female the transverse diameter of the brim only exceeded the antero-posterior by a few millimètres, and the brim index was also 91. In my perfect male pelvis the transverse diameter considerably exceeded the antero-posterior, the brim index was 85 and the form of the inlet approximated to the oval. The mean of the two males was 88, but the specimens are too few to enable one to state definitely to which of my three divisions of the pelvis this race should be referred, but in all probability it is either platypellic or mesatipellic.

The dimensions of the brim in an Esquimaux pelvis have been recorded by Dr. Struthers in a female specimen. He gives the conjugate diameter as (4⅝ inches) 117 mm. and the transverse as (6 inches) 153 mm., which furnish a brim index of 76, and show a pelvis which must have had a markedly transversely oval inlet. M. Verneau records the transverse diameter of the brim in his male pelvis as 124 mm., but it was too much damaged to enable him to obtain the conjugate dimension. In my two specimens (Table VII.) the brim index, 88 in the male and 84 in the female, closely corresponded to the mean index in Europeans of both sexes. It is probable that the Esquimaux therefore belong to the platypellic (platylekanic) group.

The two male Laplanders whose pelvic measurements are recorded by M. Verneau had a mean transverse diameter, 122 mm. and a mean conjugate diameter, 101, so that the brim index was 83. In my male specimen the transverse diameter was much smaller, both absolutely and relatively to the conjugate, and the brim index was 93. In my female, again, the transverse diameter of the brim was considerably in excess of the conjugate, and the pelvic index was only 72·5. The mean brim index of the three males was 88, and it is not unlikely that the male Lapp pelvis may, when additional observations are recorded, be found to be in the higher term of the platypellic group.

The Hindoo pelves recorded in Table V. had a brim index of 89 in the male and 93 in the female. A third Hindoo skeleton, that of a male,[1] which has been presented to

[1] This man was a Hindoo by religion, and believed to be a native of Bengal. In stature, as will be seen on p. 104, he was above the average height. See also remarks on p. 118.

the Anatomical Museum by Dr. John Anderson since Table V. was in type, had a transverse diameter, 133 mm., and a conjugate diameter, 117, giving a brim index 88. In the Sikh recorded in Table V. the index of the pelvic brim was 90 ; in the male Sikh, "Bariam Singh," measured by Barnard Davis, the transverse diameter of the brim was 125, the conjugate diameter 102 mm. and the pelvic index 81. In a male Bhutea, also measured by Barnard Davis, the transverse diameter of the brim is said to be 114 mm., the conjugate 112 mm., and the brim index 98. In a male pelvis described by M. Broca as a "black Hindoo," from the neighbourhood of Madras, the transverse diameter of the brim was 101 mm., and the conjugate 81 mm., the index therefore was 80 ; in a female from the same place the transverse diameter was 120 mm., the conjugate 117 mm., and the brim index 97·5. In a female Coolie described by Dr. Maurel the transverse diameter was 117 mm., and the antero-posterior 100 mm., the brim index being 85. The mean brim index of the five male natives of India was 87, *i.e.*, they were platypellic ; whilst the mean of the three females was 91·8, *i.e.*, mesatipellic. The specimens were too few in number on which to frame an average, but in all probability when a large average is obtained both males and females will prove to be platypellic.

The Mongolian race is represented in my measurements in Table V. by a single Chinese pelvis, which, from the label attached to it, I have described as a male, though in the open subpubic angle, 76°, it approximated to the female character. Apparently only five Chinese pelves had previously been described, a female by von Franque, a male and female by Verneau, a male by J. W. Spengel, and a male in the Dresden Museum by A. B. Meyer and E. Tüngel. Verneau in addition gives an account of a male Annamite. Von Franque pointed out that it was scarcely possible to distinguish the pelvis of his Chinese woman from that of a European ; the transverse diameter of the brim was 133 mm., and the conjugate 104 mm., so that the brim index was 78. Verneau stated that the inlet in the Chinese woman was very enlarged, very prominent, and had the form of a heart on a playing card ; the transverse diameter of the brim was 140 mm. and the conjugate 89 mm., so that the brim index was only 64, being the lowest pelvic index recorded in his series of measurements. In his male Chinese the transverse diameter was 115 mm., the conjugate 93 mm., and the brim index was 81. Spengel's male had a transverse diameter, 112 mm., a conjugate diameter, 95 mm., pelvic index 85 ; the Dresden male had a transverse diameter, 114 mm., and a conjugate 92 mm., with an index 80·7. In my specimen the corresponding index was 85. All the six Chinese pelves now recorded, viz., four males and two females, had an index considerably below 90, so that there can, I think, be no doubt that the Chinese pelvis is platypellic. Verneau's Annamite male pelvis had an inlet 110 mm. in its transverse and 88 mm. in its antero-posterior diameter, with an index of 75, which strengthens the view that the Mongolian pelvis is platypellic (platylekanic).

Dönitz,[1] from the study of seven female Japanese pelves, came to the conclusion that two different types were to be found in them, the one with a round or heart-shaped inlet, the other with a transversely oval or wide brim. Those with a round or heart-shaped inlet Wernich regarded as belonging to the Malayan race, whilst those with a wide brim, approximating to the Europeans, he held to be a product of a cross between the Aïnos, the original inhabitants, and the Malays. If the conjugate diameter be regarded as equal to 100, the wide-brimmed pelves have a transverse diameter equal to 125, whilst in Europeans the corresponding diameter is equal to 127, but the pelves with a round or heart-shaped brim have a transverse diameter equal only to 107. Scheube[1] has measured a male Aïno pelvis and has given the transverse diameter of the brim as 113 mm. and the conjugate as 115 mm., which give a brim index 102. Barnard Davis's measurements of the pelvis of an Aïno woman were, transverse diameter 102 mm., conjugate diameter 117 mm., pelvic index 97. In the single specimen of each sex the brim index was above 95, so that it is possible that the Aïnos are dolichopellic. If these measurements of the Aïno pelvis are to be regarded as expressing the character of the race, it is difficult to see how a people with apparently dolichopellic proportions, by crossing with a race in which the conjugate diameter is also proportionately great, could produce a pelvis with a wide inlet.

The male Malayan pelvis recorded in my Table V. had an inlet which was ovoid in the antero-posterior diameter, and the brim index, 105, showed it to be highly dolichopellic. In von Franque's female Malay the transverse diameter was 126 mm., the conjugate 116 mm., and the brim index 92; the form of the inlet as in my specimen was antero-posteriorly oval. A female Kubu from Sumatra, probably of the Malay race, measured by J. G. Garson, had the brim 117 mm. in transverse diameter, and 122 mm. in the conjugate, with a brim index therefore 104·3, so that it was greatly elongated antero-posteriorly. The two male Javan pelves measured by Barnard Davis are, however, stated to have had a pelvic index of 83 and 81 respectively, i.e., they were platypellic. In a female Javan pelvis measured by Verneau this index was 90. Zaaijer, from his analysis of the pelvic measurements of twenty-six Java women, stated that the form of the inlet was not uniform, in sixteen it was round, the transverse diameter being to the conjugate as 100 to 90 or under; in ten it was longish-oval, the transverse diameter being as 100 to more than 90. H. Fritsch has measured five female Malay pelves, and has described the pelvic inlet as round, with a relative predominance of the conjugate diameter. C. Martin has described the conjugate diameter as very long, the inlet round, in many examples oval. From the series of female Malay pelves described by Zaaijer, H. Fritsch, and himself, C. Martin has obtained a mean transverse diameter of 119 mm.

---

[1] Quoted by Ploss in *Archiv f. Anthropologie*, Bd. xv. p. 265, 1884, and by Wernich in *Archiv f. Gynäkologie*, Bd. xii. p. 293, 1877.
[2] Also quoted by Ploss.

and a mean conjugate of 109 mm., from which a brim index of 91·6 can be computed, so that they are mesatipellic (mesatilekanic). This is a high index for the female sex, and as experience has shown that in each race the brim index is as a rule distinctly higher in the male pelvis than in the female, it is not unlikely that the male pelves are dolichopellic, and the high index in my male specimen is probably a key to the dolichopellic (dolicholekanic) character of these people.

I have had no opportunity of examining any pelves of the Indian tribes of either North or South America. Very little, indeed, appears to be known of the pelvis in the North American Indians. Von Franque has described a male and female pelvis of Flathead Indians from Vancouver Island, and from his measurements the brim index in the male was 76 and in the female 84·5. Barnard Davis gives the measurements of the pelvis of a male Illinois Indian, which had a transverse diameter, 127 mm., a conjugate, 110 mm., pelvic index 86. Verneau describes a female Mexican[1] with a transverse diameter 130 mm. and a conjugate 104 mm., the brim index being 80. The mean of the two males was 81, and that of the two females 82, so that both sexes were platypellic.

Weber, Barnard Davis and Verneau have all described specimens of the pelvis in various tribes of South American Indians. Weber figures the pelvis of a male Botocudo Indian, the transverse diameter of the brim in which was 4 in. 7 lines, the conjugate diameter 4 inches, which gave an index 85; also a female Botocudon, the transverse diameter in which was 4 in. 3 lines, the conjugate 4 in. 6 lines which give a pelvic index 107. He places the male in his group of pelves with an oval inlet, the female in his cuneiform group. Barnard Davis found a male Puelche Indian to have both the transverse and conjugate diameters of the brim equal at 116 mm., with an index therefore of 100, and an ancient male Peruvian with the transverse diameter considerably in excess of the conjugate, and with an index of 81. Verneau gave the transverse diameter of the brim in a male Charruan Indian as 122 mm. and the conjugate as 115 mm., the index being 94; also the transverse diameter of a male Botocudon as 123 mm. and the conjugate as 91 mm., the index being 74; also the transverse diameter of a male Goytacazen 119 mm. and the conjugate 89 mm., with an index 75, and of a female with an index 86; also the mean transverse diameter of two male Peruvians 135 mm. and the conjugate 91 mm., with a mean index 67, and three females with a mean index 83; also a male Bolivian with a transverse diameter 116 mm. and a conjugate 105 mm., the index being 90·5. The males measured by Verneau varied in the brim index from 67 in the Peruvians to 94 in the Charruan, with a mean on the six specimens of 80. The females were much more uniform in the brim index, with a mean on the four specimens of 84·5. They presented this peculiarity that the mean pelvic index in the female was higher than in the male, and that therefore the transverse diameter was not proportionally so much in excess of the conjugate. Carl Martin, from

---

[1] Although he refers to a male Mexican pelvis in the Museum, yet he does not give its measurements.

his own observations and those of von Franque, has given in his latest paper the mean transverse diameter of the brim in American aboriginal women at 127 mm. and the mean conjugate at 115, from which an index of 90·5 can be computed, which is considerably higher than the mean obtained from Verneau's measurements. The mean of the whole series of South American Indians, calculated from the specimens referred to in this paragraph, is 83·3 for the males and 91·6 for the females, so that the males are platypellic, the females mesatipellic. The mean dimensions of the pelvic brim in the Fuegians, as obtained by Garson's measurements of four male pelves of the Yahgan tribe, is transverse diameter 121·5 mm., and conjugate diameter 98 mm. The index therefore is 80·6, so that these islanders, like the male aborigines of the South American continent, are platypellic (platylekanic).

I shall now classify in three parallel columns the people or races whose pelvic brim index I have analysed in the preceding pages, both from my own observations and from those of other anatomists. For reasons to which I have already referred, I have not included the female pelvis in this classification and have based it entirely on the measurements of the male pelvis, though, as will be seen from the frequent references which I have made to the brim index in the female, I consider that it assists one in arriving at a conclusion as to the group in which the pelvis of each race should be placed. In those cases in which, from the few pelves which have been measured, or from the wide variations in the brim index, there is a doubt as to the group in which a people or race should be ranked I have appended a query.

TABLE VIII.

DOLICHOPELLIC or DOLICHOLEKANIC. Brim Index above 95.	MESATIPELLIC or MESATILEKANIC. Brim Index 90–95.	PLATYPELLIC or PLATYLEKANIC. Brim Index below 90.
Australians	Negros	British
Bushmen	Tasmanians	French
Hottentots	New Caledonians	Germans
Kaffirs	Melanesians ?	Europeans generally
Andaman Islanders	...	Guanche ?
Malays	...	Esquimaux ?
Polynesians ?	...	Laplanders ?
New Zealanders ?	...	Natives of India
Ainos ?	...	Chinese
...	...	Mongolians generally
...	...	American Indians
...	...	Fuegians

How greatly the female pelvis is modified in the proportions of the pelvic brim in relation to the special sexual requirements is shown from the fact that in none of the people or races, whose pelvic dimensions are analysed in sufficient numbers to enable one to obtain an average, does the female pelvis attain, in the mean of each race, dolichopellic proportions. Thus in the Australians and Andaman Islanders, and probably the Malays, whilst the males are dolichopellic the females are mesatipellic. In the Bush race the males are dolichopellic, the females platypellic. In the Kaffirs the males are dolichopellic, the females mesatipellic or platypellic. In the Negros and New Caledonians the males are mesatipellic, the females are platypellic. Amongst the Europeans with a platypellic male index the females are also platypellic. In the South American Indians, on the other hand, whilst the males are platypellic the females are mesatipellic. These modifications all signify that in each race or people the transverse diameter of the brim, the cavity, and the outlet is as a rule relatively, and indeed for the most part absolutely, wider in the female pelvis than in the male.

c. *Sacrum.*

A comparison of the several indices in the various tables will show that great variety existed in the relative length and breadth of the sacrum in the pelves measured. These variations may be expressed numerically by computing a sacral index by multiplying the breadth of the bone by 100, and dividing by the length. When the index was above 100 the breadth of the sacrum was greater than its length, whilst, when the index was below 100 the sacrum was longer than broad. I propose to employ certain descriptive terms to express these differences in the relations of the length and breadth of this bone. As the Greek word ἱερόν is the equivalent of the Latin sacrum, the term *dolichohieric* would express a sacrum which was longer than broad, whilst *platyhieric* would express a sacrum in which the breadth exceeded the length. The highest index in the series was found in the male Esquimaux, which reached the remarkable number 139, whilst in one of the Negresses the index was as low as 89. But the differences in the sacral index are not to be looked at only as regards their value in the pelvis in individuals, either male or female, but with reference to the question whether in some races of men the sacral index is not as a rule considerably higher than in other races. In the consideration of this question, as in that of the brim index, it is important to bear in mind that sex modifies the relative proportions of the parts, and that in women the sacrum as a rule is broader in proportion to its length than in men.

Amongst Europeans M. Verneau has given, in sixty-three men, the mean length of the sacrum as 105 mm. and the mean breadth at the base as 118 mm., and in thirty-five women the mean length as 101 mm. and the mean breadth as 116 mm. If an index be computed from these figures the males will be found to possess a sacral index of 112·4 and the females one of 114·8. From Görtz's measurements of the length and breadth of the sacrum in European women I have calculated an index of 118·9. Dr. Garson states

101 mm. as the mean length of the sacrum in fourteen European women, and the mean breadth as 118·3, which yield an index of 116·8, slightly higher than that furnished by M. Verneau's measurements, but not so high as those of Görtz. But from Carl Martin's measurements of sixteen pelves, presumably German, the sacral length was 100 mm., the breadth 105 mm., and the index therefore only 105. Weisbach in his essay, already referred to, on the pelvis of the men of the Austrian empire, has given the dimensions of the sacrum. As he measures the breadth of that bone at its base, on the level of the ilio-pectineal line, he does not select that part of the base which has the greatest breadth, and consequently the sacral index computed from his measurements is less than if the widest part of the base had been chosen, wherever it may happen to be. The sacral index in his specimens, on his mode of measurement, is as follows :—Czechs 102·6, Italians 100·9, Ruthenians 100·8, Magyars 99·1, Gipsies 97·3, South Slavs 96·5, Germans 95, Poles 94·9, Roumanians 94·5, Slowaks 90. The index in all these cases is undoubtedly lower than would have been the case if the sacral breadth had been taken in the same way as that which I have employed, so that I have little doubt that the great bulk of these pelves had, according to my mode of measurement, a sacral index above 100.[1] In Europeans, therefore, both males and females, the mean diameter of the base of the sacrum was greater than that of its long axis ; or in other words it was platyhieric.

In the Australians, again, an opposite relation prevails. In only one of the six adult males measured in Table I. was the breadth of the sacrum at the base greater than its length, in two these diameters were equal, and in the remaining three the length exceeded the breadth. The mean sacral index, therefore, of the males was only 98, and in the single adult female this index was only 101. In a male measured by Keferstein the index was 88, in one by Barnard Davis 90, and in five males measured by Spengel it was 111, 106, 97, 89, and 111 respectively. In the single male Australian measured by Verneau the sacral breadth at the base is stated to be 105 mm. and the length only 87 mm.; but the latter diameter is so small for an adult male of this race, that one is disposed to think there must be either some error in the table, or that the sacrum could not have been normal; the index furnished by these measurements, 120, is therefore exceptionally high. The sacral index of a female measured by Barnard Davis was 89, and the mean index computed from the two females measured by Verneau was 105·9, and the mean sacral index of the five women measured by Garson was 114. Excluding, therefore, M. Verneau's male pelvis for the reason given above, it is clear that in the Australian men the breadth of the sacrum was small in relation to its length, so that in a considerable proportion the index did not exceed 100, and the mean of the thirteen males was 98·5, i.e., they were dolichohieric. In the women, again, the sacrum was

[1] I have tested this by the measurement of several pelves, both European and Australian. In the Europeans the greatest width of the sacrum was from 2 to 9 mm. more than the width opposite the iliopectineal lines ; in the Australian pelves the greatest width varied from 5 to 8 mm. more than the width opposite these lines.

relatively broader than long, though it did not attain the proportions reached in the European, for if we take the mean of the nine female pelves measured by B. Davis, Verneau, Garson, and myself, the sacral index was only 102·5.

The proportions of the sacrum have been recorded in two Bushmen by G. Fritsch; in the one the length was 95 mm. and the breadth 91 mm., the sacral index being 95·8, in the other[1] the length was 94 mm. and the breadth 83 mm., the sacral index being 88. These two specimens, conjoined with the sacral index, 98, of the male recorded in my Table VI., give the mean sacral index of three males as 94. Verneau's two Bushwomen had a mean sacral index of 100; Görtz's Bushwoman, Afandy, had a sacrum 87 mm. long and 90 mm. broad, the index being 103; whilst in an adult female recorded by G. Fritsch the sacral length was 97 mm. and the breadth 79 mm., the index being only 81. The mean of these four females was 94·7. There can, I think, be little doubt that it is the rule in the Bush race for the male sacrum to be longer than broad, i.e., dolichohieric. It is not, however, quite so clear as to the relative proportion in the female, for although the mean of the four specimens is only 94·7, yet it will be observed that this low index is due to one of the specimens being only 81.

G. Fritsch has also recorded the sacral length and breadth in the pelves of some Hottentots and Kaffirs from which indices may be computed. In a Hottentot woman the length of the sacrum was 95 mm., its breadth at the base 81 mm., and its index was 85. In one male Korana Hottentot the sacral length was 95 mm., the breadth 90 mm., and the index 94·7; in another the length was 105 mm., the breadth 79 mm., and the index only 75. In Wyman's male Hottentot the sacral index was only 82. In all these specimens, therefore, the length of the sacrum exceeded the breadth, and the mean index of three males was 83·9. In the six male Kaffirs measured by Fritsch the highest sacral index was computed to be 106 and the lowest 82, the mean of the series being 92·8. In the single female the sacral length was 86 mm., the breadth 92 mm., and the index 107. In the male Kaffirs, therefore, the sacrum is as a rule longer than broad, and both in them and in the Hottentots it is dolichohieric.

In all the Negro pelves measured in my Table III. the breadth of the sacrum exceeded the length, and the mean sacral index of the four males was 114; but though in one of the Negresses the sacrum was longer than broad, in the other the relation was reversed, and the mean index in the two specimens was only 99. In one of Spengel's male Negros the sacral index was 114, in the other 97; whilst in a Negro from the Gaboon measured by Barnard Davis it was only 87. If we take, however, the series of twenty-two males described by M. Verneau from Guadeloupe, Mozambique, Nubia, or of unknown locality, the proportions are such as to give a mean sacral index of 97, whilst the seven females either from Guadeloupe or an unknown locality had a mean sacral index 105·5. In the Negress measured by G. Fritsch the sacral length was 93 mm., the breadth 86 mm., and

---

[1] This Bushman pelvis has had some of its characters described by Johannes Müller.

the index 92. The mean of the twenty-nine males measured by Verneau, Spengel, B. Davis, and myself gave a sacral index 106, i.e., they were platyhieric. The mean of the ten females measured by Verneau, Fritsch, and myself was only 98·8 ; so far, therefore, as these specimens show, in the Negro race the sacrum presents the exceptional arrangement of being in the female not so broad in proportion to its length as in the male.

In the only adult male Andaman Islander, as well as in the three adult females in my Table IV., the breadth of the sacrum exceeded the length ; the sacral index of the adult male was 114, that of a young male was 106 ; the mean index of the three adult females was 111 and the index of a young female was 96·5. In the series of eight male Andaman Islanders measured by Professor Flower the mean sacral length was 97·1 mm. and the mean width was 91·3 mm., the index being 94, and in the series of nine females the mean length of this bone was 89·7 mm. and the mean breadth was 95·2 mm., the index being 106. In the single male specimen described by Barnard Davis the sacral breadth was so much less than the length that the index was only 77. It is clear, therefore, that the high sacral index in my male pelvis was an individual peculiarity, and that it is the rule in the male Andaman Islander for the length to exceed the breadth, so that the bone in them is dolichohieric, but in the women it is platyhieric.

In the Negrito skeleton from Luzon in the Dresden Museum the sacral length was 98 mm. and the breadth 107 mm., the index being 109 ; and in the Igorrote pelvis also from Luzon in the same collection, the length was 100 mm. and the breadth 112 mm., with an index of 112. In M. Hamy's Aëta Negrito the sacrum was 76 mm. long, and 93 mm. wide, but it is noted that the diminished length was due to an anomalous form of the 5th vertebra, which was sensibly less than in a normal sacrum ; the sacral index was 122. These skeletons were from women and the index was platyhieric.

In Fritsch's Nikobar Islander the sacral length was 101 mm. and the breadth 90 mm., the index therefore was 89, or dolichohieric.

The three male Tasmanians measured by Barnard Davis had a sacral index respectively of 92, 86, and 114, giving a mean of 97, so that the sacrum was dolichohieric ; but in the single female the index was 104.

Winckel has measured seven sacra in the collection of Papuan bones in the Dresden Museum obtained by A. B. Meyer from Rubi, New Guinea, three of which were regarded as males and four females ; one of the males had six vertebrae in the sacrum, so that I have disregarded its measurements, the other two were in length 99 and 112 mm., and in breadth 100 and 101 mm., the sacral index of these specimens being respectively 101·3 and 89. The females varied in length from 97 to 105 mm.,[1] and in breadth from 92 to 103 mm., the indices being respectively 87·6, 93, 94·8 and 100. In a male New Guinea pelvis recorded by M. Verneau the sacral index was 111·6. The mean sacral index of

---

[1] Winckel says (p. 87), 97 to 112, but from the tables (pp. 80, 90) 105 is the highest measurement recorded of the length of the sacrum.

the above three male pelves was 100, and of the four females 93·8. The females were dolichohieric, and the males slightly platyhieric.

In each of my five female pelves from Oahu, Sandwich Islands, the sacral breadth exceeded the length, and the mean index was 113, and in the Tonga Islander the index was 115. In M. Verneau's two Sandwich Island men the mean sacral index was also 113, and in his male Tongan it was 100. In his male Mangarevan the sacral index was 100·9, and in his Noukahivan it was 99. In Barnard Davis's male Tannese this index was 100. In each of my two male New Zealanders the sacral index was 96, but in the young, probably female, Maori measured by Meyer and Tüngel it was 110. In Verneau's male Loyalty Islander the sacral index was 107·7, and in Barnard Davis's male pelvis it was 103. In Verneau's series of New Caledonians the mean sacral index in the males was 102 and in the females 120. In this series of Pacific Islanders, the mean sacral index of the males was 102, and of the females 114, so that the sacral breadth is as a rule greater than the length, and the proportion of that bone is platyhieric. As has already been pointed out in the chapter on the pelvic brim (p. 40) it is difficult to differentiate which of the specimens are pure Melanesians, or pure Polynesians, or how far they are a mixture of the two races.

In my two male Guanche pelves the mean sacral index was 108·5, and in M. Verneau's male this index was 102. In my male Esquimaux the sacrum had the abnormal index of 139, whilst this index in the female was 106. In my male Laplander the sacral index was 106, in the female 112; but the mean index in M. Verneau's two male Lapps was only 92·6. The number of pelves of the Guanche, Esquimaux, and Laplanders is too small to form an average, but I think it not unlikely it will be found, that in each of these races it is the rule for the sacrum to be broader than long.

Of the natives of India the sacral index of the male Hindoo in Table V. was 109. The dimensions of the sacrum in the tall male Hindoo presented to the museum by Dr. Anderson were—length 110 mm., breadth 122 mm., the index being 111; in the female Hindoo the index was 127. In all therefore the sacrum was platyhieric. In my Sikh the sacral index was 124·5, but in a male Sikh, "Bariam Singh," measured by Barnard Davis this index was only 91. In a male Bhutea, also measured by B. Davis the sacral index was 93·6.

The Chinese measured in Table V. had a sacral index 98. In von Franque's female specimen the length and breadth of the sacrum were equally 111 mm., and the index was therefore 100. In Verneau's female pelvis the sacral index was 120, but in his male, owing to the great length of the sacrum, 134 mm.,[1] this index was only 78. In

---

[1] Verneau states that in the Annamite and male and female Chinese pelves the sacrum consists of six pieces. The Chinese woman, notwithstanding this, has a relatively broad sacrum; but if he has included the sixth piece in his measurements of the Chinese man and of the Annamite the low sacral index is accounted for. It is not unlikely that Spengel's specimen may have had a similar arrangement.

Spengel's male the sacrum had a still greater length, 139 mm., and its breadth was 108 mm., the index being 77·7. In Meyer and Tüngel's male Chinese in the Dresden Museum, the length was 102 mm. and the breadth 106 mm., the index being 104. The mean index in the two females was 110, and in the four males 89·4. Owing to the paucity of the specimens, and the wide diversity in the relative proportions of this bone in the pelves measured, due probably to certain of the specimens possessing six vertebræ in the sacrum, it would be difficult to state, even approximately, the mean sacral index; but from the information at present before one it is possible that in the male Chinese the length of the sacrum may exceed the breadth, though in the two males, in which only five vertebræ were in each bone, the mean index was 101. In Verneau's male Annamite, also, the sacral index was only 87·5, but here also the bone had six vertebræ.

The female Aino in the Barnard Davis collection had a sacral index 91; whilst in the male Aino, measured by Scheube, the length and breadth of this bone were equal at 115 mm. and the sacral index was 100.

In my male Malay the sacral index was 93. In von Franque's female the sacral length was 102 mm. and the breadth 100 mm., the index being therefore 98. In Barnard Davis's two male Javanese the sacral index was respectively 96 and 88, but in Verneau's female, owing to the remarkable shortness of the sacrum, 72 mm., this index rose to 145. Of the twenty-six Javanese female pelves, measured in Zaaijer's Table I., the length of the sacrum exceeded the breadth in eleven specimens, it was less than the breadth in fourteen specimens, and in one these two dimensions were equal. As it is the rule in the female pelvis for the sacrum to be relatively broader than in the male, there can, I think, be little doubt that, in the Malay race, the male sacrum is longer than it is broad, and that this bone is dolichohieric.

Of the North American Indians von Franque gives the length of the sacrum in the male Flathead as 112 mm. and the breadth as 114 mm., the index being 101·8; whilst in the female the length was 107 mm. and the breadth 108 mm., the index being 100·9. In Barnard Davis's male Illinois Indian the sacral index was 115·8, and in Verneau's female Mexican it was 108. Probably, therefore, in the North American aborigines the average breadth of the sacrum is more than the average length.

The dimensions of the sacrum have been recorded in a few more specimens of South than of North American Indians. In a male Puelche measured by Barnard Davis the sacral index was 95·8, and in a male ancient Peruvian it was 92. From Verneau's table of sacral measurements I have computed the sacral index in a male Charruan at 108, in a male Botocudon 117, in a male Bolivian 93, the mean of two male Peruvians 128, in a male Goytacazen 119; whilst the mean of three female Peruvians was 121·7, and in a female Goytacazen it was 110·5. Of the eight males three had a sacral index below 100, but the others were so much above 100 that the mean sacral index of the series was 107·5, and the mean of the four females was 116. The measurements recorded by

J. G. Garson of four male Yahgans from Tierra del Fuego gave a mean sacral length 103·2 mm., and a mean sacral breadth 112·2 mm., the mean sacral index being 109, and in each specimen this index was above 100. In the South American Indians, therefore, I have little doubt that the mean breadth of the sacrum exceeds the mean length, so that the aborigines both in the north and south of that continent, as well as the Fuegian Islanders, are platyhieric.

From this analysis of my own measurements and of those of other anatomists it is clear that the proportion of the length to the breadth of the sacrum varies in different races of mankind. In some it is the rule to find it longer than broad, in others broader than long. Although additional observations are still greatly needed, especially on some of the races, yet it seems possible to make a provisional arrangement of the races of men into two groups, according as the sacral index is below or above 100, and in Table IX., as in the preceding one based on the index of the pelvic brim, the proportions are estimated on the measurements in the male sex.

A comparison of Table VIII., framed on the index of the pelvic brim (p. 45), with Table IX. will show that in many instances a dolichopellic brim is conjoined with a dolichohieric sacrum. For example, this is the case in the Australians, Bushmen, Kaffirs, Andaman Islanders, Aïnos, and Malays. Again, a platypellic brim is conjoined with a platyhieric sacrum, as in the Europeans, American Indians, and probably the Guanches, Lapps, and the Esquimaux. The pelves which I have arranged in the mesatipellic, or

TABLE IX.

DOLICHOHIERIC. *Sacral Index below* 100.	PLATYHIERIC. *Sacral Index above* 100.
Australians	Europeans
Bushmen	Negros
Hottentots	Melanesians ?
Kaffirs	Polynesians ?
Andaman Islanders	Hindoos
Tasmanians	Guanches ?
Malays	Esquimaux ?
Chinese ?	Lapps ?
Aïno ?	North American Indians
...	South American Indians
...	Fuegians

intermediate division, partly belong, as regards the proportions of the sacrum, as in the Negros, to the platyhieric group, and partly, as in the Tasmanians, to the dolichohieric group. As the width of the pelvic brim is materially influenced by the breadth of the sacrum, it was only to be expected that a platypellic pelvis would have a relatively wide sacrum, and that a dolichopellic pelvis would have a relatively narrow sacrum. There are three races which have an anomalous position in these two tables, viz., the Chinese, the Melanesians, and the Polynesians. The Chinese with a platypellic brim, it will be observed, are placed with pelves in which the sacrum is longer than broad. The position, however, which the Chinese occupy in Table IX., can only be regarded as provisional, and when a larger series is examined, on the basis of only five sacral vertebræ being measured, it is not unlikely that their position in the table of sacral proportions will have to be altered. The position of the Melanesians and Polynesians in Table VIII. is also provisional, as a wider series of observations may require them to be transferred to another column in that table.

In connection with the relative dimensions of the conjugate and transverse diameters of the pelvic brim, and those of the length and breadth of the sacrum in the different races of men, a few words may appropriately be written on the corresponding relations in the pelvis in other mammals, at least in those which possess five vertebræ in the sacrum. In the Anthropoid Apes the length of the sacrum is considerably greater than its breadth. In two orangs, which I have measured, the mean sacral index was 87; in two chimpanzees the mean was 77, in a gorilla the index was 72, and in a gibbon 89. In an ox the sacral index was 87, and in a camel it was 89. In all these mammals the sacrum is hyperdolichohieric. The mean index of the pelvic brim in two chimpanzees was 133, and in two orangs 126; whilst in a single gorilla the index was 144, and in a gibbon 151. In an ox the pelvic index was 110, and in a camel it was 110·8. In these animals the conjugate diameter of the pelvic brim was materially greater than the transverse, i.e., the index was hyperdolichopellic. When a human pelvis therefore is dolichopellic, and also dolichohieric, it corresponds in these characters with the more usual type of mammalian pelvis; and, as compared with the relations of parts met with in the Europeans, it possesses a degraded or animalised arrangement.

In the Australian from Perth the first coccygeal vertebra, and in that from Manly Cove the entire coccyx, was fused with the sacrum.[1] In the Bush pelvis two coccygeal vertebræ were fused with the sacrum, the anterior concavity of which was also slight. In the Sikh, one of the female Andaman Islanders, a Sandwich Island woman, the Guanche pelves, and the female Laplander, the first coccygeal vertebra was fused with the sacrum. In none of the Australian pelves did the sacrum possess more than a slight concavity anteriorly. As a rule, indeed, the whole series of sacra belonging to the pelves measured in the tables had a gentle anterior concavity, without much depth, but in the male Esquimaux the lowest two sacral vertebræ were more abruptly bent forward on the third sacral, so that the bone had a deep concavity in front. The change in the direction of

[1] To avoid any misunderstanding as regards my measurements of the length of the sacrum, I wish to state that when one or more coccygeal vertebræ were fused with the sacrum they were not included in the length of that bone.

the sacrum which produced the anterior concavity was usually in the body of the 3rd or 4th sacral, or in the plane of their junction, but more commonly in the 3rd vertebra. In two Sandwich and in two Andaman Islanders, however, the bend took place in the 2nd sacral vertebra. That the anterior concavity of the sacrum is slighter in the black races than in Europeans has been recognised by previous observers. Sir Richard Owen referred to it in his comparison of the spine of a European with those of a Negro and Australian.[1] M. Bacarisse had directed attention to it in his work on the sacrum,[2] and M. Hamy has spoken of it in his description of the skeleton of a Negrito woman.[3]

3. Minor Peculiarities in the Pelves.

I may now refer to some minor points in the anatomy of these pelves. The late Professor Kilian of Bonn, in an essay entitled Das Stachelbecken (pelvis spinosa, Akanthopelys),[4] described a condition of the pelvis occasionally occurring in European women, in which the ilio-pectineal line was raised into a knife-like edge, or had a distinct pointed process projecting from it. I examined my series of pelves with reference to this condition and found a sharp pectineal spinous process projecting upwards in a Sandwich Island woman, in a female Andaman Islander, and in a male Laplander. A similar projection, but blunted at the apex, was present in the Manly Cove and Riverina Australians, in the Sikh, and in a Negress; whilst a sharp pectineal line occurred in the Queensland Australian, a Negro, a male Hindoo, a female Andaman Islander, and one of the Guanche pelves. The pectineal spinous process projected from the ilio-pectineal line immediately internal to the pectineal eminence. In its position this process corresponded with the pectineal tubercle present in the pelves of Marsupials and Monotremes.

Professor Zaaijer, in his memoir on the pelvis in the women of Java, already so frequently referred to, has called attention (p. 28) to a sulcus situated immediately anterior to the auricular surface of the ilium for articulation with the sacrum, which he has named *sulcus præauricularis*. It was present in twenty-three of his specimens and was wanting only in three, but it varied both in breadth and depth. On examining forty-one European iliac bones he found it present but not strongly developed in seven specimens, just indicated in four bones, and entirely wanting in thirty specimens. He considers that it is associated with the attachment of the anterior sacro-iliac ligaments. In my series of pelves I find it present in most of the Australian pelves, in the Bush, Sandwich Islanders, one of the New Zealanders, a Negro, Hindoo, Chinese, Malay, in the Andaman Islanders, Guanche, Laplanders, and Esquimaux. I have also seen it in several

---

[1] *Trans. Zool. Soc. Lond.*, vol. iv. p. 113.
[2] I regret that I have been unable to obtain a copy of M. Bacarisse's thesis on the sacrum; my knowledge of it is therefore solely derived from references in the writings of other anthropologists.
[3] Étude sur un Squelette d'Aeta; *Nouvelles Archives du Muséum*, ser. 2, t. ii., Paris, 1879.
[4] Schilderung neuer Beckenform, Mannheim, 1854.

European pelves, without being able, however, to state its relative frequency. It varied in its distinctness in different pelves; sometimes it was a narrow, shallow, vertical groove, so faint as to be just recognisable, in others the groove had considerable depth; sometimes it was widened out into a shallow fossa, but in others the fossa was deep. The most distinct examples of the sulcus præauricularis were found in the pelves of the Sandwich Island women. From its presence in so many races it cannot be regarded as a special character of any particular race.

Comparative views of the pelvis in various races of men have been figured by Vrolik, Weber, von Franque, G. Fritsch, and Verneau, but it has not been the custom to represent the different specimens figured according to a uniform plan, so that it is difficult to compare the figures of one observer with those of another. It would be very desirable therefore to establish some uniform method of representing the pelvis, so that, in the absence of the specimens themselves, a comparison may be instituted between the published figures of this part of the skeleton. The most natural position in which to place the pelvis for purposes of illustration would obviously be that which it occupies in the erect position of the human body. Professor G. H. Meyer, of Zurich, who has carefully inquired into this matter,[1] states that, in the erect attitude, the anterior superior spines of the ilium, along with the spines of the pubic bones, lie in the same vertical plane. This view of the normal position of the pelvis in the erect attitude has been confirmed by Dr. Prochownick of Hamburg, who has controlled it by measurements on living persons. Although it is possible that these spines may possess individual variations, as regards the vertical plane, within certain limits amongst Europeans, or between Europeans and other races, yet it is obviously an advantage to have in the illustrations of the pelvis a certain fixed standard of comparison.

The series of figures of the pelvis which illustrate this Report (Plates I., II., III.) have therefore all been made from pelves which have been so placed that both the pubic and antero-superior iliac spines were in the same vertical plane. The drawings are all strictly comparable with each other, and an inspection of them will show not only the modifications in the inclination of the ilium and in the form of the pelvic brim but some other differences. The cotyloid cavity, for example, varies in its inclination. As a rule it is directed outwards and concealed by the os pubis, but in the pelvis of the Andaman Islander, the Esquimaux, Guanche, Laplander, and Bushman it partly appears from under cover of the pubis, and in the Sandwich Island woman it comes very considerably into view. The direction of the pubic arch also is not uniform. In the male Australian, Negro, Sikh, and Andaman Islander, for example, the rami are in this position —that of the erect attitude—so directed backwards, that but little of the arch is visible; whilst in the female Sandwich Islander, the male Malay, and Esquimaux the arch approaches nearer to the vertical and is much more seen. Differences in the direction

[1] Lehrbuch der Physiologischen Anatomie des Menschen, p. 119, Leipzic, 1856.

and inclination of the sacrum in certain of the pelves are also well marked. Compare for example, the pelvis of the Scotsman with that of the Australian, and the pelvis of the Sikh with that of the Malay. It will also be noticed that the apex of the sacrum is on a much higher plane, as regards the upper border of the pubic symphisis, in certain pelves than in others; compare, e.g., the Scotsman and Sikh with the Oahuan. I direct attention to these various points so that those who may have additional specimens for examination may test in how far they are racial, or only individual characters.

4. Age Characters of Pelvis.

Various anatomists have pointed out that when the pelvis of the new-born infant, or the child, is compared with that of the adult of either sex, important differences in the form and proportions of the pelvic brim can be seen. In the child the lateral boundary of the brim is not so concave relatively to the rest as in the adult, the opposite sides are more nearly parallel to each other, and the transverse diameter is proportionally less than the conjugate. From the observations of Litzmann on the pelvis in European children it would appear that, up to the age of thirteen, the transverse diameter of the brim very slightly exceeds, and indeed is occasionally less than the conjugate, but after that age it is constantly greater. He has given the following comparative statement of the differences in the proportions in the new-born infant and adult in the two sexes, the conjugate diameter being regarded as equal to 1·00; transverse diameter in male infant 1·11, in male adult 1·294; transverse diameter in female infant 1·07, in adult 1·292. Differences also occur at the base of the sacrum, in which bone the wings grow proportionally more than the body of the bone. Litzmann states that whilst in the new-born child the wings of the 1st sacral vertebra are scarcely half as broad as its body (male 0·45 to 1, female 0·46 to 1); in a man the mean proportion is 0·56 to 1; in a woman 0·76 to 1. During growth the body of this vertebra increases not quite three times in width, whilst the wings in a woman increase nearly five times, and in a man three and a half times. The sacrum in the adult has its base projected further forward than in the child, and its anterior surface is more concave, the beginning of the curvature being usually in the middle of the 3rd vertebra.

In the skeletons of the coloured races described in this Report I have estimated the proportion of the breadth of the body of the 1st sacral vertebra to the greatest breadth of that bone. The mean breadth of the sacrum in the six male Australians was 103·6 mm., and the mean breadth of the body of the 1st sacral vertebra was 49 mm., so that the latter had to the former the proportion of 47·2 to 100. In the single female the proportion was remarkably small, being only 37 to 100. In the five Sandwich Island women the mean breadth of the sacrum was 112·6, and that of the body of the 1st sacral vertebra 51·4, the proportion between the two being 45·6 to 100. In the Tonga Islander the proportion was 40·5 to 100, and the mean of two Maoris was 48 to 100. In the Negros the proportion was 45·4 to 100, and in the Negresses 49 to 100. In the adult male Andaman Islander the proportion was 40·6 to 100, and the mean in the females was the same. In the male Bush the proportion was 53 to 100. The mean proportion in two male Hindoos was 45·6, and in a single female 43·6 to 100. In the Sikh it was 47·9, in the Malay 47, and in the Chinese 53·7 to 100. In the male Guanche the proportion was 44, and in the female 40·5 ; in the male Esquimaux 49, and in the female 38·8 ; in the male Lapp 54·9, and in the female 48 to 100. In not a single skeleton did the proportion of the breadth of the body of the 1st sacral vertebra to the entire breadth equal the mean proportion in the Europeans as given by Litzmann, and in the majority of cases fell much below it.

The changes in the form and proportions of the pelvis during its growth have been ascribed to various forces acting upon the bones when in a comparatively flexible and plastic condition, e.g., the downward pressure of the weight of the trunk on the sacrum, the pressure of the heads of the femora on the cotyloid cavities when the body is standing erect, the action of the muscles attached to the bones, and the pressure on the pelvic walls of the viscera which are developed in the pelvic cavity. Of these forces the first two are without doubt those which operate most efficiently. It would be out of place to discuss in this Report their mode of operation as two opposing forces, and the more so as the argument has been stated with great clearness and force by Dr. J. Matthews Duncan in his Researches in Obstetrics.[1] I would merely add as corroborative of his statement that the heads of the thigh bones exercise an inward and upward pressure on the walls of the pelvis in the region of the acetabula, that in a number of pelves, both European and exotic, I have seen a distinct bulging of the pelvic wall towards the cavity immediately internal to the acetabula, so that the transverse diameter of the cavity at this spot is diminished by several millimètres.

In the adult pelvis the greatest transverse diameter of the inlet is at a point between the anterior border of the base of the sacrum and a vertical transverse plane through the middle of the acetabula, but somewhat nearer the sacrum than the acetabula. If my tables of measurements of the various pelves be examined, it will be seen that the transverse diameter of the brim exceeded the greatest breadth of the base of the sacrum in the great majority of the specimens. Sometimes, however, in a male pelvis the sacral breadth was more than that of the transverse diameter of the inlet. This was the case in one Australian, two Negros, a young Andaman Islander, and one Bushman. In a male Hindoo the two dimensions were equal.

In all my adult pelves in which the conjugate diameter exceeded, or was almost the same as the transverse, i.e., in the dolichopellic and mesatipellic series, the pelvic inlet approximated more closely to the infantile form than was the case in the platypellic series ; and in such black races as the Australians and the Bush, the pelvic inlet was

[1] Edinburgh, 1868. See especially his chapter on the Development of the Pelvis.

more child-like than in the Europeans. This lack of proportional expansion in the transverse diameter was more strongly shown in the men than in the women; so that in the passage of the pelvis from the infantile to the adult stage of growth an opposite condition prevails to that presented by the skull, in which the man departs more widely from the infantile condition than does the woman.

But, as has been previously stated (p. 53), a pelvis with a conjugate diameter relatively long when compared with the transverse has a more animal form than one in which the opposite condition exists. In a quadruped the downward pressure exercised by the weight of the trunk on the sacrum is necessarily not of the same intensity as in the biped; though in the quadruped the upward pressure of the hind limbs, acting as pillars of support against the side walls of the pelvis in the region of the acetabula, must exercise an influence, in controlling the expansion of the pelvis in the transverse diameter, during its growth and when flexible and plastic. In the Anthropoid Apes also, in which the position of the body is intermediate between the quadruped and the erect attitude of man, the pressure of the weight of the trunk on the sacrum would, when the animal is standing, be diminished owing to the upper limbs being so frequently used as organs of support and progression.

The question therefore arises, is there anything in the habits and mode of life of the black races in their aboriginal state, which, by operating during childhood, could modify the vertical pressure of the weight of the trunk, and thus diminish the effect of one of the chief forces concerned in increasing the transverse diameter of the pelvic brim. It may be difficult to answer this question, but I would suggest the following as a not improbable explanation. A favourite attitude of many savages is that of "squatting," i.e., with the ankles, knees and hip-joints acutely flexed, with the trunk bent forward, with the back of the thigh supported by the calf of the leg, or with the nates resting on the heels.[1] In this position the arms are conveniently supported on the knees in front of the thighs. The aboriginal Australian does not "squat," but sits directly on the ground, bending his trunk forwards and embracing his knees with his arms. The trunk so long as this position is maintained would have a portion of its weight supported by the upper limbs, and the pressure on the sacrum and pelvis would be diminished so as to approximate the conditions somewhat to those of the Anthropoid Apes. But further, the savage when in pursuit of game often assumes a stooping or crouching attitude, in which the trunk is bent forward and its weight is directed obliquely backwards and downwards on to the base of the sacrum. Hence, both when at rest and when in active movement, his spine is made to bend forward, and its axis is not retained so much in the vertical position as in the white man, who, whether sitting, standing, or walking, erects the axis of his spine upon the pelvis.

[1] In Scotland and the north of England this attitude is designated by the expression "to sit on his hunkers." It is a favourite attitude with miners, and is named by them "hunkering down," and they are able to remain in it for a considerable length of time without fatigue.

SPINAL COLUMN.

In the chapter on the pelvis I have described the characters of the sacrum in forty specimens. In thirty of the skeletons tabulated in that chapter, the portion of the spine formed by the movable vertebræ was, with few exceptions, complete, so that I have been enabled to examine the vertebræ in the cervical, dorsal and lumbar regions, with the view of ascertaining if they presented any peculiarities either in form, arrangement, or manner of development. I shall now summarize the results of this examination.

Peculiarities of Individual Vertebræ.

The cervical region was to a large extent free from variations from the recognised arrangements based on the study of the skeletons of Europeans as described in the text books, but occasional departures from the usual description were met with. To these I shall now refer. In the Otago skeleton, the Chinese, two Hindoos, two Negros and two Andaman Islanders, the spine of the 6th cervical approximated in length to that of the 7th, and like it was not bifid. In the female Hindoo it was not bifid, but had no unusual length; in the female Lapp it was rudimentary and not bifid. In the Bushman the spines of the 3d, 6th, and 7th cervicals were not bifid, those of the 3d and 6th were short and stunted, that of the 7th as usual prominent. In a Negress only the spine of the axis was bifid and in a Negro the 3d, 4th, and 7th cervical spines were not bifid. In one of the Oahuan skeletons the 7th cervical spine was bifid. That in the lower races of men a tendency exists for the spines of the cervical vertebra to be more simple than in Europeans was recognised by Sir Richard Owen, who refers to the non-bifid character of the five lower spines in the skeletons of a Bushman and an Australian.[1] M. Hamy, in his memoir on the skeleton of a Negrito, states [2] that the spine was not bifid in the 6th cervical in some skeletons of the Oceanic and African black races, and that in an Australian a similar condition was met with as high as the 4th cervical: moreover, the skeletons of a Bushwoman, a Hottentot, and a Negress had only the spine of the axis bifid, and in the Aëta Negrito an almost similar arrangement was present.[3] The lengthening of the spine of the 6th cervical in many skeletons of the lower races of men has not had much attention given to it, though Owen states that in an Australian the 6th cervical spine was of greater length than the 5th.

In the Sikh skeleton the right vertebral groove on the atlas was bridged over by a bar of bone, and in two Hindoos and a Negress this groove was deepened by a pro-

---

[1] See his Memoir on the Vertebral Column of *Troglodytes* and *Pithecus*, in *Trans. Zool. Soc. Lond.*, vol. iv.
[2] *Nouv. Archives du Muséum*, ser. 2, tom. ii. 1879.
[3] Since this Report was in type Dr. D. J. Cunningham has published (*Journ. of Anat. and Phys.*, July 1886), observations on the comparative frequency of want of bifidity in the cervical spines in different races of men.

jection from the superior articular process. In an Australian the axis and 3d cervical were conjoined, also the 6th and 7th. In another Australian the left anterior transverse process of the 5th cervical gave off a descending process which articulated with the anterior transverse process of the 6th cervical. In the female Lapp the left half of the neural arch of the atlas was imperfect, owing to a defect in the ossification of the lamina. No skeleton possessed a movable cervical rib.

The dorsal region was, amongst other points, examined with reference to the costal articulations on the sides of the bodies of the vertebræ. In five Australians, two Hindoos, two Negresses, three Andaman Islanders, two Oahuans, two Esquimaux, a Malay, a Negro, a female Lapp, and the right side of the Sikh, the 12th, 11th, and 10th dorsal vertebræ articulated laterally, each with the head of only one rib, the facet on the 10th vertebra being for the lower part of the head of the 10th rib, the upper part of which articulated with the 9th vertebra. In two Negros, a Bush, a Maori, a Chinese, a Hindoo, an Andaman Islander, a male Lapp, and the left side of the Sikh, the 9th, 10th, 11th, and 12th dorsals articulated laterally, each with the head of only one rib; the facet on the 9th vertebra being for the lower part of the head of the corresponding rib, the upper part of which articulated with the 8th vertebra. In one Australian skeleton, only the 10th and 11th vertebræ had a single costal facet on each side, and the vertebra which represented the 12th, although with rudimentary transverse processes, had no costal facet on either side. In the great majority of the skeletons the inferior costal facet on the side of the body in the upper and middle series of dorsal vertebræ was raised from the general surface of the body as a *costal process*, but the superior facet was more in the general plane of the side of the body of the vertebra. In several skeletons, more especially the Australians, the transverse process of the 10th dorsal had no articular facet for the tubercle of the rib.

The mammillary processes were present in the 12th dorsal vertebra of each skeleton, and in many of the specimens these processes were larger than is the rule in Europeans, though sometimes one finds them very distinct in a European skeleton. In several Australians, the Maori, Chinese, Sikh, a Hindoo, Negro, Andaman Islander and Oahuan they were also distinct in the 11th dorsal, and in the Maori skeleton they could be seen as high as the 9th dorsal. Accessory processes were also recognised in many of the skeletons on both the 11th and 12th dorsals.

In three skeletons, viz., two Australians and an Esquimaux, an additional vertebra was interposed at the junction of the dorsal and lumbar regions. In the Eucla Australian it had a small articular facet on the side of each pedicle, obviously for the head of a rudimentary 13th rib. Its transverse processes were stunted as in the 12th dorsal, and there was on each side a large mammillary and a rudimentary accessory process. Its spinous process was shaped like the spine of a lumbar vertebra, and whilst its superior articular processes were shaped like those of a dorsal, its inferior pair were after the pattern of a lumbar vertebra. In the West Victoria Australian skeleton the supernumerary vertebra had a small articular facet on the side of the right pedicle, for the head of a supplementary rib, but none on the left side. The transverse processes were stunted as in the 12th dorsal, and there was a distinct mammillary process. The spinous process was like that of the 12th dorsal but somewhat larger; both the upper and lower articular processes were like those of a lumbar vertebra. In the female Esquimaux the additional vertebra had a relatively large facet for the head of a rib on the left pedicle, and a smaller facet on the right pedicle. The transverse processes were stunted, and there were large mammillary and rudimentary accessory tubercles. The spine was transitional in shape

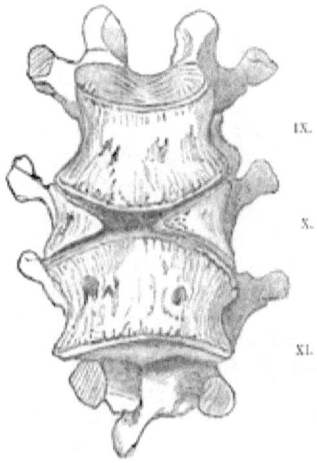

FIG. 1.—Anterior surface of the bodies of the 9th, 10th and 11th dorsal vertebræ of a Maori skeleton, to show the imperfect development of the body of the 10th dorsal.

between those of the 12th dorsal and 1st lumbar; the superior and inferior articular processes had the lumbar character.

A most remarkable anomaly in the development of the dorsal vertebræ occurred in the Maori skeleton from Otago (fig. 1). The 10th dorsal vertebra showed a great defect in the ossification of the body, which was divided by a mesial cleft into two lateral parts, the right of which was somewhat bigger than the left. The cleft passed from the anterior surface through the body to the spinal canal, also from the upper to the lower surface, and was 18 mm. wide in front and only 2 mm. wide behind. Each part of the body consisted of a wedge-shaped bar of bone, sloping both from without inwards and from above downwards, the apex of the wedge being anterior. The wedge was continuous by its base with the pedicle of its own side, and was marked laterally by the articular facet for the head of the 10th rib. The bodies of the 9th and 11th dorsals had a greater vertical diameter in front than is usual, so as partially to occupy the cleft between the separated parts of the body of the 10th, but the rest of the interval had doubtless been occupied in the recent spine by intervertebral disc. Owing to this defect in the body of the 10th dorsal vertebra it is probable that a slight posterior or angular curvature had been present during life in the lower dorsal region.

There can of course be no doubt that in the 10th dorsal vertebra of this skeleton each of the two parts of its body had developed from a distinct lateral ossific nucleus instead of from a mesial nucleus, according to the normal arrangement; and the lateral centres must have been separated by a considerable interval in the foetal spine, so as to allow of the relatively wide gap between the two wedge-shaped parts of the bone. It is possible that in the foetal cartilaginous spine the cartilage also may have been divided into two lateral parts not united mesially. This remarkable anomaly in the ossification of a vertebra is very rare, but the case is not unique. Rokitansky has described[1] the 12th dorsal vertebra in a woman, age 55, as divided into two triangular rudiments, inserted laterally between the 11th dorsal and 1st lumbar vertebra, with their points directed inwards, and in consequence of the mesial defect in the body of this vertebra the column was bent backward at a very obtuse angle. Humphry saw in a specimen of spina bifida in the Berlin Museum[2] several of the vertebral bodies consisting of two halves with an opening between the two. Ahlfeld also refers[3] to a case observed by Ammon, in which the bodies of the 12th dorsal and 1st and 2nd lumbars consisted of two lateral halves. An approximation to this condition existed also in the vertebral columns described by Sandifort,[4] Otto,[5] and Rokitansky,[6] in which only one lateral half of a particular vertebra was developed; in both Sandifort's and Otto's cases the half of the vertebral body which was present is described as wedge-shaped.

The lumbar vertebræ had, as a rule, well-marked mammillary processes, but those on the 5th lumbar were not, for the most part, so large as on the four others. Accessory processes were usually present, but their relative size varied in the different skeletons. In the Malay, a Hindoo, and a Lapp, they were strongest in the 1st lumbar; in an Australian, Hindoo, Oahuan, and two Andaman Islanders, they were best marked in the 3rd lumbar, in a Negro in the 4th lumbar. In some of the skeletons the four upper lumbars, in others only the three upper had them distinctly marked. The size of both the mammillary and accessory processes is, without doubt, correlated with the development of those deep muscles of the back which are attached to them.

---

[1] Pathological Anatomy, Syd. Soc. Trans., vol. iii. p. 232.
[2] Die Missbildungen des Menschen, p. 296, 1882.
[3] Seltene Beobachtungen, zweite Sammlung, § 15.
[4] Human Skeleton, p. 124.
[5] Museum anatomicum, vol. iv. p. 74, Tab. clxxviii. fig. 2.
[6] Op. cit., p. 231.

The transverse processes of the 1st lumbar vertebra were short and rudimentary in an Australian, a Sandwich Islander, and the Malay. These processes were relatively short in the four upper lumbar vertebræ of the Chinese. In the spine of the Sikh these processes in the 3rd lumbar were very long. In one of the Andaman Islanders and two Australians one or both transverse processes of the 5th lumbar articulated with the base of the sacrum. In another Andaman Islander the inferior articular process of the last lumbar was prolonged outwards, especially on the right side, so as almost to reach the transverse process.

In the Queensland skeleton the body of the 5th lumbar had been modified in its development, though not to the same extent as the 10th dorsal vertebra in the Maori skeleton from Otago (fig. 1). Its anterior, upper, and lower surfaces were grooved a little to the left side of the mesial plane, so as to give the appearance of a division of the body into a right and left lateral wedge-shaped portion, of which the right was the larger. These divisions had, however, fused together, so that they were not separated by a mesial cleft; the body had thus the appearance of having been developed from two originally distinct lateral centres, which had subsequently fused together.

Imperfections in the development of the neural arch of the 5th lumbar vertebra were not unfrequent. In a male Andaman Islander, and in the Chinese, the right and left halves of the lumbar spine had not united mesially. In five skeletons the part of the neural arch which formed the two laminæ, the spine and the inferior pair of articular

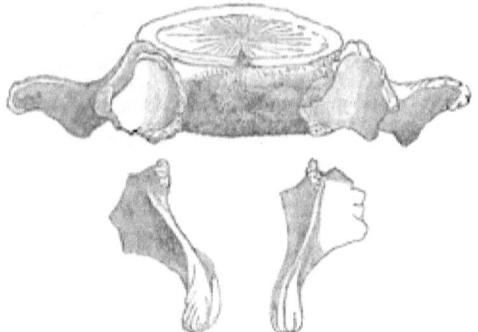

FIG. 2.—Fifth lumbar vertebra from a Malay skeleton, showing the divided condition of the laminar part of the arch.

processes, had been developed independently of the part of the arch which formed the two peduncles, the transverse processes and the superior pair of articular processes. This irregular development was seen in its most pronounced form in the Malay skeleton, in which not only the lamina and inferior articular process on each side formed a plate of bone quite separate from the peduncle, transverse process, and superior articular process; but the two laminæ, not united mesially and posteriorly into a single spine, were separated from each other by a mesial cleft (fig. 2). In both the Bushman and the male Esquimaux the laminæ had united posteriorly into a mesial spine, but they and the inferior articular processes were not fused with the pedicles, so that the posterior part of the neural arch formed a separate piece of bone. The very imperfect spine of a Sandwich Islander, recently presented by Dr. G. W. Parker of Waiahia, Oahu, which is not included in the preceding thirty skeletons, exhibited a defect in the neural arch of the 5th lumbar, similar to that seen in the Bushman and Esquimaux. In one of the Negro skeletons the right half of the neural arch was normal, but the left lamina, with its inferior articular process, had remained distinct and separate from the spine, as well as from the pedicle of its own side. These five specimens show that the laminar part of the neural arch had arisen in them from a pair of ossific centres, quite distinct from the centres from which the pedicles took their origin; and that whilst the inferior articular processes belonged to the laminar part, the superior belonged to the peduncular part of the vertebra. As this condition was only seen in the 5th lumbar vertebra the question naturally arises, does the neural arch of this bone on each side normally develop from two ossific centres, laminar and pedicular, which subsequently fuse with each other, though in these five skeletons they had remained distinct; whilst in the other four lumbar vertebræ only a single pair of ossific centres are formed for the production of both the peduncular and laminar part of the arch. It is known, for instance, that the anterior division of the transverse process (parapophysis) in the 7th cervical vertebra is developed from a distinct centre, which may sometimes acquire the form and dimensions of a cervical rib, whilst the parapophysis in each of the other six cervical vertebræ arises by an extension into its cartilage of ossific material derived from the primary centres of ossification of the bone, so that this process in the cervical series does not develop uniformly in all the vertebræ. It is possible that the neural arch of the 5th lumbar vertebra may normally develop on a different plan from that of the other lumbars, so as to permit of such a separation of the laminar part of the arch as was found in these specimens. The development of the neural arch in this bone is worthy, therefore, of special investigation by the embryologist.

In the General Summary of the characters of the aboriginal Crania described in the First Part of this Report, I pointed out (p. 118) that a larger proportion of important variations from the usually described arrangements occurred in them than would have been found in a corresponding number of the skulls of the white races. With equal truth a similar remark may be made on the variations in the Spinal Column which I have just described. I am not able to state, numerically, the proportion in the white races in which variations in the form of the spinous processes of the cervical vertebræ, the occurrence of a supernumerary vertebra in the dorsi-lumbar region, or the development of the laminar part of the neural arch independently of the pedicular part occurs, for observations on a sufficiently large number of specimens have not yet been systematically conducted. But this may without doubt be affirmed, that in a series of spinal columns from white races equal in number to those analysed in this chapter, and like them taken without selection, there would not have been found so large a proportion in which the 6th cervical spine was not bifid and nearly equal in length to the spine of the 7th cervical; or three skeletons with a supernumerary dorsal vertebra; or seven specimens of irregularity in the development of the neural arch of the 5th lumbar vertebra.

The Lumbar Curve of the Spinal Column.

In the course of the investigations into the characters of the skeletons described in this Report, I have measured the bodies of the lumbar vertebræ with the view of ascertaining if modifications existed in their vertical diameter, anteriorly and posteriorly, which might affect the lumbar curve of the spine.

Anatomists are in the habit of teaching that the human spine is convex forward in the lumbar region, so that a lumbar convexity is interposed between the thoracic and sacral concavities, and contributes to the alternating series of concavo-convex curves of the spinal column, which are associated with the erect attitude of man. My belief in the universality of the view that the lumbar vertebræ themselves invariably produce a forward convexity in that region was disturbed some years ago, when Charles Robertson, Esq., of the Oxford Museum, showed me the skeleton of an aboriginal Australian in that museum, which he had articulated in 1873. Mr. Robertson told me that the skeleton was that of an adult male of the Tomki tribe of the Richmond River, N.S.W. In it there was a continuous curve, concave forwards through both thoracic and lumbar regions. As the skeleton was, however, artificially articulated, the question naturally arose in one's mind if this modification in the lumbar curve might not have been produced by some peculiarity in the method of articulation, and was not therefore natural to the spine. Since I saw this skeleton, however, Mr. Robertson has written to tell me of another adult male from Port Augusta, South Australia, articulated in 1878 with great care and with especial attention to the lumbar curve, which exhibited a similar concavity in the lumbar region, and that the articulated skeletons of a Gilbert Islander and a male Andaman Islander have a similar lumbar concavity, though not so well marked. Before I had heard, however, of these later specimens in the Oxford Museum, I had examined the lumbar vertebræ in the series of spines at my disposal in Edinburgh, and had obtained some interesting results.

Two important factors contribute to the curve in the lumbar region, viz., the vertebral bodies and the intervertebral discs. The exact share contributed by each of these parts can only be ascertained with precision by applying to the vertebral column in the different races of men the method of observation which Professor D. J. Cunningham of Trinity College, Dublin, has employed in the study of the spine in the Irish race, viz., the making of longitudinal mesial sections through the long axis of the spine in frozen bodies, and then carefully measuring the relative thickness both of the vertebral bodies and the discs. In the absence, however, of the fresh bodies of Australians and other Aborigines, I have been precluded from obtaining any information on the thickness of the discs, and have been restricted to the examination of the vertebræ themselves, so far as they have been preserved in the skeletons which have reached me. I have measured, therefore, the vertical diameter of the body of each lumbar vertebra, both in front and behind, and have noted the difference in each vertebra, and in the series of lumbar vertebræ in each spine.[1]

In order to obtain some data for comparison, I measured the lumbar vertebræ in twelve adult European spinal columns, the great majority of which were males, and found that the vertical diameter of the anterior surface of the bodies of the five vertebræ in each spine was collectively greater than the vertical diameter of the posterior surfaces in the same spine. The maximum difference between the collective depth of these surfaces in the series of five vertebræ was 11 mm. in one skeleton, and the minimum difference was 1 mm. in another skeleton. The mean collective depth of the five vertebral bodies in the twelve European skeletons was 137 mm. for the anterior, and 131·4 for the posterior surface, the mean difference therefore was 5·6 mm. in favour of the anterior surface. If we were to assume that in these spines each intervertebral disc had been of equal thickness throughout, then the greater thickness of the vertical diameter of the bodies in front than behind in each spine would have given a slight convexity forwards to the spinal column in the lumbar region. But we know that these differences in the vertical diameter in the lumbar region of Europeans are not limited to the vertebral bodies, and that some of the discs also are thicker anteriorly than posteriorly, so that the anterior convexity would therefore by their interposition be increased.

In the individual lumbar vertebræ in each of these European spinal columns, with only two exceptions, the body of the 1st lumbar vertebra was deeper behind than in front, in one instance 6 mm., in another 4 mm., but usually not more than 1 or 2 mm.; in the exceptional cases the anterior and posterior vertical diameters were equal. The body of the 2nd lumbar was deeper behind than in front in six spines; they were equal in depth in four spines, and the anterior surface was deeper than the posterior in two spines. The body of the 3rd lumbar was deeper in front than behind in ten spines, and in two they were equal. The body of the 4th lumbar was deeper in front than behind in eleven spines, and deeper behind than in front in one specimen. The body of the 5th lumbar was deeper in front than behind in all the specimens. From these spinal columns it is

[1] When my paper on the lumbar curve was published in the *Journal of Anatomy and Physiology*, April, 1886, vol. xx., I was not aware that Dr. Cunningham had given an abstract of his researches in *Nature*, 18th February of the same year. He has since kindly directed my attention to this abstract, and I have now incorporated in this Report many of the facts contained in it.

REPORT ON THE BONES OF THE HUMAN SKELETON. 67

evident that, whilst in the 1st and 2nd lumbar vertebræ the body was deeper behind than in front in a considerable proportion of the specimens, in the 3rd and 4th lumbar the reverse occurred, until in the 5th lumbar the bodies of all the specimens had a greater vertical diameter anteriorly than posteriorly, and this indeed is a character of the 5th lumbar that has long been recognised by the descriptive human anatomist. The vertical diameter of the body of the 4th lumbar in the twelve skeletons amounted to 336 mm. for the anterior surfaces collectively, and to 313 mm. for the posterior surfaces collectively. In the 5th lumbar the vertical diameter of the anterior surfaces collectively amounted to 337 mm., and the posterior surfaces to 281 mm.; the mean anterior depth was 28 mm., the mean posterior 23·4, and the mean difference in favour of the anterior surface was 4·6 mm. Hence it follows that of all the lumbar vertebræ the 5th had much the greater proportional depth at the front as compared with the back of its body, and that it contributed more than any of the others to the anterior convexity of the lumbar region, so far as that is produced by the bodies of these vertebræ.

For the purposes of comparison of the lumbar region in Europeans with the same region in the spines of other races of men, it may be well to frame a general lumbar index for the entire region, and a special index for the body of each vertebra. If we assume the vertical diameter of the bodies of the five vertebræ anteriorly to be = 100, then the formula $\frac{\text{posterior diameter} \times 100}{\text{the anterior diameter}}$ would give the *general lumbar index*, and by a similar formula the *special index* of each vertebra may be obtained.

In Table X. the mean index of each lumbar vertebra in the series of twelve European spines is given, from which it will be seen that the index diminished from 106·8, that of the 1st lumbar vertebra, to 83·6, that of the 5th. The mean general index of the series of five lumbar vertebræ was 96. Dr. Cunningham in the abstract of his researches on

TABLE X.—LUMBAR INDICES.

Mean special Index of	12 Europeans.	5 Australians (4 ♀, 1 ♂).	2 Andaman Islanders.	3 Negros (2 ♀, 1 ♂).	3 Oahuans, Sandwich Islands.
1st Lumbar vertebra,	106·8	114·4	111·3	108·8	114·6
2nd ,, ,,	101·5	112·3	105·6	104·2	108·0
3rd ,, ,,	95·4	108·0	102·0	100·0	108·2
4th ,, ,,	93·0	103·7	91·8	93·0	101·5
5th ,, ,,	83·6	91·4	84·2	89·0	87·7
Mean general Lumbar Index,	96·0	105·96 = 106·0	98·98 = 99·0	99·0	104·0

the lumbar curve which he has recently published has given the mean lumbar indices in seventy-six European skeletons, the general results of which accord very closely with those which I have obtained from my more limited number of skeletons. The mean index in his series was 95·8, and the mean index of the individual vertebræ ranged from 106·1 for the 1st lumbar to 81·6 for the 5th. He also pointed out that the two sexes differed in the proportional depth of the anterior and posterior surfaces of the bodies of the lumbar vertebræ, so that they did not have the same mean lumbar index. The average in twenty-one Irish men he found to be 96·2, and in twenty-three Irish women 93·5, from which it is evident that in the women the anterior vertical diameter of the five lumbar bodies collectively was proportionally greater than in the men, and the lumbar spine in them was more convex.

During the past few years I have collected the skeletons of seven adult aboriginal Australians—six men and one woman. In four of the men the lumbar spine is complete, in one the last lumbar vertebra has been lost, in another the 3rd, 4th and 5th lumbars are absent; in the woman all the lumbars are present. In each of the five skeletons in which the lumbar spine was complete, the vertical diameter of the bodies of the five vertebræ collectively was deeper behind than in front; the maximum difference observed in three male skeletons was 9 mm., the minimum in the woman was 2 mm. The mean collective depth of the five vertebræ in the five perfect Australian skeletons was 112·2 mm. for the anterior surface of the bodies, and 118·8 mm. for the posterior surface; the mean difference, therefore, was 6·6 mm. in favour of the posterior surface. In the skeleton in which the 5th lumbar was absent the collective diameter of the four lumbars was 3 mm. greater behind than in front. In the relation of the vertical diameter of the posterior surface to the anterior surface the opposite condition prevailed to that which was found in the Europeans. Before, indeed, I had measured the vertebræ in these Australians, I found that, when the bodies of the lumbar vertebræ in each spine were placed in apposition with each other, without the interposition of artificial discs, they produced a concave curve forward, and not a convex curve as in the European spine, so that I was not surprised to see, when the bodies were measured, that collectively they were deeper posteriorly than anteriorly.

When the measurements of the individual lumbar vertebræ in the series of Australian spines were compared, it was seen that the body of the 1st lumbar vertebra in every instance was deeper behind than in front, in four skeletons as much as 4 mm. The body of the 2nd lumbar was with one exception deeper behind than in front, in two specimens as much as 4 mm.; in the exceptional vertebra the depth in front was 1 mm. greater than behind. The body of the 3rd lumbar in four skeletons was deeper behind than in front; in one skeleton they were equal, and in another—the adult female—the anterior diameter was 1 mm. deeper than the posterior. The body of the 4th lumbar was deeper behind than in front in three skeletons; these diameters were equal in one, and in two the anterior diameter was greater than the posterior. The body of the 5th lumbar was deeper in front than behind in all the five complete skeletons, the maximum difference between the two surfaces being 3 mm.

When these dimensions are compared with those obtained from the European spinal columns, it will be seen that in the 1st, 2nd, and 3rd lumbars the body was more constantly deeper behind than in front in the Australians than in the Europeans. In the 4th lumbar, whilst it was the exception in the Europeans for the body to be deeper behind than in front, in the Australians one-half the skeletons exhibited this relation. In all the Australians, as in the Europeans, the body of the 5th lumbar was deeper in front than behind; the mean vertical diameter of the anterior surfaces was 23·2, and of the posterior 21·2, a difference of 2 mm. only in favour of the anterior surface; whilst in the Europeans the anterior surface was on the average 4·6 mm. thicker than the posterior.

In Table X. the mean index of the five Australian skeletons in which the lumbar spine was complete is given. The mean index of the separate vertebræ diminished from 114·4 in the 1st lumbar to 91·4 in the 5th, and the mean general index of the entire series was 106. Dr. Cunningham has stated in his abstract the mean lumbar indices in seventeen Australian spines, and obtained from them a mean index 107·8, which was somewhat higher than in my measurements. The range in his series was from 119·8, the mean index of the 1st lumbar, to 90·4, the mean index of the 5th. In his series six males had a mean lumbar index of 110·1, and four females of 103·1.

In my single male Bush skeleton the collective vertical diameter of the bodies of the five lumbar vertebræ was 108 mm. anteriorly, and 115 mm. posteriorly. In the 1st, 2nd, and 3rd lumbars the posterior diameter exceeded the anterior; in the 4th these two diameters were equal, and in the 5th the anterior diameter was 1 mm. greater than the posterior. The proportions in this skeleton closely corresponded to what was seen in the Australians. The general lumbar index was 106, and the index of the 5th lumbar vertebra was 95. Dr. Cunningham has given 106·6 as the mean lumbar index of three Bushmen, whilst the mean index of the individual vertebræ ranged from 115·9 in the 1st lumbar to 95·3 in the 5th.

In my series of Andaman Islanders' skeletons only two had the lumbar vertebræ complete. In one the vertical diameter of the five vertebræ collectively was 113 mm. anteriorly, and 112 mm. posteriorly; in the other 125 mm. anteriorly, 124 mm. posteriorly. The 1st and 2nd lumbars in both skeletons were thicker behind than in front. The 3rd lumbar in one skeleton was of equal diameter on both aspects, and in the other was 1 mm. thicker behind than in front. In both skeletons both the 4th and 5th lumbars were thicker in front than behind, in the one skeleton the anterior surface of the 5th lumbar being 3 mm., in the other 5 mm., thicker than the posterior. The mean index in the two skeletons diminished from 111·3 for the 1st lumbar to 84·2 for the 5th (Table X.); the mean general lumbar index of the two skeletons was 99. Dr. Cunningham has given the mean lumbar index of the twenty-three Andaman Islanders, which he has measured as 104·8, which was considerably higher than the average of my two specimens. Fourteen of his skeletons were males with a mean lumbar index 106·3, and nine were females with a mean lumbar index 102·4.

In three Negro skeletons I was able to measure the vertical diameter of the bodies of the lumbar vertebræ both in front and behind. In each of the three skeletons the collective vertical diameter of the five lumbar bodies was slightly greater in front than behind; the maximum difference, however, was only 2 mm. The mean collective depth of the five vertebræ in the three Negro skeletons was 121 mm. for the anterior surfaces, and 119·6 mm. for the posterior surfaces; the mean difference, therefore, was 1·4 mm. in favour of the anterior surface. In all three skeletons, both the 1st and 2nd lumbars were slightly deeper behind than in front; the 3rd lumbar was equal in depth both anteriorly and posteriorly, whilst both the 4th and 5th lumbars were somewhat deeper in front than behind. The mean index in the three skeletons diminished from 108·8 in the 1st lumbar to 89 for the 5th, and the mean general lumbar index of the five vertebræ was 99. Dr. Cunningham obtained from the measurements of ten Negros a mean lumbar index of 105·4; his series of skeletons consisted of seven males with an index of 106, and three females of 103·4; whilst my skeletons were two females and one male, which may perhaps in some measure account for the mean general lumbar index being lower in my specimens than in his.

In a Maori skeleton, from Otago, the vertical diameter of the series of five vertebræ was the same both in front and behind, viz., 101 mm. The 1st and 2nd lumbars were slightly deeper behind than in front, the 3rd and 4th were equal in depth on both surfaces, and the 5th was 3 mm. deeper in front than behind. The general lumbar index was 100, and the index of the 5th lumbar vertebra was 85.

In each of two female skeletons from Oahu, in the Sandwich Islands, and in the spine of a third skeleton, apparently a male, the collective vertical diameter of the five lumbar bodies was greater behind than in front; in one skeleton the difference was 7 mm., in another 4 mm., in the third 3 mm., in favour of the posterior surface. The mean collective depth of the five vertebræ in the three skeletons was 121·6 mm. for the anterior, and 126·3 mm. for the posterior surfaces; the mean difference, therefore, was 4·7 mm. in favour of the posterior surface. In both female skeletons the bodies of the 1st, 2nd, 3rd, and 4th lumbars were all deeper behind than in front, whilst the 5th lumbar was deeper in front than behind. In the male the 1st, 2nd, and 3rd were deeper behind than in front, but the 4th and 5th were deeper in front than behind. The mean index in the three skeletons diminished from 114·6 in the 1st lumbar to 87·7 in the 5th. The mean general lumbar index of the five vertebræ was 104.

Dr. Cunningham has stated the mean lumbar index of three Tasmanian skeletons to be 107·2; two of these were males and their mean index was 108·5, whilst the lumbar index in the female was 104·7. The mean index of the individual vertebræ ranged from 115·1 in the 1st lumbar to 92·4 in the 5th.

In one of three Hindoo skeletons, the tall male presented by Dr. John Anderson, the vertical diameter of the series of five lumbar bodies was 137 mm. anteriorly, and 146 mm. posteriorly. The 1st, 2nd, and 5th lumbars were deeper behind than in front, the 3rd was 1 mm. deeper in front than behind, and in the 4th these two diameters were equal. The general lumbar index was 106, and the index of the 4th lumbar vertebra was 107. In the two other Hindoo skeletons, a male and a female, the vertical diameter of the bodies of the five lumbars was somewhat deeper in front than behind, and the mean lumbar index was 97·3. In each of these skeletons the vertical diameter of the 5th lumbar vertebra was deeper in front than behind, and the mean index was 89. In the skeleton of a male Sikh, the vertical diameter of the five lumbar bodies was 130 mm. anteriorly and 133 mm. posteriorly, being a difference of 3 mm. in favour of the posterior diameter. In this skeleton the 1st and 5th lumbar bodies were deeper behind than in front, but the 2nd, 3rd, and 4th were each of equal diameter on both aspects. The lumbar index was 102, and the index of the 5th lumbar vertebra was 108·7.

In a Chinese skeleton the vertical diameter of the five lumbar bodies was 145 mm. anteriorly, and 123 mm. posteriorly. In each vertebra, except the 1st, the vertical diameter was deeper in front than behind, and in the 1st the two diameters were equal. The general lumbar index was 84·8, and the index of the 5th lumbar vertebra was 70. In a male Malay skeleton, the vertical diameter of the five lumbar bodies was 127 mm. anteriorly, and 125 mm. posteriorly. In the 1st, 2nd, and 3rd the posterior diameter was deeper than the anterior; in the 4th and 5th the anterior diameter was deeper than the posterior. The general lumbar index was 98, and the index of the 5th lumbar vertebra was 77·7.

In a female Esquimaux the vertical diameter of the series of five lumbar bodies was the same in front and behind (127 mm.), so that the general lumbar index was 100. In a male skeleton the vertical diameter of the bodies anteriorly was 120 mm., and posteriorly 116 mm., and the general lumbar index was 96·6. Both in the female and male the 1st and 2nd lumbars were deeper behind than in front, but the 4th and 5th lumbars were deeper in front than behind. The index of the 5th lumbar vertebra in the female was 81, and in the male 71. In a male Laplander the vertical diameter of the five lumbar vertebræ was 111 mm. anteriorly and 110 mm. posteriorly, and the general lumbar index was 99. In a female Laplander the vertical diameter was anteriorly 121 mm., and posteriorly 118 mm. and the general lumbar index was 97·5. In both skeletons, whilst the 1st lumbar vertebra was deeper behind than in front, both the 4th and 5th lumbar were deeper in front than behind. The index of the 5th lumbar in the male was 86, and in the female 88.

From the observations which have been made both by Dr. Cunningham and myself, working quite independently of each other, and on two distinct series of skeletons of various races of men, it is obvious that differences exist amongst them in the relative thickness of the bodies of the lumbar vertebræ anteriorly and posteriorly. The production of bone in the bodies of the lumbar vertebræ of these races has been so adjusted that they are collectively thicker in front than behind in the white races, and behind than in front in the black races. If the spinal column consisted only of the osseous vertebræ in direct articulation with each other, both by their articular processes and bodies, the lumbar region would then be concave forward in the black races, and convex forward in the white races. But the spine, in addition to the osseous vertebræ, contains an intercalated series of intervertebral elastic discs, and these discs may perhaps be so adjusted in the black races as to be collectively thicker in front than behind in the lumbar region, and thus to compensate for the want of development in depth of the anterior surface of the vertebral bodies, and to give to the column a forward convexity in that region as in the white races, although not perhaps in so well-marked a degree. Should this be the case, it would follow that in the course of the development and ossification of the spinal column in the lumbar region in these races, important differences would arise anteriorly and posteriorly in the proportion of that mesoblast tissue which becomes cartilage and bone, and that which becomes intervertebral disc. We have no information, however, on the thickness of the discs in the black races, either relatively or absolutely, so that this interesting question is not in a position to be definitely answered.

Putting on one side, therefore, for the present, the question of modifications in the relative thickness of the discs, and limiting ourselves to the consideration of the influence which the bodies of the vertebræ themselves would have on the curvature of the spine, we find a very considerable range of variation in the vertical diameter anteriorly and posteriorly of the series of five lumbar vertebræ. These differences are expressed numerically by the general lumbar index. In my series of skeletons the lowest index was in a Chinese, 84·8, and the highest both in a Bushman and in a male Hindoo, 106, but Dr. Cunningham has obtained, as the mean of two male Tasmanians, an index as high as 108·5, and of ten male Australians, 110·1. Without at present taking into consideration the compensatory arrangements in the living body which might modify these relative differences in thickness, the lumbar spine—so far as represented by the bodies of its vertebræ, and with the lower surface of the body of one vertebra in contact with the upper surface of the body of the vertebra next below—might present one or other of three forms in different races of men. It might be convex forwards, or straight, or concave forwards, and to each group an arbitrary numerical limit might be assigned, based on the general lumbar index. We might assume that such a series of vertebræ, with the general lumbar index calculated only from the vertical diameters of the lumbar bodies, and ranging from 98 to 102, both inclusive, formed a straight spine, *Orthorachic* (ὀρθός, straight, ῥάχις, spine); one with a general index above 102 had the lumbar curve concave forwards, *Koilorachic* (κοῖλος, hollow); one with a general lumbar index below 98 had the curve convex forwards, *Kurtorachic* (κυρτός, arched, convex).

The data now before us are sufficiently large to enable one to state with certainty that the lumbar vertebræ in Europeans are collectively convex forwards, since the mean general lumbar index is between 95 and 96; and from the low index in my single Chinese skeleton it is probable that the mean of this race may also be very distinctly kurtorachic.

On the other hand, in the Australians, the mean general lumbar index is in my series 106·0, and in that of Cunningham 107·8; so that the vertebræ are collectively deeper behind than in front, and there can, I think, be little doubt that the two Australian skeletons in the Oxford Museum articulated by Mr. Charles Robertson will, when measured, also show a corresponding relation in the vertical diameter of the lumbar bodies. A similar arrangement prevails in the Bush race in which the mean general lumbar index of four skeletons, measured by Cunningham and myself, was 106·0. From the measurements of my three Oahuans, yielding a mean index of 104, it is probable that the Sandwich Islanders are also koilorachic, and the same would apply to Cunningham's Tasmanians.

The limited series of Negro and Andaman skeletons at my disposal gave a mean index in each case of 99, which would have placed them in the orthorachic category, but the more numerous measurements of Cunningham have shown that they possess a higher mean lumbar index, which he states to be 105·4 for the Negros, and 104·8 for the Andaman Islanders, so that both these races are, without doubt, koilorachic. My single Maori, with an index 100, possibly also the Hindoos, Sikh, Laplanders, and Esquimaux, may be orthorachic, but the specimens are too few in number to enable one to state with certainty the mean general lumbar index in these races.

As regards the 5th lumbar vertebra, in all the skeletons which I have measured, with two exceptions, the vertical diameter of the anterior surface of the body was greater than that of the posterior. There are, without doubt, differences in the relative depth. The anterior diameter was proportionally greater than the posterior in the Chinese, Malay, Esquimaux, Lapps, Europeans, and Andaman Islanders, than was the case in the Australians, Bush, Negros, and Hindoos. But in a single Hindoo skeleton, and in the Sikh, the posterior diameter of this vertebra was greater than the anterior; these, however, were probably individual exceptions, and this greater depth would assist in giving the high lumbar index to these two skeletons.

In order, in the absence of the discs, to put the lumbar vertebræ approximately into the position which they might have had when the discs were in position, I then had the vertebræ articulated with each other in several of those spines in which the posterior vertical diameter of the bodies markedly exceeded the anterior. In making this articulation the upper border of the superior articular facet of the vertebra below was placed in the same transverse plane as the upper border of the inferior articular facet of the vertebra above. The gaps left between the vertebral bodies probably approximated therefore to the size and form of the intervertebral discs, and the lumbar curve which was produced bore, without doubt, a relation to the curve in the living person. In the Bush spine (fig. 3) the anterior concavity of the dorsal region was continued down to as far as the lower border of the body of the 4th lumbar and the interval between it and the 5th, which, along with the upper border of the body of the 5th lumbar, were the

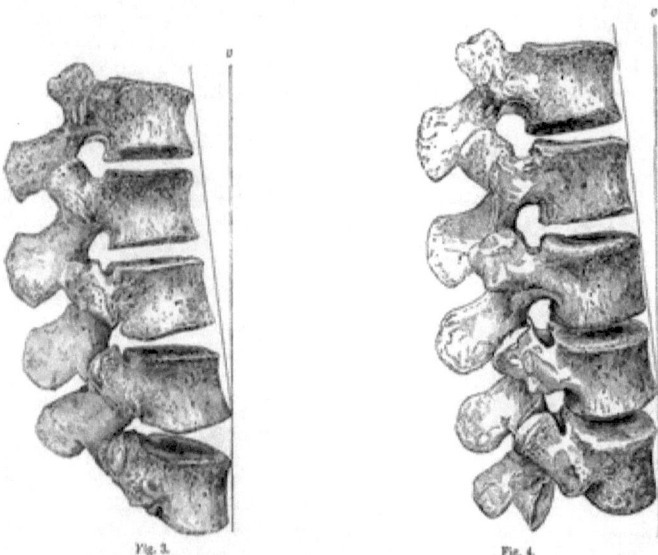

Fig. 3. Fig. 4.

Fig. 3.—Profile view of lumbar spine of Bushman articulated as described in text. The neural arch as formed by the laminæ and spinous process of the 5th lumbar was separate from the pedicles, and is not represented in the figure. v, vertical line.
Fig. 4.—Profile view of lumbar vertebræ of a male Australian from Perth, Western Australia. Both these figures are from photographs.

most projecting parts of this region. The body of the 5th lumbar vertebra was directed downwards and backwards from this most anterior projection. The interval for the disc between the 4th and 5th lumbar bodies had a very definite wedge-shaped form, with the narrow end of the wedge directed backwards.

In the Perth Australian (fig. 4) the lumbar spine above the lower border of the 4th vertebra was faintly concave forwards, but not to so great an extent as in the

Bushman, and the anterior part of the 5th vertebra was almost in the same vertical plane as the lower border of the 4th. The interval between the bodies of these two bones was not so strongly wedge-shaped as in the Bush skeleton. In the Eucla, Manly Cove, and West Victoria skeletons, the lower border of the body of the 4th lumbar was also the most prominent point in the lumbar region, and the body of the 5th lumbar inclined backwards and downwards from this point. But in these three skeletons the anterior convexity showed itself at the body of the 3rd lumbar vertebra. This was apparently also the case in the Queensland Australian, but the defect in the development of the body of the 5th lumbar described on p. 63, and some osseous outgrowths from the sides of the bodies of the other lumbar vertebræ, gave a twist to this part of the column which interfered with accurate observation.

In one of the Oahuan skeletons the most prominent point in the lumbar region was either the lower border of the body of the 4th lumbar or the upper border of the body of the 5th lumbar, and from the dorsal region downwards to this point the curve of the spine was concave forwards, whilst the body of the 5th lumbar sloped downwards and backwards from it. In another Sandwich Islander the form was somewhat modified, owing to the body of the 2nd lumbar projecting somewhat in front of both the 1st and the 3rd lumbars.

Variations in the anterior curvature of the spine in the lumbar region would in all probability affect the outline of the back of the body in that region, as one would expect the loins to have a deeper hollow when the spine possessed a strong anterior convexity, than when it did not have a well-marked lumbar curve. Luschka had, indeed, some years ago pointed out[1] that a strong concavity in the loins was a character of the body of a well-formed woman, in whom, as has already been stated, the lumbar spine is more convex forwards than in men. How far these departures in the lower races of men from the proportions of the front and back of the vertebral bodies, as seen in the higher races, may serve to modify the curvature of the lumbar spine in the erect attitude can only be definitely settled when the intervertebral discs, as well as the vertebral bodies, have been measured, and when the influence exercised by the discs on the production of the anterior lumbar convexity has been accurately determined.

The upper and lower surfaces of the body of a lumbar vertebra are parallel to each other only in those bones in which the vertical diameters anteriorly and posteriorly are equal, but as this is the exception and not the rule, it follows that in the lumbar spine it is customary for these surfaces not to be parallel, but to approximate in their antero-posterior diameter to the form of a wedge. My observations show that the surfaces of the body are either parallel, or approach most closely to it, either in the 2nd or 3rd lumbar, whilst they diverge most widely from it in the 1st and 5th lumbar. Aeby, in his examination of the European spine, found[2] the 2nd lumbar to be the vertebra in

[1] Die Anatomie des Menschen, Bd. ii. p. 80, 1863.   [2] Archiv für Anatomie, p. 91, 1879.

which the vertical diameters in front and behind were usually equal, whilst the 1st lumbar had the anterior diameter 0·4 mm. less than the posterior, and the 5th lumbar had the anterior diameter 6·2 mm. greater than the posterior. Aeby regards, therefore, the change from the concavity of the thoracic part of the spine to the convexity of the lumbar to take place at a point between the 2nd and 3rd vertebræ, which opinion is substantially corroborated by my observations. It is, therefore, at the two ends of the lumbar series of vertebræ that the wedge-shaped form of the bodies is most distinct, the 4th and 5th vertebræ having the narrower part of the wedge directed backwards to the spinal canal, whilst in the 1st it is directed forwards to the front of the spine. This statement applies to the individual vertebræ, both in the black and white races; but, as in the Australians, for example, the upper three lumbars were more constantly deeper behind than in front, and the lower two lumbars were proportionally less thick in front than behind than in Europeans, the general effect was to produce, so far as the depth of the vertebral bodies themselves and without the intermediate discs can influence the curvature, a lumbar spine, in the one race concave forwards, and in the other convex forwards.

The question now arises, at what period of life do the bodies of the lumbar vertebræ assume the wedge-shaped form? From the measurements, both of Aeby[1] and Ravenel,[2] it would appear that in the new-born child neither the vertebral bodies nor the discs are wedge-shaped, and that in all the regions of the spine the anterior and posterior vertical diameters are equal, so that the spine, the sacral region being excepted, is almost straight. In a boy of three months, measured by Ravenel,[3] the lumbar region, including apparently both bodies and discs, was 6 mm. higher anteriorly than posteriorly, and in one of two years 1 cm. higher. In the spine of a child, apparently in its second year, measured by myself, the bodies of the lumbar vertebræ were collectively 4 mm. thicker in front than behind, and the half of the increase was in the body of the 5th lumbar. It is obvious, therefore, that the anterior vertical diameter of the lumbar region increases with the assumption of the erect posture, and with the formation of the convex forward curve in the lumbar spine. Some years ago Ravenel measured in Bern the spine in twenty-two adult Europeans, eleven of either sex. The mean proportions of the lumbar part of the column—the anterior surface of the entire column being estimated as = 100— was in men 30·5 for the anterior surface of the lumbar spine, and 26·4 for the posterior surface; whilst in women it was 31·9 for the anterior, and only 22·2 for the posterior surface. The difference, therefore, for the two sexes was 4·1 in favour of the anterior surface in the men, and 9·7 in the women, so that the lumbar spine was considerably more convex in the latter sex. Ravenel also stated that in women the posterior surface of the whole spinal column was 6 per cent. shorter than in men, which, for the most part,

[1] Der Bau des menschlichen Körpers, Leipzig, 1871, p. 159. Die Altersverschiedenheiten der menschlichen Wirbelsaule, *Archiv für Anatomie*, p. 77, 1879.
[2] Die Maassverhaltnisse der Wirbelsaule, *Zeitschr. für Anat. und Entwicklungsgeschichte*, Bd. ii., 1877.
[3] *Op. cit.*

was due to the diminished proportion in the lumbar region. The observations of the brothers Weber,[1] made many years ago on a European skeleton, gave to the series of anterior surfaces of the bodies of the five lumbar vertebræ a height of 6·7 mm. above the posterior surfaces, with which my measurements closely approximate; whilst the height of the anterior surfaces of the discs (including those from the 12th dorsal to the 5th lumbar vertebræ) was 11·9 mm. above the posterior, but if the disc between the 5th lumbar and 1st sacral be also taken into account, then the anterior surface of the collective series of discs was 21·1 mm. more than the posterior, so that the discs contributed about three times more to the anterior convexity than did the bodies. There can, indeed, be no doubt that it is the rule in the adult European spine for the disc between the 5th lumbar and the 1st sacral vertebra to be very materially thicker in front than behind. The existence of an anterior convexity in the lumbar spine shows that the growth proceeds more rapidly in front than behind, and in this growth, both the vertebral bodies collectively and the discs participate in the European spine.

If we were to assume that in the black races the lumbar spine possessed a forward convexity equal to the average convexity of Europeans, it would then be necessary, owing to the diminished depth of the anterior surfaces of the vertebral bodies as compared with the posterior, for the discs to be very much thicker in front than behind, either throughout the lumbar region or in a part of its extent, so as to throw the bodies forward. Were this the case then in the lumbar spine the elastic discs would make up an even larger proportion of this region of the column than in the white races, and their growth would necessarily have been much more active in front than behind. The brothers Weber pointed out long ago that whilst the form of the articular processes of the lumbar vertebræ interfered with lateral flexion and rotation in this region, yet that the lumbar spine had great flexibility from before backwards through the interposition of these elastic discs. But even should the lumbar region be less convex forwards in the black races than in the Europeans, it is not unlikely that the proportion of elastic disc to inelastic bone may be greater in the former than in the latter; greater flexibility would thus be given to the spine, and the body would more easily be enabled to assume those positions during rest and in motion which have been already referred to in the section on the age characters of the pelvis, as more frequently adopted by man in his wild and native state than when living under the influences of civilisation.

[1] Mechanik der menschlichen Gehwerkzeuge, pl. viii. p. 92, Göttingen, 1836.

STERNUM.

The sternum was present in thirty of the skeletons. As a rule the præ- meso- and xiphi-sternal segments were not united to each other, and the xiphi-sternum had usually been lost. In the following specimens this rule was departed from. In the Perth Australian and the Sikh, the præ- was fused with the meso-sternum, but the xiphi-sternum was free. In an Andaman Islander and the Malay the xiphi-sternum was ossified and fused with the meso-sternum, but the manubrium was free. In an Andaman Islander, in which the epiphyses of the long bones were not fully ossified to the shafts, the præ-sternum was fused with the first segment of the meso-sternum, but the latter was not ankylosed to the second segment, and in the lowest segment of this division of the bone the two lateral halves were imperfectly united mesially. In the Chinese the first segment of the meso-sternum was free, but the second, third, and fourth segments were fused together, and the xiphoid was ossified but not fused with the meso-sternum; this skeleton, from the ossification of the long bones, apparently belonged to a man from twenty to twenty-four years of age. In the Manly Cove Australian, although all the segments of the mesosternum were ankylosed together, yet a distinct fissure marked the plane of fusion of the first and second segments.

In the Bush skeleton, the Malay and the male Lapp, the meso-sternum was perforated by a hole, large enough to admit a quill, situated at the junction of its third and fourth segments; in the Malay the first pair of costal cartilages were ossified on the surface. A meso-sternal hole due to defect in the ossification of the cartilaginous sternum is sometimes seen in Europeans.

These sterna do not throw much light on the question whether the manubrium or the xiphi-sternum unites first with the meso-sternum, for whilst there are two cases of fusion of the xiphi-sternum, without ankylosis of the manubrium, there are also two cases of fusion of the manubrium without ankylosis of the xiphi-sternum. There is also one remarkable instance of fusion of the manubrium with the first segment of the meso-sternum before the meso-sternum itself had completed its ossification, but this is quite exceptional. It is without doubt the rule for the manubrium not to fuse with the meso-sternum until comparatively late in life. The Malay skeleton and one of the Oahuan women show that ossification of the costal cartilages may have considerably advanced without the præ- and meso-sternum having become ankylosed together. The condition of ossification of the sternum does not, I think, afford any accurate guide to the age of the skeleton, and in this respect my observations conform with those of Dr. Thomas Dwight.[1]

[1] The Sternum as an index of Sex and Age, Journ. Anat. and Phys., vol. xv. p. 327, 1881.

CLAVICLE.

In the series of skeletons the clavicle presented various modifications in length, thickness, degree of curvature, and prominence of the ridges and processes for attachment of muscles and ligaments. These modifications were apparently in great measure to be associated with sex, and with the degree of muscular development. It was especially observed, in the majority of the bones, that the groove on the under surface for the subclavius muscle was either absent or very faintly marked.

Measurements of the Clavicle.

I took the length of the clavicles in each skeleton, with the view of ascertaining their absolute length, if differences existed between the bones on opposite sides of the same skeleton, and the proportionate length of the clavicle to the humerus.

The length of the clavicle was measured in a straight line between the sternal and acromial ends of the bone; 150 mm. may be taken as expressing the mean length of the clavicle in the men of the British Islands, and 140 mm. the mean length in the women.

The maximum clavicle in my series of male Australians was 160 mm. in the Riverina skeleton, the minimum 121 mm. in the Perth skeleton, and the mean 142·2 mm. The contrast in shape between the elongated, curved clavicle of the man from the Riverina and the short thick clavicle of the Perth Australian was very marked. In the female Australian the length was 118 mm. The Bush clavicles, notwithstanding the diminutive stature, were each 147 mm. long, and were slender curved bones. Six Oahuan clavicles varied from 117 mm. to 153 mm., and the mean was 139 mm. The clavicle in the Andaman Islanders ranged from 112 to 126 mm., and the mean was 119·3 mm.; the bones were not strongly curved and were slight. In two Negresses the maximum clavicle was 150 mm. and the minimum 134, whilst the mean was 141·7 mm.; in three Negros the longest was 160 mm., and the shortest 140, the mean being 149·4 mm. In the Otago skeleton the clavicle was 134 mm. In the three Hindoos the clavicle ranged from 118 mm. in the women to 165 mm. in the tall male. In the Sikh the longer clavicle was 164 mm., in the Malay 158 mm., and in the Chinese 132 mm. In the female Lapp the longer bone was 122 mm., and in the male 148 mm. In the female Esquimaux the longer clavicle was 147 mm., and in the male 142 mm.

In eight skeletons the right clavicle was longer than the left, in the Malay skeleton by as much as 6 mm. In fifteen skeletons the left clavicle was longer than the right; in an Andaman Islander and the female Esquimaux by 6 mm., and in the Riverina Australian by 7 mm. In Dr. Anderson's tall Hindoo the left clavicle was 18 mm. longer than the right, but the difference was so great that I am led to think the shorter bone probably did not belong to this skeleton.

Many years ago the late M. Paul Broca[1] compared the length of the clavicle with that of the humerus in the same race, and came to the conclusion that in the Negro this bone was, like the radius, longer in proportion to the humerus than in the European. If the humerus be regarded as = 100 then he found that the clavicle in five European men had the proportion 44·3, and in four European women 45·0, whilst in nine Negros it was 45·8, and in seven Negresses 47·4.

The mean length of the clavicle in my six male Australians, as I have just stated, was 142·2, and the mean length of the humeri, in the same skeletons, was 335·7, and the proportion of the clavicle to the humerus, which may be termed the *claviculo-humeral index*, was 42·3 to 100, which is less than M. Broca obtained in male Europeans. In my Bushman's skeleton, owing to the length of the clavicle, the claviculo-humeral index was 51·4, whilst in the so-called Hottentot Venus, a female of the Bush race, this index, from Broca's measurements, was only 42. The mean length of the humeri in my three Negros was 341·8, and that of the clavicles 149·4, so that the claviculo-humeral index was 43·7, which is below the mean obtained by Broca both for his Negros and Europeans; the mean length of the humeri in my two Negresses was 314·5, and that of the clavicles 141·7, the claviculo-humeral index was 45, which is almost the same as the mean in the European women as obtained by Broca, but considerably below the mean of his seven Negresses. M. Broca also gives the proportion of the length of the clavicle in an Esquimaux skeleton as 43·8. In my male Esquimaux skeleton the claviculo-humeral index was 41·5, and in my female 44·6.

It seems doubtful if the relation between the length of the clavicle and the humerus is sufficiently definite to permit it to be employed with certainty as a race character. At any rate it is obvious that a much larger number of skeletons than I have before me, or the claviculo-humeral proportions of which have yet been recorded by anatomists, would require to be measured before the mean ratio of the clavicle to the humerus for each race can be obtained.

[1] Sur les proportions relatives du Bras, de l'Avant-bras et de la Clavicule chez les Nègres et les Européens, *Bull. de la Soc. d'Anthropologie*, April 3, 1862, t. iii. p. 162, 1862. Observations by M. Emile Pasteau in a Thesis entitled Recherches sur les proportions de la Clavicule dans les Sexes et dans les Races, Paris, 1879, a notice of which is in the *Revue d'Anthropologie*, p. 150, 1881, would seem to give support to Broca's conclusions regarding the relative lengths of the clavicle and the humerus in Negros and Europeans, but as regards other races no positive result was apparently obtained.

SCAPULA.

The scapulæ belonging to the skeletons from which the pelves were obtained, were examined with reference to their form and proportions. In all, twenty-nine pairs were under observation, and with the exception of the male and female Laplanders they were not the scapulæ of Europeans.

In the Australians the scapulæ were as a rule smaller than in Europeans of the same sex; the axillary border was somewhat more concave, and the borders of the infraspinous fossa sloped more rapidly to the inferior angle. The suprascapular notch was distinct in each bone, although in the Riverina and Perth skeletons it was shallow. Both the acromion process and spine were well developed. The small size of the scapulæ in the Bush skeleton conformed with the diminutive stature of the race. In the right bone the suprascapular notch was present, though shallow, but in the left bone, in which the supraspinous fossa was deep anteriorly, the notch was converted into a foramen by a broad plate of bone. The right acromion and spine were present, but on the left side they were absent, either through non-development or removal early in life.

In four of the Negro skeletons the suprascapular notch was distinct, and in one of these especially so; but in a fifth skeleton the superior border of each scapula was deeply falciform, and the suprascapular notch was not differentiated.

In the Andaman Islanders the scapulæ were small, slender, and with the muscular impressions not strongly pronounced. In three skeletons a shallow suprascapular notch had been differentiated at the root of the coracoid, but in the fourth the superior border of the scapula was falciform and the notch was not specialised. This latter character of the scapula in these islanders was observed by Prof. Flower, who states that in only three of the large series which he examined was a distinct notch present, and that, especially in the females, the superior border was deeply excavated.

In the Maori from Otago the axillary border was falciform, owing to a broad process projecting forwards from it at the anterior limit of attachment of the teres major; the infraspinous region therefore presented considerable breadth near the inferior angle, and the plate-like character of the bone was increased. The superior border of the right scapula formed a continuous concavity, and was without a suprascapular notch; but in the left bone an oblique foramen pierced the supraspinous fossa close to the base of the coracoid, and had without doubt transmitted the suprascapular nerve; the notch therefore in this bone was crossed by an osseous bridge. The scapulæ of the Sandwich Island women from Oahu were thin and light; in the one the suprascapular notch was shallow, in the other it was of ordinary depth.

In the female Hindoo the scapulæ were slender, and in them and those of the smaller male the suprascapular notch was shallow; but in the tall male these bones were much more massive, and in the left scapula the notch was almost completely converted into a foramen by the ossified suprascapular ligament. In the Sikh, also, the bones were massive, in the one the suprascapular ligament was completely ossified, in the other partially so. In the Chinese, owing to the deep concavity of the superior border of the scapulæ, the area of the supraspinous fossa was greatly diminished and the notch was not specially differentiated at the base of the coracoid. In the Malay the suprascapular notch was fairly well marked.

In the female Lapp the superior border of the scapulæ was deeply concave, and the suprascapular notch scarcely differentiated; in the male the concavity of this border, though not so great, had the notch equally indistinct. In the male the axillary border was somewhat falciform. In each scapula of the Esquimaux the suprascapular notch was present, and the bones in one skeleton were pointed at the inferior angle.

Measurements of the Scapula.

The study of the modifications in the form and proportions of the scapula in the different races of men, based on exact measurements, with the view of establishing an anthropological character by the use of the numerical method, dates from the publication, in 1878, of M. Paul Broca's memoir on the scapular index, so that the literature of this subject is both recent and comprised in a small compass.

BROCA, PAUL, Sur les indices de largeur de l'omoplate chez l'homme, les singes et dans la série des mammifères. *Bull. de la Soc. d'Anthrop. de Paris*, February 21, 1878, ser. 3, t. i. p. 66, 1878.

HAMY, E. T., Étude sur un Squelette d'Aëta des Environs de Binangonan, Luçon. *Nouvelles Archives du Muséum d'Histoire naturelle*, sér. 2, t. ii. p. 181, 1879.

LIVON, MARIUS, De l'omoplate et de ses indices de largeur dans les races humaines. *Thèse inaugurale*, Paris, 1879.

FLOWER, W. H., and GARSON, J. G., The Scapular Index as a Race Character in Man. *Journ. of Anat. and Phys.*, October 1879, vol. xiv. p. 13, 1880.

M. Broca obtained the length (height) of the scapula by measuring in a straight line the distance from the superior to the inferior angle; and the breadth of the scapula by measuring from the middle of the outer border of the glenoid cavity to the point where the spine of the scapula intersects the vertebral border. The latter dimension is in the fundamental morphological axis of the scapula, and corresponds closely to the line of attachment of the spine, and the bone attains a greater or less length by growth in the direction of either the supra- or infraspinous fossa. With these measurements he computed a scapular index as follows: $\frac{\text{breadth} \times 100}{\text{length}}$, length = 100. When the index is high the scapula is broad in proportion to its length, and vice versa. Again, he measured the distance from the inferior angle to the point where the scapular spine intersected the vertebral border, and obtained the relations between the breadth of the scapula and the

REPORT ON THE BONES OF THE HUMAN SKELETON.

infraspinous length, by the following formula: $\frac{\text{breadth} \times 100}{\text{infraspinous length}}$. The product obtained is the infraspinous index of the scapula. M. Livon and Messrs. Flower and Garson have, in their inquiry into the scapular and infraspinous indices, adopted Broca's measurements.

As these measurements, with the indices derived from them, give the relations both of the entire length of the scapula and of its infraspinous length to the breadth of that bone, and thus fix certain important proportions, I have also employed them in this investigation. As Broca has shown, the scapular index is at its minimum in bipeds and at its maximum in quadrupeds, for whilst the length of the scapula exceeds the breadth in man, the reverse is the case in quadrupeds. An increase, therefore, of the scapular index in the human bone is an indication of a form of scapula more closely approaching to the ordinary mammalian type than when the index is low. The relation of the infraspinous index to the scapular index will vary with the variations in the relative length of the supra- (præ-) and infra- (post-) spinous fossæ. When the supraspinous fossa has a relatively great length to the infraspinous, then the infraspinous index is high, which is the normal mammalian proportion, but when the infraspinous index is low, as in the human scapula, then the infraspinous fossa dominates over the supraspinous.

Europeans.—The mean length of fourteen adult scapulæ of Frenchmen, measured by M. Broca, was 160·5 mm., the mean breadth was 105·7 mm., and the mean infraspinous length was 120·5 mm. M. Livon's measurements of seventy-three Frenchmen yielded a mean length of 168 mm., a mean breadth of 105·9, and a mean infraspinous length of 124·3 mm.; whilst in fifty-one Frenchwomen the corresponding dimensions were 135, 91·1 and 102·5. Messrs. Flower and Garson's measurements of 200 European scapulæ give the mean length 155·5 mm., mean breadth 101·4 mm., and mean infraspinous length 113·6 mm. These dimensions are smaller than those obtained by M. Broca, which is to be accounted for by their series containing a proportion of female scapulæ. In Broca's Frenchmen the mean scapular index was 65·9, and the mean infraspinous index was 87·7. The mean scapular index in M. Livon's Frenchmen was 63, and the mean infraspinous index was 85·4, whilst in the Frenchwomen the mean scapular index was 67·4, and the mean infraspinous index was 88·8, so that in women the scapula is broader in proportion to its length than in men. In Flower and Garson's Europeans of both sexes the mean scapular index was 65·2 and the mean infraspinous index was 89·4.

Australians.—I have examined twelve scapulæ belonging to six male skeletons. The maximum length of this bone was in the Queensland skeleton 168 mm., and the minimum in the West Australian from Perth 138 mm. In only one skeleton, that from Swan Hill, was the length of the right and left bones the same, and in the Perth skeleton they varied as much as 7 mm. The maximum breadth was, in the right scapula of the Riverina skeleton, 109 mm., and the minimum in the scapulæ of the Manly Cove skeleton, 88 mm. The breadth of the scapulæ in the same person was more frequently the same, or nearly the same, than was the length. The maximum infraspinous length was 130 mm. in the Queensland specimen, and the minimum was 102 mm. in the Eucla scapulæ. As a rule, the scapulæ were somewhat smaller that in male Europeans, for the mean length was 154·5 mm., the mean breadth was 97·3 mm., and the mean infraspinous length was 113·6 mm. The mean scapular index was 63, and the range was from 57 to 69·9; the mean infraspinous index was 87, and the range was from 74 to 101. In the two Australian males measured by M. Livon the mean scapular index was 63, and the mean infraspinous index was 86. In the twelve Australian scapulæ measured by Messrs. Flower and Garson the mean scapular index was 68·9 and the mean infraspinous index was 92·5. In their specimens these indices were materially higher than in M. Livon's and in mine, and a comparison of the two series showed this peculiarity, that whilst in theirs the scapular and infraspinous indices were higher than in Europeans, in mine they were distinctly below the European standard. My specimens and those of M. Livon were all males. It is possible that a majority of those measured by Flower and Garson may have been females, and if in the Australians the females have, as is the case in Europeans, higher indices than in the males, then the discrepancies in our respective measurements may be accounted for. Six Tasmanian scapulæ measured by the last-named anatomists had a mean scapular index, 60·3, and a mean infraspinous index, 81·4.

African Blacks.—In my Bush skeleton the right scapula was 133 mm., the left 137 mm. long, whilst their respective breadths were 96 and 95 mm. The scapular index in the one bone was 72, in the other 69, and the mean was 70·5. In the female measured by M. Livon the mean scapular index was 61·6, whilst Flower and Garson obtained a mean of 66·7 from six scapulæ. The two scapulæ in my skeleton yielded a mean infraspinous index of 102·5, those of Flower and Garson a mean of 90·7, and those of Livon only 76. In a Hottentot measured by M. Livon the mean scapular index of the two bones was 60, and the mean infraspinous index was 82. In four Negro skeletons, which I measured, the scapular index ranged from 63 to 78·9, and the mean of the eight bones was 70; in two Negresses the range was from 57 to 81, and the mean of the four bones was 68·5. In twenty-nine Negros measured by M. Livon the mean was 69, and in eight Negresses it was 71; in Broca's series of twenty-five skeletons, which may also have been included in Livon's measurements, the mean scapular index was 68; in six scapulæ measured by Flower and Garson the mean was 71·7. The infraspinous index in my specimens ranged from 80 to 115 in the Negresses, the mean being 97, and from 97 to 117 in the Negros, the mean being 105. In M. Broca's series of skeletons the mean index was only 93·8, in M. Livon's it was 96 both for the men and the women, and in Messrs. Flower and Garson's series it was 100·9.

Andaman Islanders and Negritos.—In three Andaman Islanders I found the scapular index to range from 66 to 75·8, with a mean of 70·6, which is almost in accordance with the mean of 69·8 obtained by Flower and Garson from twenty-one scapulæ. The infraspinous index in my six scapulæ ranged from 94 to 115, and the mean was 102, whilst the mean in Flower and Garson's series was 92·7. In the Aëta Negrito measured by M. Hamy the scapular index was 64·9, and the infraspinous index was 88·6.

Pacific Islanders.—In my two Oahuan skeletons the mean scapular index was 78·8, and in my Maori from Otago it was 63·9. In thirteen Melanesians measured by M. Livon the mean was 69·8, and in sixteen Polynesians 66·6. Messrs. Flower and Garson give the mean index of two Papuan scapulæ as 64·5, and of two Tahitian as 70·3. The mean infraspinous index in my Oahuans was 117, and in the Otago Maori 88·5. M. Livon's Melanesians had a mean infraspinous index of 93·3, and his Polynesians of 89·4. In Flower and Garson's Papuan the mean infraspinous index was 87·6, and in their Tahitian 95·6.

Asiatics.—In my tall male Hindoo the mean scapular index was 68·9, and the mean of six Hindoos measured by M. Livon was 68·3. In my male Sikh the mean index was 68·5. In my Chinese the mean index was 66·8; the mean of three Chinese in M. Livon's table was 66·6, and of a single Japanese 64·9. In my Malay the mean scapular index was 64, and in M. Livon's Table the mean of two Malays was 74; in Flower and Garson's Table the mean of two Bornean scapulæ, possibly Malays, was 64·8; and in a Kubu from Sumatra, measured by Garson, this index was 72·9. The infraspinous index in my Hindoo was 95, and in Livon's series 92; in my Sikh it was 107; in my Chinese it was 88, and in Livon's series 90·8; in my Malay it was 93, in Livon's series it was 98·7, and in Flower and Garson's Bornean 89·8.

Lapp and Esquimaux.—In my two Lapps the mean scapular index was 59·5, in Livon's skeletons 63·7, and in Flower and Garson's skeleton 64·8. In my two Esquimaux skeletons the mean scapular index was 60·5, and in a similar number measured by Flower and Garson it was 61·6, whilst in a pair of Samoyed scapulæ it was 62·1. In my Lapps the mean infraspinous index was 85, in Livon's 83·7, and in Flower and Garson's 89·1. In my Esquimaux the mean infraspinous index was 82·2, in Flower and Garson's it was 80·5, and in a pair of Samoyed scapulæ it was 89·5.

I have not myself examined the scapulæ of any American Indians, but M. Livon has measured seventeen male and six female Peruvians, from which he has obtained a mean scapular index 66·5, and a mean infraspinous index 89·6. Dr. Garson, from the measurements of his Yahgan Fuegians, has obtained 64·3 as the mean of four men, and 66·2 as the mean of one woman.

It may now be convenient to give in a tabular form (Table XI.) the mean scapular and infraspinous indices obtained, by including the measurements by myself and other observers of the series of adult scapulæ referred to in the preceding paragraphs in one common average, the males and females not being differentiated from each other.

If we exclude the single Hottentot skeleton, where only two scapulæ were measured, we shall find that the mean scapular index ranged from 60·3 in the Tasmanians, to 70·2 in the Andaman Islanders, and that the Europeans stand midway between these extremes at 65·3. From the very large number of Europeans which have been measured, it may

TABLE XI.

Race and Number of Scapulæ.	Scapular Index.	Infraspinous Index.
Europeans (462),	65·3	87·8
Australians (28),	64·9	88·5
Tasmanians (6),	60·3	81·4
Bush (10),	66·2	89·7
Hottentots (2),	60·0	82·0
Negros (about 100),	69·7	98·5
Andaman Islanders (27),	70·2	97·3
Negrito (2),	64·9	88·6
Melanesians (Livon, 26),	69·8	93·3
Polynesians (Livon, 32),	66·6	89·4
Hindoo and Sikh (16),	68·5	98·0
Chinese (8),	66·7	89·4
Malay (10),	68·9	93·8
Lapps (8),	62·6	85·9
Esquimaux (8),	61·0	81·3
Peruvians (Livon, 46),	66·5	89·6
Fuegians (9),	65·0	...

safely be assumed that this figure expresses accurately the European mean, though in the other races, excepting perhaps the Negro and the Andaman Islanders, it is doubtful whether the number of scapulæ measured in each race is sufficient to give a reliable average. For I gather both from my own measurements, and those of other observers, that the range of variation in the relative length and breadth of the scapula is very considerable in the same race, so that it needs a large number of bones to enable one to obtain an accurate idea of the mean of any race. Taking, however, the table as it stands, it will be seen that the Lapps, Esquimaux, and Tasmanians fall considerably below the European average; the Negros, Andaman Islanders, Melanesians, and Malays rise considerably above it, and the Australians, Bush, Polynesians, Peruvians, and Fuegians are in close approximation to the Europeans. As in the Anthropoid Apes and in mammals generally, the scapular index is higher than in man, it follows that the higher this index is in the human scapula, the more does it approach the ordinary mammalian standard, and it shows that the scapula has grown in breadth at a greater ratio than in length. If the averages of the black races given in the table are approximately correct, then considerable diversity exists amongst them in the relative length and breadth of the scapula, for whilst the Andaman Islanders, Negros, and Melanesians closely approach the mean of the chimpanzee or gorilla,[1] the Australians and Bushmen are more like the Europeans, and the Tasmanians again are still further removed than the Europeans from the pithecoid proportions. The Lapps and the Esquimaux are also considerably below the European standard, so that in their scapular index, as well as in the tibio-femoral index, as will be shown in a subsequent chapter (p. 108), these extreme northern races are amongst the least pithecoid in their proportions.

Although I have given in the table the infraspinous index, yet I am doubtful if much value can be attached to it as a race character, for its range of variation in the same race is so extensive. Thus in the Australian scapulæ, which I measured, this index ranged from 74 to 101, and in the Negros from 80 to 117, and a difference of from 5 to 8 in the infraspinous index in opposite scapulæ of the same skeleton was not uncommon.

M. Livon in his thesis on the scapula, so frequently referred to, did not limit himself to such measurements as enabled him to compute the scapular and infraspinous indices, but determined the distance between several other points of the bone, and also calculated a supraspinous index. Although I have made the measurements for the determination of this index, I have not thought it necessary to incorporate them in this Report.

As, in the Anthropoid Apes, the relatively greater supraspinous fossa is associated with an obliquity of the spine of the scapula, much more marked than in the human scapula, in which the axis of the spine approaches to a right angle with the vertebral border of the bone, I was desirous of ascertaining if modifications in the direction of the spine of the scapula existed in the different races of men to such a degree as to establish a race character. I accordingly devised a goniometer which would, I thought, enable me to determine the angle which the axis of the spine formed with the vertebral border. I found, however, that this border had not unfrequently projections and depressions in it, which gave a degree of uncertainty to the base line, and made it difficult at times to determine, with precision, the angle which the axis of the spine formed with it. In twenty-five European scapulæ this scapulo-spinal angle ranged from 73° to 91°, and the mean of the series was 82°·5. In eleven Australian scapulæ the range was from 67° to 86°, and the mean of the series was 78°·2. In four scapulæ of chimpanzees the mean scapulo-spinal angle was 50°·5, and the mean of two orangs was 66°·5. On these measurements, therefore, the Australians were intermediate between the Europeans and Anthropoid Apes in this relation. But in stating this result it is right that I should say, for the reason already given, that I was not always satisfied with the accuracy of the angle obtained, though the mean probably furnishes a fair approximation to the relation of the two lines with each other.

[1] Messrs. Flower and Garson give 69·9 as the mean scapular index in the chimpanzee, and 72·2 as that of the gorilla ; M. Livon states the index to be 71 in the chimpanzee and 70 in the gorilla.

If one compares the scapula with the pelvis one recognises that the latter fulfils in man a much more important office than the former. The pelvis presents both a surface for the attachment of important muscles, and is also the part of the skeleton through which the weight is transmitted to the lower limbs. The forces exercised on it are therefore more varied and more powerful than those which bear on the scapula. For the latter bone lies comparatively free in the flesh, and has its surfaces and processes developed essentially in relation to the various muscles which are attached to it, and it is not in man concerned in the transmission of weight. The external forces operating on the human scapula, which might lead to a modification in its form and proportions, would therefore be mainly, if not exclusively, in connection with its muscular attachments, more especially those muscles which are engaged in the abduction and elevation of the upper limb, and the rotatory muscles of the humerus. Should there be anything in the habits of one race of men which might require a particular group of scapular muscles to be used and developed to an extent far greater than in another race, then it is not unlikely that the area of attachment of those muscles in that race would be widened or lengthened to an extent greater than is the case in those races in which the same group is not similarly exercised, and the proportions of these parts of the scapula to the rest of the bone would in so far be modified. The arboreal habits of the ape require that it should use its upper limbs for purposes of climbing, and for swinging itself from one branch of a tree to another, so that the muscles engaged in the elevation of the upper limb require to be powerful; which would account for the greater development of the supraspinatus muscle and supraspinous fossa, and would probably lead also to the greater obliquity of the scapular spine than is the case in man. In a similar manner one would expect to find in those races of men, as the Australians, who climb trees in quest of food, or those natives of the interior of New Guinea, whose houses are built in the upper branches of lofty trees, a commensurate development of the elevatory muscles of the upper limb and of their respective areas of attachment. But in connection with this development the additional area might perhaps be obtained, either by an addition to the length or breadth of the surface, or perhaps both to its length and breadth.

SHAFT OF THE SUPERIOR EXTREMITY.

As a general rule, the bones of the upper limb of the aboriginal skeletons which I have examined had not the ridges and processes for the attachment of muscles of especial magnitude, so that they did not express great muscular development. In many instances the bones were slender and with smooth surfaces. This character was especially noticed in the Australian, Chinese, Andaman Islanders, Hindoo, and Negress skeletons. In the male Sikh the bones were much more powerful, and in the Te Aroha New Zealander, Bush, male Laplander, and Esquimaux they had a robust appearance. In no specimen was a supra-condyloid process or foramen present. An intercondyloid (supra-trochlear) foramen existed in both humeri of the Queensland Australian, left humerus of Sikh, left humerus of each of the Oahuans, right humerus of a female Andaman Islander, and all the humeri of two other Andaman Islanders, left humerus of Bushman, the humeri of the two Negresses, right humerus of one Negro, and both humeri of the larger male Hindoo. Of the fifty-eight humeri examined in these skeletons, the intercondyloid foramen existed, therefore, in eighteen specimens, being at the rate of 31 per cent., which is a very much larger proportion than one finds in the humeri of modern Europeans, in which it has been estimated by MM. Hamy and Sauvages as from 4 to 5 per cent.[1] Observations on its frequency in several aboriginal races have now been put on record. Thus M. Broca found it to be frequent in the humeri of the people of the stone period.[2] Professor Wyman states that in the Mound builders of the United States it has been seen in 31 per cent.,[3] and M. Topinard gives the proportion in Polynesians as 34 per cent., in Melanesians 14 per cent., in Negros 21 per cent., and in natives of the Grand Canary Islands as 25·6 per cent.[4] Professor Flower found it very common in female Andaman Islanders, occurring in eleven out of seventeen humeri, whilst it was only five times present in sixteen humeri of males. This defect in the ossification of the humerus, it may be noted, occurs frequently in races many of which exhibit, in the weight and massiveness of their crania, evidence of an almost exuberant ossification in that part of the skeleton.

In the Chinese and the female Hindoo, the upper epiphysis of the humerus and the lower epiphysis of both radius and ulna, were not fully fused with the shafts of their respective bones, for the line of demarcation between shaft and epiphysis was visible on the surface of each bone.

---

[1] Quoted by M. Topinard, reference below.
[2] *Bull. Soc. d'Anthropologie*, 1865.
[3] *Reports of Peabody Museum*, 1871.
[4] Éléments d'Anthropologie générale, 1885, p. 1015.

Measurements of the Bones.

The length of the bones of the shaft of the upper limb was taken on a Broca's osteometric board, made by M. Collin, Paris. I measured the maximum length of each humerus from the top of the head to the most projecting part of the trochlear surface. In each radius I measured the length from the top of the radius to both the base and the tip of the styloid process, and in each ulna from the summit of the olecranon to both the inferior articular surface and the tip of the styloid process. The measurement to the tip of the styloid process in both radius and ulna gives the maximum length of each of those bones. In taking these measurements I was desirous of ascertaining the absolute length of each bone, the relative length of the corresponding bones in opposite limbs of the same skeleton, and the proportionate length which the bones of the forearm bore to the bone of the upper arm in the same limb.

The longest humerus was in the right arm of one of the Negro skeletons, in which it measured 372 mm.; the longest humerus in each of the two other Negros was 339 and 324 mm., and in the two Negresses 331 and 307 mm.[1] In the male skeleton, presented by Dr. Anderson as a Hindoo, the left humerus was 370 mm. long; in the other male Hindoo each humerus was 318 mm., and in the female the right humerus was 285 mm. In the Sikh the right humerus was 354 mm., in the Chinese 298 mm., and in the Malay the left humerus was 307 mm. In the male Australians the maximum humerus was 352 mm., in the Riverina skeleton; then followed 348 mm. in the Queensland, 335 in the Manly Cove, 334 in the Eucla, 330 in the Perth, and 325 mm. in the Swan Hill skeleton; whilst in the female from West Victoria the right humerus was only 287 mm. The right humerus of the male New Zealander from Te Aroha was 335 mm., and the left in the Otago skeleton was 326 mm. In the one female Oahuan the maximum humerus was 311 mm., in the other 267 mm. In the male Esquimaux the right humerus was 343 mm., in the female 326 mm. In the male Lapp the right humerus was 299 mm., in the female 280 mm. In the Bushman the right humerus was 288 mm. long. The longest humerus in the Andaman Islanders was 281 mm. in one skeleton, 278 in another, 253 in a third, and 248 in a fourth.

The longest radius, the length of which was 287 mm., was in the right arm of the Negro skeleton which also had the longest humerus. In the other Negros the maximum radius was 273 and 258 mm., and in the Negresses 245 and 242 mm. In Dr. Anderson's male Hindoo the maximum radius was 282 mm., in the other male Hindoo 257, and in the female 233 mm. In the Sikh the longest radius was 267, in the Malay 250, and in the Chinese 227 mm. Both radii of the Queensland and the left radius of the Riverina skeleton measured 270 mm., and the maximum radius in the

---

[1] In Table XIV., p. 109, the maximum lengths of the humerus and radius in thirty of the skeletons which I have measured is recorded.

Eucla, Manly Cove, Swan Hill, and Perth skeletons was respectively 264, 259, 252, and 246 mm.; in the female the maximum length was 222 mm. The Otago skeleton had the longest radius in the New Zealanders, 263 mm., whilst in the Te Aroha specimen it was 252 mm. In one female Oahuan the maximum radius was 234 mm., in the other 211 mm. In the male Esquimaux the maximum radius was 239 mm., in the female 251 mm. In the male and female Lapp the longest radius was 207 mm. In the Bushman the right or longer radius was 220 mm. In one Andaman Islander the maximum radius was 225, in another 223 mm. The usual length of the styloid process in these specimens was 3, 4, or 5 mm.; but in the longest radius in the Negros, in the shorter male Hindoo, and in an Andaman Islander, it was 7 mm., and in another Negro it was 9 mm.

The longest ulna was in Dr. Anderson's male Hindoo, which measured 305 mm.; in the other male it was 273 mm., and in the female 248 mm. In the Sikh the maximum ulna was 297, in the Malay 265, and in the Chinese 247 mm. In the Negro, with the long humerus and radius, the maximum ulna, the right, was 301 mm.; in the other Negros 298 and 272 mm., and in the Negresses 261 and 258 mm. The Queensland skeleton, amongst the Australians, had the longest ulna, 292 mm., and then followed the Riverina 287, Eucla 280, Manly Cove 275, Swan Hill 264, and Perth 259 mm., whilst in the female from Victoria the right ulna was 232 mm. The right ulna from Te Aroha, New Zealand, was 279, and the left from Otago 278 mm. In one Oahuan the ulna was 258, in the other 230 mm. In the female Esquimaux the maximum ulna was 277, and in the male 265 mm. In the female Lapp the maximum ulna was 226, and in the male 220 mm. In the Bushman the right or longer ulna was 234 mm. In one Andaman Islander the longer ulna was 241, in another 239 mm. In many of the skeletons, as the Eucla, Perth, and Manly Cove Australians, the Malay, Andaman Islanders, and male Lapp, the Negros, Negresses, and Hindoos, the styloid process did not project more than 1, 2, or 3 mm. beyond the inferior articular surface; but in the Riverina skeleton it projected 6 mm., and in the Sikh 7 mm. beyond it.

I shall now speak of the relative length of the corresponding bones in the opposite limbs of the same person. The right humerus was longer than the left in the Sikh, Chinese, Manly Cove, Riverina, Perth, Swan Hill, and West Victoria Australians, in both Oahuans, the Bush, four Andaman Islanders, both Lapps, both Esquimaux, the female Hindoo, two Negros, and two Negresses. The left humerus was longer than the right in the Eucla and Queensland Australians, the Otago skeleton, a Negro, and Dr. Anderson's male Hindoo. The humeri were equal in length in the other male Hindoo. The differences in length on the two sides sometimes did not exceed 1, 2, or 3 mm. But in the Sikh, Manly Cove, an Andaman Islander, the male Lapp, and an Esquimaux it was 6 mm., in an Oahuan and Negro 7 mm., in the Negro with the longest humerus 8 mm., in the female Australian 10 mm., and in the female Lapp 12 mm.

The right radius was longer than the left in the Sikh, the Chinese, the Manly Cove, Perth, and Swan Hill Australians, both Oahuans, the Bush, two Andaman Islanders, the female Lapp, the three Hindoos, the male Esquimaux, two Negros, and one Negress. The left radius was longer than the right in the Riverina, Eucla, and West Victoria Australians, the Otago skeleton, male Lapp, female Esquimaux, and one Negro. The two radii were of equal length in the Queensland and an Andaman skeleton. The difference between the two radii was usually 1, 2, or 3 mm., but in one Negro it was 6 mm.; in another, viz., the one with the longest radius, it was 8 mm., and in the Otago skeleton 9 mm.

The right ulna was longer than the left in the Sikh, Chinese, Manly Cove, Perth, Queensland, and West Victoria Australians, one Oahuan, the Bushman, two Andaman Islanders, both Lapps, the male Esquimaux, the three Hindoos, a Negro, and a Negress. The left ulna was longer than the right in the Malay, Eucla Australian, Otago skeleton, female Esquimaux, a Negro, and a Negress. The bones were equal in length in the Swan Hill Australian, an Andaman Islander, and a Negro. The difference between the lengths of the two bones was usually not more than 1, 2, or 3 mm., but in the Chinese, Otago skeleton, and Bushman it rose to 6 mm.

That differences existed in the relative lengths of the forearm and the upper arm in the races of men was pointed out by Charles White at the end of the last century in a comparative study of the Negro and the European,[1] in which he found that the forearm in the former was longer in proportion to the upper arm than in the latter. Prof. Humphry also recorded, in his treatise on the Human Skeleton, a similar observation. M. Broca subsequently made more extended inquiries into this subject,[2] and showed that if the humerus were regarded as equal in length to 100, the mean length of the radius in fifteen Negros was 79·4, and in nine Europeans 73·9. I have, in estimating the proportionate length of the forearm to the upper arm in the same limb, in my series of skeletons, selected, when the bones were uninjured, the right limb, and have compared the maximum length of the humerus with that of the radius, the styloid process being included.[3] On the assumption that the length of the humerus was = 100, the proportionate length of the radius was obtained by the formula $\frac{\text{radial length} \times 100}{\text{humeral length}}$, the product is the radio-humeral or antebrachial index.

To furnish a standard of comparison for these exotic skeletons, I shall in the first instance state the indices obtained by the measurements of the bones of the shaft of the upper limb in Europeans as recorded by Humphry, Broca, Hamy, Topinard and Flower. Prof. Humphry's measurements of twenty-five skeletons gave a mean radio-

---

[1] An Account of the regular gradation in Man and in different Animals, &c., London, 1799.
[2] Sur les proportions relatives du Bras de l'Avant-bras, &c., in Bull. de la Soc. d'Anthropologie, April 3, 1862, t. iii.
[3] In Table XIV., p. 109, I have given the maximum length both of humerus and radius in my series of skeletons, the dimensions in most cases having been taken from the right limb.

humeral index 72·4. M. Broca[1] obtained 73·9 as the mean radio-humeral index of nine Europeans, five men and four women. M. Hamy,[2] who measured the maximum length of the humerus, obtained a mean of 72·1 in European skeletons. M. Topinard gives[3] the mean radio-humeral index of one series of eighty-five European male skeletons as 72·5, of another series of fifty-five as 73, and of a third series of ten as 74·7; the mean of the whole being 73·4; whilst the mean in twenty-six European women was 72·4. Professor Flower[4] states that the mean of fourteen European skeletons which he measured was 73·9, and this number corresponds exactly with the results obtained by M. Broca from the measurements of his nine skeletons.

In my series of six male Australians the radio-humeral index varied from 78 in the Eucla skeleton to 74 in that from Perth, and the mean of the series was 76·5, whilst in the single female the index was 77. The mean index of three Australians recorded by Topinard was 76·6, that of eleven skeletons measured by Flower was 76·5, that of four skeletons measured by Spengel in the Blumenbach collection in Göttingen was 76·4, in Ecker's young Australian the index was 73, and in Keferstein's old skeleton 79. From the measurements, therefore, of the above twenty-seven skeletons, we are in a position to state with some certainty that the mean radio-humeral index in the aboriginal Australians lies between 76 and 77, and that in this race, as in the Negros, the radius is longer in proportion to the humerus than in Europeans.

The radio-humeral index in two of the Oahuan female skeletons which possessed the upper limbs was 79 and 75 respectively, the mean being 77; and in two male New Zealanders it was 75 and 78, with a mean of 76·5. The measurements of the bones of the upper limb of some Pacific Islanders have also been taken by M. Topinard, who gives the mean radio-humeral index of eight New Caledonians at 76, and five Polynesians also at 76. Barnard Davis has given the radio-humeral index of a male Loyalty Islander as 77, of a male Tannese as 83, and Spengel[5] has recorded this index in an "Alfuru" as 79·7. Spengel has also given the mean lengths of the humerus in Fijians[6] as 315·5 mm., and that of the radius as 264 mm., which yield an index 83·6. E. Tüngel states[7] that the mean length of the humerus in the skeletons collected by Dr. A. B. Meyer in the neighbourhood of Rubi, at the south end of Geelvink Bay, New Guinea, was 313·8 mm.,

---

[1] M. Broca measured the length of the humerus from the head to the radial articular surface, which is somewhat less than the maximum length; so that the radio-humeral index which he obtained is a little higher than when the maximum length is taken.

[2] Les proportions du Bras and de l'Avant-bras in Revue d'Anthropologie, t. i. p. 91, 1872.

[3] Anthropology, English Translation, 1878, and Éléments d'Anthropologie generale, Paris, 1885.

[4] The references to authorities on the Bones of the Limbs, except when otherwise stated, are the same as those given in the Bibliography of the Pelvis, pp. 3, 4, 5.

[5] See Table, p. 96, in Supplement to Thesaurus Cranium, by Barnard Davis.

[6] Journal der Mus. Godeffroy, Heft. iv., 1873. I quote the mean length of the humerus and radius from Tüngel's Memoir, which yield the index stated above, though Tüngel himself places the relation of the radial to the humeral length as 79·2.

[7] Messungen von Skeletknochen der Papuas, Mittheil. aus dem K. Zoolog. Museum zu Dresden, Heft. i., 1877.

and the mean length of the radius was 233, which gave a radio-humeral index 74·2. It should be stated, however, that the specimens examined by Tüngel were not such as to furnish very accurately the proportion of the radius to the humerus, for though thirteen humeri were present there were only four radii, and it was not certain to which humeri they corresponded.

Two Tasmanian men measured by Topinard had a mean index of 78·7, whilst in two women the index was 78·6; in one Tasmanian woman measured by Barnard Davis the index was 80, whilst three Tasmanian men had a mean index 81; the average of the eight specimens being 79·6.

The radio-humeral index in my male Bushman was 76, and in a Bushman measured by G. Fritsch it was 74·5. In two Bush women measured by M. Topinard the mean index was 73·9, and in one measured by G. Fritsch it was only 68. From Professor Humphry's measurements of three Bushmen I have calculated an index 76·8. The mean of eight skeletons of both sexes was 73·8. The mean index in four male Kaffirs measured by G. Fritsch was 78·7, the range of variation in these skeletons being from 74·5 to 81; in a Hottentot woman examined by the same author the index was 71.

The mean radio-humeral index in my three Negros was 78·5, the range being from 77 to 80·5; the mean of my two Negresses was 76. From Professor Humphry's measurements of twenty-five Negros, probably skeletons of both sexes, an average index of 77·7 can be calculated. M. Broca obtained 79·4 as the mean index of fifteen skeletons, nine men and six women. M. Hamy states that the twenty-five skeletons which he measured gave a mean index 78·2. M. Topinard gives the mean of thirty-two Negros as 79, and of ten Negresses as 78·3. The mean of two Negros in the Blumenbach collection measured by Spengel was 82·8; and the Balumba Negro in the Barnard Davis collection had an index 85·7.

The mean index of my three Andaman Islanders, in which the bones of the forearm were preserved and fully ossified, was 81·2; in one Andaman woman measured by M. Topinard it was 81·7; and in twenty-nine skeletons of Andaman Islanders, measured by Professor Flower, this index was 80·6, being 81·5 for the men and 79·7 for the women.

In one of the two Negrito women measured by Meyer and Tüngel the radio-humeral index was 85, in the other 86; in the woman of the Aëta tribe, measured by Hamy, this index was 80; the mean of the three specimens was therefore 83·7.

In my two male Hindoos the mean radio-humeral index was 78·9, and in the female it was 81·7. M. Topinard gives 77·2 as the mean of four Hindoo men, and 75 as the mean of three Hindoo women. The mean index in my male Sikh was 75, in Barnard Davis's "Bariam Singh" it was 76, and in his Bhutea skeleton it was 77.

In my Chinese skeleton the radio-humeral index was 76; in a Chinaman measured by Meyer and Tüngel it was 80·5; in five Chinese and Annamite men measured by

M. Topinard it was 78, and in two Chinese and Japanese women it was 77·9; in a male Chinese recorded by Spengel it was 79·2; the mean measurements by Barnard Davis of two male Japanese was 82, and in a female Aino the index was 75. The radio-humeral index in my Malay skeleton was 81, in a male Banda Islander in the Göttingen collection, recorded both by Keferstein [1] and by Spengel, it was 78·2, and in the Kubu skeleton measured by Garson it was 74·1.

In the male Esquimaux, which I measured, the radio-humeral index was 69·6, and in the female 76, whilst in a male Esquimaux measured by M. Topinard this index was 69·8. In a male Samoyed, also recorded by Topinard, this index was 72·9. In my male Lapp the radio-humeral index was 68, and in the female 74.

I have not myself had the opportunity of measuring the bones of the shaft of the upper limb in any skeleton of the American aborigines. Barnard Davis has given the radio-humeral index in an Illinois Indian as 80, in a South American Puelche Indian as 75, and in an ancient Peruvian also as 75. M. Topinard has recorded the radio-humeral index of five male South American Indians as 77·4, and of six females also as 77·4. Dr. Garson, in his recent memoir on the Yahgan tribe of the inhabitants of Tierra del Fuego, has placed the radio-humeral index of five male skeletons at 81·3.

From this general review of the results which have been obtained by those anatomists who have measured the relative lengths of the radius and humerus in different races of men, it is evident that an appreciable disparity exists in the lengths of these two bones, and that the forearm, in proportion to the upper arm, is longer in some races than in others. In estimating, however, what this disparity is, one experiences a similar difficulty to that which one had to contend with in the study of race differences in the pelvis, viz., the comparatively small number of specimens of some of the races which have as yet been measured, so that it is impossible to speak with certainty of the average index in them. Sufficient material, however, seems to have been collected to enable one to make a provisional grouping, based on these differences, in the radio-humeral index. At one end of the series we find the natives of Western Europe, with the Lapps and the Esquimaux, possessing a low index, and at the opposite end the Andaman Islanders, Negritos, and Yahgan Fuegians with a high radio-humeral index; whilst the most important and most numerous of the black races, some of the yellow races, and probably the Continental American Indians, occupy an intermediate position. The extremes are so far asunder that it seems possible to make three groups, as follows:—those in which this index is below 75, those in which it is 80 or upwards, and those in which the radio-humeral index ranges from 75 to 79·9, both inclusive. Those with a low index, i.e., with a relatively short forearm, may be called *brachykerkic* (κερκίς, radius); those with a high index, i.e., a relatively long forearm, may be called *dolichokerkic*; whilst those

[1] Bemerkungen über das Skelett eines Australiers, Dresden, 1865.

whose index is intermediate are *mesatikerkic*. Table XII. embodies this provisional arrangement, but, from the queries appended, it will be seen that I do not speak with confidence of the position of several of these races.

TABLE XII.

DOLICHOKERKIC. Index 80 or upwards.	MESATIKERKIC. Index 75 to 79.	BRACHYKERKIC. Index below 75.
Andaman Islanders. Negritos. Fuegians. Melanesians ?	Australians. Tasmanians. Polynesians. Melanesians ? Kaffirs. Negros. Hindoos. Sikh. Chinese. Malays ? American Indians.	Europeans. Lapps. Esquimaux. Samoyed ? Bushmen ?

Professor Humphry pointed out several years ago, in his treatise on the Human Skeleton, that the Negro presented more numerous approximations to the proportions of the fœtal than to those of the adult European, and that in the fœtus the forearm has greater relative dimensions than the upper arm. M. Hamy has measured[1] the upper limb in sixty-two European fœtuses and children from $2\frac{1}{2}$ months to $13\frac{1}{2}$ years, and has found a gradually decreasing proportion in the length of the radius to the humerus as the age advanced. In a fœtus of $2\frac{1}{2}$ months, the proportion of radius was 88·8, the humerus being equal to 100; the mean proportion of radius in six fœtuses from 4 to 5 months was 80·4, and from 5 to 7 months 77·6; the mean in eleven new-born infants was 76·2; the mean in seven infants from 21 to 30 days was 74·5; and the mean in six children from 5 to $13\frac{1}{2}$ years was 72·3. Those races, therefore, in which the adults have dolichokerkic proportions, approximate, in the relations of the forearm to the upper arm, to the embryo of a European before the end of the 5th month; those whose proportions are mesatikerkic to embryos after the 5th month and to new-born children; whilst those with brachykerkic proportions are like European children above 5 years of age and European adults.

[1] Recherches sur les proportions du Bras et de l'Avant-bras aux différents ages de la Vie, *Revue d'Anthropologie*, t. i. p. 79, 1872.

SHAFT OF THE INFERIOR EXTREMITY.

Both the femur and the tibia were examined in the several skeletons to see if any peculiarities existed in the shape of the bones. M. Broca directed attention some years ago to some femora in which the middle third of the shaft was prismatic and triangular, the lateral surfaces being concave, and the linea aspera projecting posteriorly as a strong raised ridge. Bones of this shape were termed *femur à pilastre* or *femur à colonne*. The femora from Cro-Magnon, near Les Eyzies, and those of the Guanches in the Museum of the Anthropological Society of Paris, were illustrative of this shape of femur, and M. Topinard has found the femora of the New Caledonians to possess a similar form.

In my series of Australian skeletons this variety of femur was seen to great advantage in those from the Riverina, Eucla, Manly Cove, and Queensland. In the Riverina skeleton the transverse diameter of the middle of the shaft of the right femur was 25 mm., and the antero-posterior diameter was 33 mm., which gives an index of 132; in the Eucla, Manly Cove, and Queensland skeletons this index was respectively 120, 120, and 127. In almost all the Australian femora the ridge from the linea aspera to the great trochanter to which the gluteus maximus is attached, was strongly marked; in some it was raised so as to form a low trochanter tertius, and the projection was accentuated by an elongated depression parallel to its outer side. In one adult Andaman Islander the prismatic form of the femoral shaft was very pronounced, and the same character was seen in the Oahuan, Esquimaux, and Lapp skeletons. I have also sometimes seen the shaft of the femur in Europeans in my dissecting room prismatic in shape. In five of seven New Zealand femora a peculiar flattening of the upper third of the anterior surface of the shaft immediately below the great trochanter was recognised. This was associated with, and apparently due to the projection outwards of an infra-trochanteric ridge, extending downwards from below the outer side of the great trochanter; but in these bones the middle of the shaft was not prismatic. A similar flattening was also observed in an odd femur, which, though it was presented to the museum along with some New Zealand bones, was said to be Australian. In the femora from a skeleton, which I obtained a number of years ago in a cave at Oban, Argyllshire, an equally well-pronounced flattening of the upper third of the shaft was seen, and the infra-trochanteric ridge formed a definite bulging quite distinct from and in front of the ridge leading from the great trochanter to the linea aspera.[1] The linea aspera was strong, but not so projecting as in the Australians. In the Oahuan femora, and in the Lapp and Esquimaux skeletons, the flattened anterior surface of the upper third of the shaft with the prominent external infra-trochanteric ridge was also present. In some of the

---

[1] This form of femur apparently corresponds with that found in a femur from a sepulchral cave at Perthi-Chwaren in Denbighshire, described by Mr. Busk in *Journ. Ethnol. Soc. Lond.*, January 1871. I described this Oban cave to the Anthropological Department of the British Association in 1871 (see *Reports* of Edinburgh meeting, p. 160, 1871).

femora the anterior aspect of the lower third of the shaft was raised almost into a ridge leading upwards from the outer lip of the patellar articular surface, which caused the shaft internal to that ridge to slope downwards and inwards towards the internal tuberosity. In the Lapp skeletons, in addition to the infra-trochanteric ridge, a low trochanter tertius was present. In one Hindoo skeleton and in the Malay a third trochanter was moderately developed. In the Hindoos, Sikh, and Chinese, the lateral surfaces of the shaft of the femur were not concave, and the linea aspera was not strongly ridged. The index of the relation of the antero-posterior and transverse diameters at the middle of the shaft of the femur in the tall Hindoo was 103 for the right and 111 for the left bone; in the Sikh 93 for the right and 103 for the left femur; in the Malay 104 for the left femur, the right having been broken; in the Chinese 104 for the right and 100 for the left bone. In the Bush femora the linea aspera was moderate, and the same remark applies to the Negro skeletons.

In the Anthropoid apes the linea aspera is very faintly marked, the shaft of the femur is not prismatic, but is antero-posteriorly compressed, and with the lateral aspects rounded. In an adult orang the transverse diameter of the middle of the shaft of each femur was 24 mm. and the antero-posterior diameter 18 mm., the index being only 75; in an adult chimpanzee the corresponding diameters were 27 and 21 mm., and the index was 77.

Of the femora, the indices of which have been given above, the Australians exhibit a much wider departure from the proportions of the shaft in the Anthropoid apes than do the skeletons of the Asiatics. The strength and projection of the linea aspera are to be associated with the development of the muscles engaged in retaining the equilibrium of the trunk on the thighs and hip joints, and in extending the knee joint, that is to say, groups of muscles which play an important part in the assumption and preservation of the erect posture.

The investigations both of Mr. Busk and of M. Broca demonstrated some years ago the tendency in primeval man, as shown in skeletons obtained in sepulchral caves in various parts of Western Europe, to have the shaft of the tibia laterally compressed. Conjoined with this lateral compression the posterior surface of the tibia was no longer flattened, but convex from side to side. To this form of tibia the term *platyknemic* has been applied. Similar observations have been made by Professor Jeffries Wyman on tibiæ from ancient mounds in the United States. Virchow has also called attention to the platyknemic type of tibia (although with certain differences) in an Oahuan, a native of New Britain, and in some skeletons from the Philippine Islands, including Negritos. M. Hamy recognised a lateral flattening in the tibiæ of his Aëta Negrito, although by no means so strongly as in European skeletons of the Stone Age. The occurrence of platyknemia in various races of men has recently been discussed by M. Kuhff.[1] In the tibiæ

[1] See Busk in *Trans. Internat. Congress of Prehistoric Archæology*, 1868, p. 161, and *Journ. Ethnol. Soc. Lond.*, January 1874; Broca in *Mémoires sur les ossemens des Eyzies*, Paris, 1868; J. Wyman in *Fourth Annual Report of Peabody Museum*, 1871; Virchow in *Verhandl. d. Berlin. Ges. f. Anthrop.* in *Zeitsch. f. Ethn.*, 1872, Bd. iv. s. 207, and 1880, Bd. xii. s. 112; M. Hamy in *Nouvelles Archives du Muséum*, t. ii. p. 209, 1879, also *Reliquiæ Aquitanicæ*; and Kuhff in *Revue d'Anthropologie*, 1881.

of the skeleton from the Oban bone cave, referred to in a preceding paragraph (p. 97), the shaft was decidedly platyknemic; the breadth of the middle of the shaft from the interosseous to the inner border was 19 mm., and the antero-posterior diameter at the same spot was 29 mm., the index was therefore 65·5, a proportion a little higher than that obtained by M. Broca as the mean, 64, of the tibiæ from the Caverne de l'Homme-Mort, Lozère, but not so high as the mean, 66, of the Guanche tibiæ from the Great Canary Islands.

I examined the tibiæ in my series of exotic skeletons with reference to the platyknemic form, and compared them with a well-formed European tibia. In the Oahuans, adult Andaman Islanders, and Bushman the tibial shafts were decidedly compressed, and the posterior surface convex, so that they were platyknemic, although not in the same marked degree as in the tibia from Cro-Magnon, near Les Eyzies, described by M. Broca, but more like those from Perthi-Chwaren figured by Mr. Busk. In many of the other skeletons also, as the New Zealanders, Lapps, Esquimaux, Hindoos, Sikh, and Malay, a tendency to the platyknemic form was distinctly recognisable. In some of the Australian skeletons, in one Hindoo, and in the Chinese the fibular articular area on the external tuberosity of the tibia was indistinct, and the same remark applies to the corresponding surface on the head of the fibula. In the Anthropoid apes the shaft of the tibia also possesses a certain amount of lateral compression, and the posterior surface is somewhat convex, but the anterior border of the bone is not sharp but rounded.

Measurements of the Bones.

The length of the bones of the shaft of the lower limb was taken by means of a Broca's osteometric board. In each femur I measured the maximum length of the bone between the head and the most projecting point of the inner condyle; the maximum trochanteric length from the same point of the inner condyle to the tip of the great trochanter; the length when both condyles were placed in contact with the vertical plane of the osteometric board, both to the summit of the head and to the tip of the great trochanter; these two last measurements constituting what the French anthropologists call its length in the oblique position. In each tibia I measured the length from the condylar articular surfaces both to the tip of the malleolus and to the base of the malleolus, where it articulates with the superior surface of the astragalus. The distance from the condylar articular surfaces to the tip of the malleolus I call the maximum length of the tibia. In these measurements my object has been to determine the absolute length of the femur and tibia, the relative length of the corresponding bones in opposite limbs of the same skeleton, the proportionate length which the tibia bears to the femur in the same limb, and the relative length of the femur to the humerus.

The longest femur was in the skeleton presented by Dr. Anderson as a male Hindoo, in which the right thigh bone measured in its maximum length 509 mm.; in the other male

Hindoo the left femur was 460 mm., and in the female 408 mm.[1] In the Sikh the right femur was 498 mm., in the Chinese the left femur was 420 mm., and in the Malay 450 mm. long. In the Riverina Australian the right femur was 496 mm., in the Queensland skeleton each femur was 492 mm., the maximum femur in the Eucla skeleton was 468 mm., the Manly Cove 467 mm., Swan Hill 458 mm., Perth 452 mm., and in the femur from West Victoria 404 mm. The maximum femur in the New Zealanders was 462 mm. in the left femur from Te Aroha, in the left femur from Otago 460 mm., whilst in another New Zealander the length was only 425 mm., but the bones were robust. In the female Oahuans the longest femur was 432 mm., and the shortest 391 mm. The longest femur in the three Negros was 498 mm., the shortest 464 mm., and in the two Negresses the longest was 462 and the shortest 430 mm. In the male Esquimaux the longest femur (left) was 435 mm.; in the female it was 428 mm. In the male Lapp the maximum femur was 408 mm., in the female 362 mm. In the Bushman both femora were 420 mm. In two of the Andaman Islanders the left femur attained a length of 395 mm., but in another the maximum length was as low as 363 mm.

The differences between the maximum length of the femur and the maximum trochanteric length ranged from 26 mm. in the right femur of the Riverina Australian to 6 mm. in the right femur of one of the Negros. In eighteen of the sixty-two femora measured the total maximum length exceeded the maximum trochanteric length by 20 mm. or upwards; in forty-four specimens the maximum length was less than 20 mm. in excess of the trochanteric, and in three of these, being Negro femora, it was less than 10 mm. When these two diameters approach each other, the approximation in length expresses either an elongation of the great trochanter in connection with the insertion of the muscles of the buttock; or a diminution in the angle between the neck and shaft of the femur, so that it was almost a right angle. The total maximum length exceeded the length in the oblique position by as much as 9 mm. in the two Negresses, 8 mm. in the female Esquimaux, 7 mm. in the female Oahuans, a male New Zealander, and two male Australians; in one male Hindoo and in one male Andaman Islander these two diameters were equal; as a rule the total maximum length was not more than 3 or 4 mm. in excess of the length in the oblique position, and the differences between them expressed the greater or less projection of the inner condyle beyond the plane of the outer condyle.

The longest tibia was in Dr. Anderson's Hindoo skeleton, in which the right tibia in its maximum length measured 429 mm., but in the other male Hindoo it was only 398 mm., and in the female the left tibia was 348 mm. In the Sikh the right tibia was 403 mm., the Chinese was 331 mm., and the Malay 372 mm. In the male Australians the longest tibia was 423 mm. in the Riverina, 421 mm. in the Queensland, 394 mm. in the Swan Hill, 392 mm. in the Eucla, 387 mm. in the Perth, and 384 mm. in the Manly

---

[1] In Table XIV., p. 169, the maximum length of the femur and tibia in thirty of the skeletons which I have measured is recorded.

Cove skeletons; whilst in the female from West Victoria the maximum length of the tibia was only 340 mm. The maximum tibia in the left leg of the Otago New Zealander was 401 mm., and in the skeleton from Te Aroha 365 mm. In one female Oahuan the tibiæ each measured 362 mm., in the other the maximum tibia was 332 mm. The maximum tibia in the three Negros was 419 mm., and the minimum 410 mm., and in the two Negresses the maximum was 385 and the minimum 348 mm. In the male Esquimaux the maximum tibia was 375 mm., in the female 347 mm. In the male Lapp the maximum tibia was 307 mm.; in the female each tibia measured 290 mm. In the Bushman both tibiæ measured 334 mm. In one Andaman Islander the right tibia (an odd bone) was 362 mm. long, in another 337 mm., in a third the left tibia was 336 mm., in a fourth 296 mm. In seventeen of the fifty-eight tibiæ measured the malleolus projected 10 mm. beyond the inferior articular surface of the tibia: in twenty-four specimens the projection was less than 10 mm.—the shortest malleoli being in the male Esquimaux, where the right was only 6 mm. and the left 5 mm. long; in seventeen specimens the malleolar projection was more than 10 mm., and the skeletons in which they reached their maximum were the Sikh, in which both internal malleoli were 13 mm., and the right tibia of the Queensland Australian, and the left tibia of the tallest Hindoo, in each of which the malleolus was 14 mm. long. In none of the tibiæ was the spine included in the length of the bone, as Broca's osteometric board provides for the length being taken from the condylar articular surfaces.

In the next place I shall direct attention to the relative length of the corresponding bones in opposite limbs of the same skeleton. The right femur was longer than the left in the Sikh, a male Hindoo, one male Australian, one female from Oahu, the male Lapp, and three Negros. The left femur was longer than the right in a male and female Hindoo, in the Chinese, one female and four male Australians, two New Zealanders, three Andaman Islanders, one Oahuan, a female Lapp, two Esquimaux, and one Negro. The right and left femora were equal in length in a male Australian, a New Zealander, and in the Bush skeleton. Frequently the difference in length between opposite femora was not more than 1, 2, or 3 mm.; but in the Chinese the left femur was 5 mm. longer than the right, in a Negro and male Hindoo the right femur was 5 mm. the longer, in a male Australian, a male New Zealander, and a male Hindoo the left femur was 6 mm. the longer, in an Andaman Islander the left femur was 7 mm. the longer, and in a female Australian it was 12 mm. the longer.

The right tibia was longer than the left in the Sikh, two male Hindoos, the Malay, Chinese, a male Andaman Islander, four male Australians, and two Negros. The left tibia was longer than the right in the female and two male Australians, a female Hindoo, one Oahuan, a New Zealander, two Andaman Islanders, a Lapp, and both Esquimaux. The right and left tibiæ were equal in length in an Oahuan, a Bush, a Lapp, and a Negro skeleton. Usually the differences in length were only 1 or 2 mm., but in the Riverina Australian well as those of races short in stature, the range in the length of the femur and tibia was very remarkable. The tallest skeleton was that of the male Hindoo, presented to the Anatomical Museum of the University of Edinburgh by Dr. John Anderson, in which the shaft of the right limb was 922 mm. in length. On the supposition that the stature of the individual is twice the length of the femur and tibia, then the height of this man would have been 1844 mm., or 6 feet. In the Sikh the length of the right femur and tibia was 885, which by the same rule would give 1770 mm., or 5 feet 9¾ inches, as his approximate height. In both the Riverina Australian and in one of the Negro skeletons the right femur and tibia measured 903 mm., which by the same rule would give 1806 mm., or 5 feet 11 inches, as the approximate height of each of these persons. Dr. G. More Reid, by whom the Riverina Australian skeleton was presented to me for the University Museum, told me that this man, the chief of his tribe, was 5 feet 10 inches in height. The length of the femur and tibia in the Queensland skeleton was 892 mm., but both this and the Riverina skeleton were exceptionally high for the Australian aborigines, as in none of the other four male skeletons of this race did the conjoint length of these bones exceed 845 mm., and their mean in these four males was 835 mm. In the valuable Table VI. of the stature of the races of men, compiled by the Anthropometric Committee of the British Association,[1] the mean stature of the adult male Australian aborigines is given as 5 feet 5·68 inches, or 1669 mm., which, on the basis of the stature being twice that of the femur and tibia, would require for these bones conjointly a mean length of 834·5 mm., which corresponds with the mean of the four male Australians from Manly Cove, Eucla, Perth, and Swan Hill.

The Lapps and Andaman Islanders were in striking contrast, in the length of the bones of the shaft of the lower limb, to the skeletons just referred to. In the male Lapp the left femur and tibia measured 699 mm., which by the above rule would give a stature of 1398 mm., or 4 feet 7 inches. In the female Lapp, by a similar computation, the stature would have been only 1286 mm., or 4 feet 2½ inches. In the Table of the Anthropometric Committee the mean height of the adult male Lapp is stated, on the authority of Horch, to be 1500 mm., or 4 feet 11 inches. The mean height of three males measured by Garson[2] (the thickness of the soles of the boots being deducted) was 5 feet ½ inch; so that it is clear either that my male Lapp was much below the average, or that the bones of the shaft of the lower limb do not in this race bear so definite a relation to the stature as in the Australians, and on this point I may refer to an observation by Garson, who states that the lower limbs are short in proportion to the size of the trunk as compared with Europeans generally. In the Andaman Islanders the longest shaft in one skeleton was 718 mm., in another 720 mm., in a third 650 mm., which would give for the latter a stature of 1392 mm., or 4 feet 7 inches, which is below the average of 4 feet 10

[1] *Rep. Brit. Assoc.*, 1883, p. 270.
[2] Physical Characteristics of the Lapps, *Journ. Anthrop. Inst.*, vol. xv. p. 235, 1885.

inches obtained by Dr. Bannder[1] from the measurement of fourteen men, though M. de Quatrefages[2] places the height of the males of this race at 1436 mm., or 4 feet 8½ inches.

In one of the Sandwich Island women from Oahu the maximum length of the shaft of the limb was only 712 mm., but in the other it reached 779 mm., giving a computed stature in the one case of 1424 mm., or 4 feet 8 inches, and in the other 1558 mm., or 5 feet 1¼ inch. In the Bushman the maximum shaft was 744 mm., and the computed stature was 1488 mm., or 4 feet 10½ inches, which is higher by 147 mm. than the mean stature of the race as given in the Table of the Anthropometric Committee above referred to. The computed stature of the Otago Maori was 1700 mm., of the Malay 1616 mm., of the male Esquimaux 1606 mm.; the Malay approximated to the mean of the race as given by the Anthropometric Committee, but the Maori and Esquimaux were both appreciably below the average stated in their Table VI.

From the data provided in my Table XIII. the proportionate length of the leg to the thigh in the same limb may be calculated. On the assumption that the length of the femur = 100, the proportionate length of the tibia may be obtained by the formula $\frac{\text{tibial length} \times 100}{\text{femoral length}}$, the product is the *tibio-femoral index*.

To begin with, I shall refer to the results obtained by Professors Humphry, Flower, and M. Topinard from the measurements of these bones in Europeans. Humphry measured twenty-five European skeletons, and obtained 17·88 inches as the mean length of the femur and 14·4 inches as the mean length of the tibia; the mean tibio-femoral index of these specimens was 80·5. Flower states that the average tibio-femoral index of fourteen Europeans measured by himself was 82·1. Topinard gives the mean of fifty-five European men as 81·1, and a second series of ten skeletons as 80·4; whilst the mean of seventeen European women was 80·8. The difference between the results obtained by these anatomists is doubtless due to Professor Flower including the spine of the tibia in the length of that bone, which necessarily increases the value of the index, whilst M. Topinard omits the spine from his measurements.

In computing the tibio-femoral index in my specimens, I have made the calculation from the longer of the two limbs, the measurements of which are given in Table XIII., but in addition I have obtained this index in the skeleton of the Malay, the Te Aroha Maori, an Andaman Islander, a Negro and a Negress, in which one limb only was perfect.

In my series of six male Australians the tibio-femoral index ranged from 81 in the Manly Cove to 84·9 in the Swan Hill skeleton, and the mean of the series was 82·96; whilst in the only female skeleton this index was 80. The mean index of eleven Australians measured by Flower was 84·9; the mean of three Australians recorded by Topinard was 82·1; that of four Australians measured by Spengel 83·2; the index of

[1] *Proc. Roy. Soc. Edin.*, p. 415, Session 1879-80.
[2] Étude sur les Mincopies, in *Revue d'Anthropologie*, t. i. p. 53, 1872.

Ecker's Australian was 85, and of Keferstein's 82. The mean tibio-femoral index of this series of twenty-seven Australian skeletons is therefore 83·3. It should be stated, however, that the various measurements by myself and these other anatomists have not been made in precisely the same way; for both Ecker and Flower take the maximum length of the bones, both the spine and malleolus of the tibia being included; Spengel has apparently followed the same plan; Keferstein, whilst giving the maximum length of the femur, measures the tibia between the two articular surfaces, and thus excludes both spine and malleolus; the index recorded by Topinard was obtained from the maximum length of the femur, and from the tibia between the condylar articular surface and the tip of the malleolus. For the reason stated on p. 102, I have taken a somewhat different measurement in constructing Table XIII., but I have also calculated the mean index of my six male Australians according to the method of M. Topinard, and have obtained 84 as the index.[1] It follows, therefore, that according to this method a somewhat higher index is obtained than on the plan followed in constructing Table XIII., and this index would have been yet further increased if the spine of the tibia had been included in the length of that bone. These differences in the method of measurement and in the computed indices are to be kept in mind in the comparison of my observations with those of other anatomists, though my own observations are of course comparable with each other.

The tibio-femoral index in the two female Oahuans was 83 in each skeleton. In the Otago Maori it was 86; but in the left limb of the Maori from Te Aroha it was only 77·7, the tibia being unusually short. M. Topinard's measurements of five male Polynesians yield an index of 82·2, eight New Caledonians of 83·1, and three female New Caledonians of 84·5. Barnard Davis's Loyalty Islander had an index of 82, and his Tannese 80.[2] In Spengel's "Alfuru" the index was 85·9. The mean length of the femur in the Fiji Islanders measured by Spengel was 442 mm., and that of the tibia 362·4 mm., which gave an index of 81·8. Forty-four femora and twenty-eight tibiæ of Papuans were collected near Rubi, New Guinea, by Dr. Meyer; Tüngel's measurements of these bones gave, in the adult males, the mean length of the femur as 443·45 mm., and that of the tibia as 364·6 mm., the index being 82·2.

In two Tasmanian men measured by M. Topinard the mean tibio-femoral index was 83·6, and in two women it was 82·3; in skeletons measured by Barnard Davis this index was 80 in a woman, and the mean in three men was 85.

The tibio-femoral index in my male Bushman was 78·8; in a man measured by G. Fritsch the index was 82, and in a woman 79·5; in two Bushwomen recorded by M. Topinard the mean index was 85·8; from the measurements of three skeletons (sex not stated) given by Professor Humphry an index of 86 has been computed. In four male

---
[1] The maximum lengths are given in Table XIV., p. 109.
[2] Barnard Davis's measurements record the "extreme length" both of femur and tibia, as also do those of E. Tüngel.

Kaffirs measured by G. Fritsch the tibio-femoral index ranged from 80 to 83, the mean being 81·5. In a Hottentot woman he obtained an index of 79, and from Wyman's measurements of a male Hottentot I have calculated an index of 87.

The mean tibio-femoral index of my three Negros was 85·9, and the range of variation was from 82 to 88·7; the mean of my two Negresses was 81·5. From Professor Humphry's measurements of twenty-five Negros (sex not stated) I have calculated an index of 84·7. Two Negros in the Blumenbach collection, measured by Spengel, had the indices 85·5 and 82·2 respectively, and the Balumba Negro from the Gaboon measured by Barnard Davis had an index of 85. In M. Topinard's table the mean index of thirty-two Negros is 82·9, and of ten Negresses 84·4.

The mean index of four Andaman Islanders which I have measured[1] was 81·2, the extremes being 79 and 83. In the much more numerous series of skeletons examined by Professor Flower an index of 84·4, being exactly the same in both sexes, was obtained by his method of measurement.

In a male Negrito measured by Virchow,[2] the tibio-femoral index was 87, but it should be stated that the superior spine was included in the length of the tibia.

In one of the female Negrito skeletons measured by Meyer and Tüngel, the tibio-femoral index was 74·7, in the other 88; in M. Hamy's specimen it was 86 (the malleolus being included). The mean tibio-femoral index of these four Negrito skeletons was 83·9.

In my three Hindoos the tibio-femoral index was practically the same in each skeleton, 83; M. Topinard has given 83·9 as the mean index of three female Hindoos, and 82·8 as the mean index of four "Noirs de l'Inde." The index in my male Sikh was 78·8; in Barnard Davis's skeleton it was 77, and in his Bhutea it was 78.

In my Chinese skeleton this index was 76·7; in the Chinaman measured by Meyer and Tüngel it was 80; in five male Chinese recorded by M. Topinard the mean index was 80·2; whilst Spengel's measurement of the male skeleton in the Blumenbach collection gave an index of 82·3. In six Tartars in M. Topinard's table the mean tibio-femoral index was 79·6.

The tibio-femoral index of my male Malay was 80·7; in two male Javanese measured by Barnard Davis this index was 80 and 87 respectively; in a female Javanese in M. Topinard's table it was 85·2; the index of the Banda Islander's skeleton, according to Keferstein's method, was 83, and according to Spengel's, 85; the index in Garson's Kubu skeleton was 80·7. The Aino skeleton measured by Barnard Davis was 76·8.

In my male Esquimaux the index was 85, and in the female 79·8; but in the male measured by M. Topinard it was 78·7; in his male Samoyed this index was 79·8. In my male Lapp the tibio-femoral index was only 73·8, and in the female 78.

In the aborigines of America, Barnard Davis has obtained a tibio-femoral index of

---

[1] These include a specimen not in Table XIII., in which the right femur was perfect, but the left was broken.
[2] *Verhandl. der Berlin. Ges. f. Anth.* in *Zeitsch. f. Ethn.*, Bd. iv. s. 206, 1872.

83 in a male Illinois, 81 in a male Puelche Indian, 84 in an ancient Peruvian; and M. Topinard has given 84·1 as the mean index of five South American men, and 83·1 as that of six South American women. The mean tibio-femoral index in the Yahgan Fuegians measured by Dr. Garson was 84·7.

A comparison of the several indices, computed from the measurements of the skeletons of the various races now examined, shows that considerable diversity exists in the proportionate length of the tibia and femur, so that in some the leg approaches nearer to the length of the thigh than in others. In attempting, however, to form an estimate of the disparity which exists between different races, one is met, not only with the difficulty which one experienced in comparing the proportionate lengths of the forearm and upper arm, viz., the small number of specimens of some of the races that have as yet been measured, but with the different methods of measurement which have been employed by anatomists, so that they cannot at all times be compared with each other. Hence, I do not feel prepared with the requisite data to make even such a preliminary grouping of these races, based on the proportional length of the leg and thigh, as I ventured to do, though with much diffidence, in the section on the superior extremity. As it is obvious, however, that in some races the leg is longer in proportion to the thigh than in other races, some people may be called long-legged *dolichoknemic* ($\kappa\nu\dot{\eta}\mu\eta$, tibia), others short-legged, *brachyknemic*; the word leg being used in its strict anatomical sense to express that segment of the lower limb which lies between the knee and ankle joints.

If we assume a tibio-femoral index, 83, as marking the division between the proportionally long-legged and short-legged, then we may say that those races, in which the mean index is 83 or upwards, are dolichoknemic, and amongst these we might rank the Australians, Tasmanians, Negros, Andaman Islanders, Negritos, American Indians, and Yahgan Fuegians; possibly also the Melanesians, though their exact position, as well as that of the Polynesians and Malays, is doubtful. On the other hand, when the mean tibio-femoral index is below 83, the race may be said to be brachyknemic, and in this group we might place Europeans, Chinese, Tartars, Lapps, Esquimaux, Samoyeds, possibly the other tribes occupying the most northern part of the continent of Asia, and the Mongolian race generally.

In the next instance I shall proceed to the comparison of the extreme lengths of the humerus and radius with those of the femur and tibia in the same skeleton, a line of investigation which was introduced a number of years ago by M. Broca.[1] If we assume the extreme length of femur + tibia (spine omitted) to = 100, then an *intermembral index* may be computed as follows :— $\dfrac{\text{humerus} + \text{radius} \times 100}{\text{femur} + \text{tibia}}$.

[1] Sur les proportions relatives des membres supérieurs et des membres inférieurs chez les Nègres et les Européens, &c., Bull. de la Soc. d'Anthropologie, ser. 2, t. ii. p. 641, November 21, 1867.

REPORT ON THE BONES OF THE HUMAN SKELETON. 109

To bring the facts on which this comparison is made into convenient compass, I have compiled Table XIV., in which the extreme lengths of the bones in the right upper and lower limbs are given in millimètres, though in a few instances, where the right limb was imperfect, the dimensions have been taken from the limb on the left side.

TABLE XIV.—Maximum Length of Bones of Shafts, Spine of Tibia excluded.

	Femur.	Tibia.	F. + T. Total.	Humerus.	Radius.	H. + R. Total.	Intermembral Index.
Manly Cove,	464	382	846	335	259	594	72·0
Riverina,	496	423	919	352	268	620	67·4
Eucla,	465	392	857	331	260	591	68·9
Perth,	452	385	837	330	246	576	68·8
Queensland,	492	421	913	347	270	617	67·5
Swan Hill,	457	394	851	325	252	577	67·8
W. Victoria, ♀,	404	339	743	287	221	508	68·3
Oahu, A ♀, Sandwich Islands,	391	330	721	267	211	478	66·2
Oahu, B ♀, Sandwich Islands,	432	362	794	311	234	545	68·6
Te Aroha, New Zealand,	462	365	827	335	252	587	70·9
Otago, New Zealand,	454	400	854	325	254	579	67·8
Bushman,	420	334	754	288	220	508	67·3
Negro,	464	412	876	339	273	612	69·8
Negro,	468	410	878	320	252	572	65·1
Negro,	498	419	917	372	287	659	71·8
Negress,	462	385	847	331	242	573	67·6
Negress,	434	353	787	307	242	549	69·7
Andaman,	394	337	731	278	225	503	68·8
Andaman,	388	330	718	281	223	504	70·1
Andaman,	363	290	653	248	207	455	69·6
Hindoo,	509	429	938	365	282	647	68·9
Hindoo,	454	398	852	318	257	575	67·4
Hindoo, ♀,	406	345	751	285	233	518	68·9
Sikh,	498	403	901	354	267	621	68·9
Chinese,	415	331	746	298	227	525	70·3
Malay,	450	372	822	307	250	557	67·7
Esquimaux,	434	374	808	343	239	582	72·0
Esquimaux, ♀,	425	314	770	326	250	576	74·8
Lapp,	408	304	712	299	205	504	70·7
Lapp, ♀,	360	290	650	280	207	487	74·9

(Australians bracket at left covering rows from Manly Cove to W. Victoria.)

When the intermembral index is relatively low, then the bones of the shaft of the upper limb are short in relation to the bones of the shaft of the lower limb, but when it is relatively high, then they more nearly approach them in length. Amongst Europeans the intermembral index, as estimated by Broca, from the measurements of fourteen skeletons, eight men and six women, was 69·73, and by Flower, also from the measurement of fourteen skeletons, 69·2. In my six male Australians it ranged from 72 to 67·4, and the mean of the series was 68·7 ; in the single female it was 68·3. The mean of the two Oahuans was 67·4, and that of the two Maoris 69·3.

The single Bushman had the intermembral index 67·3. In Fritsch's male I have calculated an index of 65·2, and in his female 68·5; whilst the corresponding mean index computed from Humphry's measurements of three Bush skeletons was 68·4. The mean of these six skeletons was 67·3. In Fritsch's Hottentot woman this index was 68·8, and in his four male Kaffirs it ranged from 68·6 to 70·3 with a mean of 69·4.

The mean index of my three Negro skeletons was 68·9, and of the two Negresses 68·6. From Professor Humphry's measurements of twenty-five Negro skeletons, I have calculated a mean intermembral index of 68·4, and M. Broca has given 68·27 as the mean index of the sixteen African Negros, ten men and six women, which he measured. A remarkable uniformity runs through the whole of the measurements of the shafts of the limbs in the Negro skeletons, and the intermembral index in this race obviously lies between 68 and 69. The mean index of my three Andaman Islanders was 69·5, which is higher than was obtained by Professor Flower from the measurements of twenty-five skeletons, in which the index was 68·3; that of the males being 69, and of the females 67·5. If my specimens are added to his then the mean of the entire series becomes 68·9.

The mean intermembral index of my three Hindoos was 68·1, and the highest of the series was only 68·9. In the skeleton of the male Sikh this index was also 68·9, but from the measurements given by Dr. Barnard Davis, it would seem that in his Sikh skeleton this index was only 65·8. In my Chinese the intermembral index was 70·3. From Spengel's measurements of his male Chinese I have computed an index of 67·7, the mean of the two skeletons being 69. In my Malay skeleton the intermembral index was 67·7; in one of Barnard Davis's Javanese this index was 70·4, in the other 67·4, and the mean of the three skeletons was 68·5. In Garson's Kubu skeleton the intermembral index was 70.

In both the Esquimaux and the Lapps the intermembral index was remarkably high. The mean of the two Esquimaux was 73·4, and of the two Lapps 72·8.

It would appear, therefore, that there is a certain amount of disparity in the proportion of the shaft of the upper limb to that of the lower limb in the different races of men. If we accept 69·5 as expressing the mean index in Europeans, then it is clear that the black races do not reach that mean, and that the shaft of the upper limb in them is proportionally shorter than the shaft of the lower limb. A similar proportion, if one may judge from the few specimens which have yet been measured, prevails amongst the Mongolians, Malays and natives of India. On the other hand in the Esquimaux and Lapps, and in the Yahgan Fuegians as measured by Garson, the mean index is distinctly higher than in Europeans, and expresses that the upper limb is relatively longer than the lower.

As the maximum lengths of both the femur and humerus are recorded in Table XIV., one can calculate, according to the method of M. Broca, the relative lengths of these two bones, and obtain a *femoro-humeral index* by the following formula $\frac{\text{humeral length} \times 100}{\text{femoral length}}$, the femur being regarded as = 100.

From Broca's measurements of fourteen Europeans, the femoro-humeral index was 72·2, and from Flower's measurements of eleven Europeans 72·9.

In my six male Australians this index varied from 70·5 to 73, and the mean was 71·4, in the single female it was 71. In one Oahuan this index was 68·3, in the other 72, the mean being 70. In one Maori this index was 72·5, in the other 71·5, the mean being 72.

In my Bush skeleton this index was only 68·5. I have calculated the index in Fritsch's Bushman, and find it also 68, but in his Bushwoman it was 73; whilst the mean of the three specimens measured by Humphry was 72. The mean of these six Bush skeletons was 70·3. In Fritsch's Hottentot woman this index was 72; and in his four male Kaffirs it ranged from 68·6 to 72·6, with a mean of 70·6.

The mean femoro-humeral index of my five Negro skeletons was 71·6, and from Professor Humphry's measurements of his twenty-five Negros the mean in them was 71·2, but the mean of the sixteen specimens, ten Negros and six Negresses, measured by M. Broca, was only 68·9. The mean index in my three Andaman Islanders was 70·4, and in Professor Flower's twenty-five skeletons it was 69·8, being 70·3 for the males and 69·2 for the females.

The mean index in my three Hindoos was 70·5. In my male Sikh the index was 71, and from Barnard Davis's measurements the index in his specimen was 66·5. In my Chinese this index was 71·8, and in the Chinese skeleton measured by Spengel it was 68·8. In my Malay the index was 68·2, and in each of Barnard Davis's Javanese it was 69·9. In Garson's Kubu skeleton this index was 75·2.

The mean femoro-humeral index in the two Esquimaux skeletons was 77·7, and in the two Lapps 75·4.

It is clear therefore that differences exist in the relative lengths of the humerus and femur in the different races of men. If we take 72·5 as the mean index in Europeans, then it is obvious that in the black races the mean index falls below that figure, and that in them, therefore, the humerus is shorter in relation to the femur than in Europeans. So far as one can judge from the few specimens of Mongolians, Malays, and natives of India which have been measured, a similar proportion would also appear to prevail in them. On the other hand, in the Esquimaux and Lapps the femoro-humeral index is remarkably high, so that the humerus in them is long in relation to the femur.

I may now refer to the radio-humeral, tibio-femoral, femoro-humeral, and intermembral indices obtained by the measurements of the bones of the shafts of the limbs in the Anthropoid apes.

The radio-humeral index in three chimpanzees, which I have measured, ranged from 92 to 95, and the mean was 94. From four chimpanzees measured by Professor Humphry, I have calculated a mean index 90. In a single adult orang skeleton in the Anatomical Museum of the University this index was 97·8, the mean of the two specimens in Humphry's table was 100, and a similar mean was obtained by Flower. In the three gorillas measured by Humphry the mean index was only 77·7; the mean of the three gorillas in Mr. St. George Mivart's tables[1] was 81·6, whilst Flower puts this index in the gorilla at 80. The index in the chimpanzee and orang is therefore very high, and expresses that the forearm closely approximates in length to the upper arm, so that they may be described as hyperdolichokerkic. In the gorilla, on the other hand, there is a much greater disproportion between the length of the radius and humerus, for the mean index is about 80. In this respect the Andaman Islanders and Fuegians surpass the gorilla in the relative length of the forearm to the upper arm, for the radio-humeral index in them averages between 80 and 82, so that in the proportion of forearm to upper arm they are probably the most ape-like of the races of men. Europeans again are at the opposite end of the series, for the mean radio-humeral index in them did not reach 75, whilst the Australians, Kaffirs, Negros, &c., form an intermediate series.

The tibio-femoral index in my three chimpanzees ranged from 81 to 83·5, and the mean was 82·4. Professor Humphry's four specimens gave a mean 80·6. In my single orang this index was 86, and the mean of Humphry's two specimens was 86·8. His three gorillas had a mean 81, and Mr. Mivart's specimens had the same index. In Europeans this index is about 82, whilst in the Australians, Negros, Andaman Islanders, and Fuegians it was higher, and ranged from 83 to 85 or 86, according to the mode of measurement adopted. The difference therefore in the relative length of the tibia to the femur in man, as compared with the chimpanzee and gorilla, is not very marked. In the orang, however, the index rises considerably, owing to the greater proportional length of the tibia, and it is also to be noted that in the lower races of men there is a rise in this index as compared with Europeans, so that as regards the proportion of leg to thigh they are more in accordance with what is found in the orang.

The femoro-humeral index in my three chimpanzees ranged from 94 to 100·3, with a mean of 97·7, so that the humerus sometimes exceeded the femur in length. The mean index computed from Humphry's measurements of four chimpanzees was 98, and Flower places it at about 100. In the orang the humerus is much longer than the femur, and in my specimen the femoro-humeral index was 133·4, the mean of Humphry's two specimens was 132, and Flower gives it as 130. In the three gorillas measured by Humphry the humerus was longer than the femur, though not in the same proportion as in the orang, and the mean index was 119; in Mivart's specimens the mean index was also 119, and in Flower's 120. There is thus a considerable range of difference in the relative proportions of femur to humerus in the great Anthropoid apes, for, whilst in the orang and gorilla the humerus considerably exceeds the femur in length, in the chimpanzee these bones are almost equal and as a rule the femur is somewhat longer than the humerus.

[1] On the Appendicular Skeleton of the Primates, *Trans. Roy. Soc. Lond.*, 1867.

In all the races of men the femur very materially exceeds the humerus in length, but the proportionate excess is not the same in all the races which have been measured. We may, I think, accept 72·5 as expressing the mean femoro-humeral index in Europeans. In the Lapps and Esquimaux, if I may take the four skeletons which I have measured as average samples of these races, the mean index rises considerably above the European standard, and of all the races the bones of whose limbs have been measured, they show the greatest proportion of humeral length, and approximate therefore to, though still widely removed from, the proportion in the ape. On the other hand the black races of Australia and Africa, the Pacific Islanders and the Negritos of the Andaman Islands, all have a less femoro-humeral index than the Europeans. It is probable that in the Chinese, Malays, and the natives of India, the humerus is also shorter in relation to the length of the femur than in the Europeans. It follows therefore that, in the relative proportion of femur to humerus, the European, and still more the Laplander and the Esquimaux, possess a character approaching more to the ape than those black races, which from certain other characters we are in the habit of speaking of as the lower races of mankind.

The intermembral index in my three chimpanzees ranged from 102 to 107, with the mean of 104·6, and in Professor Humphry's specimens the mean index was 103·5; the bones of the shaft of the upper limb, therefore, somewhat exceeded in length the bones of the shaft of the lower limb. In the orang these bones in the upper limb were very materially longer than those in the lower limb; in my specimen the index was 141, and the mean of Professor Humphry's two skeletons was also 141. In the gorilla the upper limb, though longer than the lower, is intermediate in its relative proportions to the chimpanzee and orang; the mean intermembral index of Professor Humphry's three specimens was 117, and the index computed from Mr. Mivart's measurements was 119.

In all the races of men the length of the bones of the shaft of the lower limb was very considerably in excess of that of the bones of the upper limb, so that the intermembral index was much below 100. But amongst these races a range of variation within certain limits was recognised. In Europeans the mean intermembral index was obviously about 69·5, but in the Lapps, Esquimaux, and Fuegians this index was distinctly higher than in the Europeans, so that in this respect these races approached nearer to the ape in this character. On the other hand this index in the black races was distinctly below the European mean, and it is probable that a similar lower ratio will be found when more extensive measurements have been made of Mongolians and Malays.

From the comparison which has now been made of the relative proportions of the bones of the shafts of the limbs, one arrives at the conclusion, that such a physical degradation as is implied by the possession of characters which approximate to those of the Anthropoid apes, is not constantly found in one particular race or group of races, as to lead one to say, that in all respects, in the proportions of their limbs, such race or group of races is constructed on a more ape-like pattern than the other races. In the relative length of the radius to the humerus, as expressed by the radio-humeral index, the Europeans, Lapps, Esquimaux, and it may be the Bushmen were furthest removed from the apes, the Andaman Islanders and Fuegians most closely approached them, whilst the Australians, Kaffirs, and Negros were intermediate. In the relative length of the tibia to the femur, as expressed by the tibio-femoral index, the Europeans, and still more the Lapps and Esquimaux were amongst the races in which the leg was the shortest in relation to the thigh. In the black races generally, more especially in the Andaman Islanders, as well as in the Fuegians, the proportionate length of the tibia increased, so that the relation of tibia to femur was almost the same as in the orang.

On the other hand in the proportion of femur to humerus, as expressed by the femoro-humeral index, the Lapps and the Esquimaux approximated most closely to the apes, the black races of men were furthest removed from them and the Europeans were intermediate. Similarly in the proportions of the bones of the shaft of the lower limb, compared with those of the upper limb, as expressed by the intermembral index, the Lapps, Esquimaux, and Fuegians most closely approximated to the apes, the Europeans were less near, and the black races were still further removed. It follows therefore that whilst the black races approached more closely to the apes than did Europeans in the relation which the two segments of the shaft in the same limb bore to each other; they were more widely removed from the apes in the relations which the bones of the shaft of the upper limb bore to those of the lower extremity.

As regards the Anthropoid apes themselves, the orang had a radio-humeral index furthest removed from man, the chimpanzee came next in order, whilst in the gorilla this index most closely approached to the mean of that of man. In the tibio-femoral index the orang was also the furthest removed from the average man, whilst both the chimpanzee and gorilla were nearer both to each other and to him. In the femoro-humeral index the orang was widely removed from the human proportion, the gorilla less so, and the chimpanzee least of all. In the intermembral index the orang was also widely removed from man, the gorilla came next, whilst the chimpanzee most nearly approached him. It follows, therefore, that in the proportions of the limbs of these Anthropoid apes, the orang was the most widely separated from man, the chimpanzee the most closely approximated, and the gorilla was intermediate in position.

I have not entered into the consideration of the characters of the skeleton of the distal segments of the limbs, the Hand and the Foot. For although their bones were more or less perfectly preserved in several of the skeletons, yet I did not think them to be sufficiently numerous to enable me to arrive at any general conclusion.

GENERAL SUMMARY.

It may now be useful to gather together into a short chapter a summary of the leading facts and conclusions, which have been stated in more or less detail in the preceding pages. As regards the conclusions, I must again guard myself by saying that in some instances they are to be looked upon only as provisional, for the number of skeletons of several of the races examined and measured, both by other anatomists and by myself, is as yet too few on which to speak in more than a tentative way.

We may take for our standard of comparison the Europeans, as illustrated especially by the French, Germans and British, whose skeletons have so frequently and in such numbers been examined and described by anatomists. The European pelvis is large and roomy. In its external dimensions its breadth materially exceeds its height, so that the breadth-height index in men is about 79, and in women 74 or 75. The pelvic inlet is considerably wider in the transverse than in the conjugate diameter; the brim index is distinctly below 90 both for men and women, and is platypellic. The sacrum both in men and women is broader than long, so that it is platyhieric. The lumbar curve of the spinal column, as estimated both by the relative depth of the front and back of the vertebral bodies, and by that of both the bodies and discs when in position, is greater in front than behind, i.e., kurtorachic. The mean scapular index is about 65. The radius is short in relation to the length of the humerus, i.e., brachykerkic. The tibia is short in relation to the femur, i.e., brachyknemic. The humerus is long in relation to the length of the femur, and the femoro-humeral index is moderately high. The shaft of the upper limb is long in relation to the shaft of the lower limb, and the intermembral index is moderately high. The skull may be either dolichocephalic, or mesaticephalic, or brachycephalic, but the face is orthognathous.

If we now examine the skeletal characters of the black races we shall find that in many particulars they differ from the Europeans, and also differ amongst themselves. In the Bush race the pelvis in its external dimensions is high in proportion to its breadth, and the ilium approximates to the vertical in direction. In the Australians again, the external dimensions of the pelvis are not unlike those of Europeans, and a similar proportion of breadth and height also exists in Negros. In the Negritos of the Andaman Islands, on the other hand, the height of the pelvis increases in relation to its breadth, and the breadth-height index is relatively high. The conjugate diameter of the pelvic brim is long in relation to the transverse diameter, and the brim index is high, or dolichopellic, in Australians, Bushmen, Hottentots, Kaffirs and Andaman Islanders; but in Negros, Tasmanians and possibly the Melanesians of the Pacific Islands the conjugate diameter is not so long in relation to the transverse, and the brim index is not so high, or mesatipellic. In all these black races except the Negros, and it may be the Melanesians, the average length of the sacrum is greater than its average breadth, and the bone is dolichohieric.

The lumbar curve of the spinal column, as determined by the depth of the bodies of the vertebræ, and without taking into consideration the influence exercised by the intervertebral discs, is concave forwards in the black races. The clavicle, at least in the Negros, may possibly be longer in proportion to the humerus than in Europeans. The scapular index in Negros, Andaman Islanders, and Melanesians, is apparently materially higher than in Europeans, which shows that the breadth is proportionally greater than the length; in the Bush and Australians, it approximates to the Europeans, and in the Tasmanians it may have been distinctly lower. The radius is longer in relation to the humerus than in Europeans, and whilst the index in the Andaman Islanders and other Negritos is dolichokerkic, in the Australians, Tasmanians, Kaffirs, and Negros it is mesatikerkic. The tibia in the black races is long in relation to the femur and the index is dolichoknemic. The humerus in the black races is short in relation to the length of the femur and the femoro-humeral index is low; similarly the shaft of the upper limb in them is proportionally shorter than the shaft of the lower limb, and the intermembral index is relatively low. The cranium is dolichocephalic and prognathous in Australians, Negros and Melanesians, dolichocephalic and perhaps mesognathous in Kaffirs, mesaticephalic and prognathous in Tasmanians, mesaticephalic and orthognathous in the Bush race.

Our information on the skeletal characters of the yellow races is, unfortunately, scanty. In the Chinese the pelvis would appear to have the transverse diameter of the brim considerably in excess of the conjugate, and the brim index, therefore, platypellic; but the relative length and breadth of the sacrum is still doubtful. The lumbar curve, estimated from the vertical diameter of the vertebral bodies, is in all probability kurtorachic. The scapular index is probably about the same as in Europeans. The radius is longer in relation to the humerus than in Europeans, it is mesatikerkic. The proportionate length of the tibia and femur is more like that of the white than of the black races, so that it is brachyknemic. The humerus is possibly shorter in relation to the femur than in Europeans, and a similar relation may prevail in regard to the shaft of the upper limb as compared with that of the lower. The skull of the Chinese belonging to the skeleton described in this Report was brachycephalic, C.I. 81·7; metriocephalic, V.I. 73·7; orthognathous, G.I. 96·8; leptorhine, N.I. 47; megaseme, O.I. 89·5; brachyuranic, P.M.I. 128.

In the Malays the conjugate diameter of the pelvic brim is, for the male sex, in all probability either greater than, or about equal to the transverse, and the brim index is dolichopellic; the sacrum is longer than broad and the bone is dolichohieric. The vertical diameter of the bodies of the lumbar vertebræ may possibly be greater collectively anteriorly than posteriorly. The scapular index is higher than in Europeans. Possibly the proportion of the radius to the humerus is higher than in Europeans. Data are wanting for giving the relative length of the tibia and femur. It is possible, however, that the Malays, like the Chinese, may have the humerus shorter in relation to the femur, and the shaft of the upper limb shorter in relation to that of the lower limb than in Europeans. The skull of the Malay belonging to the skeleton described in this Report was characterised by great parieto-occipital flattening, so that the cephalic index was abnormally high, 91, and also the vertical index, 87. It was orthognathous, G.I. 93·9; leptorhine, N.I. 41; megaseme, O.I. 95; brachyuranic, P.M.I. 127.

In the American Indians the transverse diameter of the pelvic brim decidedly exceeds the conjugate; the brim index is platypellic. The Yahgan Fuegians have a similar relation. The sacrum is broader than long both in the Indians of the American continent and in the Fuegians. The scapular index approximates to that of Europeans. In the continental Indians the radius is apparently a little longer in proportion to the humerus, and the index is mesatikerkic; but in the Fuegians its proportional length is still greater, and the index is dolichokerkic. The tibia is long in relation to the femur, dolichoknemic, both in the continental Indians and the Fuegians, and in the Fuegians the upper limb is relatively longer than the lower. The continental American Indians are, with the exception of some tribes, brachycephalic, and perhaps mesognathous; the Fuegians again are mesaticephalic and mesognathous, though individual crania have dolichocephalic proportions.

In both the Lapps and Esquimaux the index of the pelvic brim is probably platypellic, and the sacral index platyhieric. The collective vertical diameters of the bodies of the lumbar vertebræ is probably greater in front than behind. The scapular index is apparently distinctly below that of Europeans. The radius is short in relation to the humerus, brachykerkic. The tibia is short in relation to the femur, brachyknemic. The humerus is long in relation to the femur, and the upper limb is relatively long in proportion to the lower. Although in their general characters the skeletons of my Lapps and Esquimaux present many points of similarity, yet they differ materially in certain of their craniological aspects. Both the Lapp skulls are markedly brachycephalic (C.I. 86·5 male, 86·7 female), and the Esquimaux dolichocephalic (C.I. 74 male, 70·8 female). They all agree, however, in having the vertical index below the cephalic; in the two Lapps this index is 76·5 and 69·7, and in the two Esquimaux 70·8 and 68. In the male Lapp the gnathic index is orthognathous, in the female mesognathous, and the same applies to the male and female Esquimaux. In both Lapps and Esquimaux the nasal index is leptorhine. In both the Lapps, the orbital index is megaseme; in both the Esquimaux, mesoseme. In the male Lapp the palato-maxillary index is brachyuranic, in the female mesuranic; in the male Esquimaux this index is mesuranic and in the female dolichuranic.

I have not sufficient material to enable me to make a satisfactory general statement of the skeletal characters of the natives of India, but I should like to bring into the compass of a single paragraph the main features of the skeletons of the Sikh and the tall Hindoo. In both, the index of the pelvic brim was on the verge between platypellic and mesatipellic, and the sacrum was platyhieric. In both, the vertical diameter of the bodies of the lumbar vertebræ was greater behind than in front. In both, the scapular index was between 68 and 69. In both, the radio-humeral index was mesatikerkic. In the Hindoo the relative length of the tibia to the femur was somewhat greater than in the Sikh. In the femoro-humeral and intermembral indices they were almost identical. As regards their craniological characters they were both hyper-dolichocephalic, C.I. 66·5 for the Hindoo, 65·8 for the Sikh. In both, the vertical diameter exceeded the transverse breadth, the vertical index being 68·6 for the Hindoo, 71 for the Sikh. Both were distinctly orthognathous, 93 and 90·7. In the Hindoo the nasal index was platyrhine, 54, in the Sikh leptorhine, 47. In the Hindoo the orbital index was megaseme, 97, in the Sikh microseme, 71. In the palato-maxillary index both were brachyuranic, 123 and 117. Although certain differences in their proportions existed between the two skeletons, yet in their main features they corresponded so closely to each other, that although the skeleton, which throughout I have designated as the tall male Hindoo, belonged as Dr. Anderson told me, to a man of Hindoo religion, yet it is possible that he may have been a Sikh by race.

Notwithstanding the incompleteness, and consequent imperfection, of many of the data for making a detailed comparison of the skeletal characters of the several races of men described or referred to in this Report, there is sufficient information to enable one to say that racial differences are not confined to the skull, but occur also in other parts of the skeleton. The question therefore naturally arises, are these differences of such a degree or kind as to point to one race, or group of races, as being in all the relations of the skeleton more highly developed than all other races? or to another race, or group of races, as being in all the skeletal relations more lowly developed than all other races? By highly developed I mean a condition of the skeleton which is further removed either from the characters and proportions of the skeleton in mammalia other than man, or from the infantile condition of man himself; and by lowly developed, one which is either more closely approximated to the mammalian characters and proportions, or to the infantile condition of the human skeleton. In other words, is there in the different varieties or races of men such a graded condition of the skeleton as would indicate, that by successive stages a human type had been produced which in all its skeletal relations was superior to all other forms of humanity; and that the stages, through which the skeleton had passed to reach that type, were represented by the various races which either now inhabit, or at some former epoch have inhabited, the different parts of the globe.

Although our knowledge of the races which inhabited the earth in the early parts of the human period is very imperfect, researches made during the latter half of the present century, in different parts of Europe, have brought to light both skulls and skeletons, which are referred to the time when the mammoth, the reindeer, and the cave bear were the mammals of the south of Europe. Apparently at that epoch, as at the present, three different forms of human skull occurred, dolichocephalic, mesaticephalic, and brachycephalic. The dolichocephalic skulls are represented by the Neanderthal cranium and the skulls of Canstadt, Würtemberg, and of the cave-dwellers of Cro-Magnon in the valley of the Vézère; mesaticephalic skulls have been found at Furfooz in the valley of the Lesse, Belgium, and brachycephalic skulls have been discovered in gravel pits at Grenelle, near Paris, and at La Truchère.[1] As in the skulls of the present day, some of these ancient crania, in which the face has been preserved, have a prognathic condition of the upper jaw, whilst others are orthognathic. In their internal capacity many of these crania are equal to the mean of modern European skulls. The vault of the skull is in a number of specimens arched, as in all well-formed crania, though in others, as the Neanderthal skull, it is more depressed and associated with strongly projecting glabella and supraciliary ridges.

In many of the skeletons of these primitive men, especially those from Cro-Magnon, a large proportion of the tibiæ were platyknemic; the femora were prismatic, and with a strongly projecting linea aspera; and the humeri were perforated by a supra-trochlear foramen in the olecranoid fossa. As has been pointed out in the description of the skeletons of the existing races described in this Report, instances of a corresponding conformation of these bones not unfrequently occurred.

Amongst existing races of men, therefore, craniological and skeletal characters are met with similar to those which have been recognised in the most ancient human remains that have yet been discovered,[2] and the differences that exist between the skulls and skeletons of primitive man are no more, either in kind or degree, than are to be seen in the corresponding parts in the men of the present day.

In the examination of the skeletons of existing races of men, characters sometimes present themselves in certain races which one recognises as more in accordance with the ordinary mammalian arrangement than is the case in the corresponding parts of other races. For example, in adults of the black races the conjugate diameter of the pelvic brim tends to preponderate over the transverse diameter, and the forearm to be longer in proportion to the upper arm, than in adults of the white races, so that it may be said that in these respects the white man is more highly developed than the black man. In other words, the adult skeleton in the white man, in the relative proportions of these parts, is further removed from the proportions found both in lower mammals and in the infantile

---

[1] The characters of these crania have been most carefully described by MM. de Quatrefages and Hamy in their great work, Crania Ethnica.

[2] Some years ago I pointed out that skulls of the Neanderthaloid type were closely parallelled in the crania of many existing savage races as well as in modern Europeans, *Quarterly Journal of Science*, April and October, 1864. See also de Quatrefages, L'espèce humaine, and Vernean, La race de Cro-Magnon, *Revue d'Anthropologie*, January 1886.

condition of man himself, than is the case with the black man. But, on the other hand, as has indeed been already stated on p. 114, in the proportions of the shaft of the lower limb to the shaft of the upper limb, and of the thigh to the upper arm, the black races are more widely removed from the apes than are Europeans, and the tendency to produce a femur with a prismatic shaft, which is the very opposite to a pithecoid character, is more marked in the Australians than in the white or yellow races. Also, whilst the Lapps and Esquimaux, of all the races which I have measured, most closely approach the apes in the proportions of thigh to upper arm, and of shaft of lower limb to shaft of upper limb, they are amongst the races most widely removed from the apes in the proportions of forearm to upper arm, and of leg to thigh. The Yahgan Fuegians, again, whilst they are, in the proportions of forearm to upper arm, the most ape-like of men, yet possess a platypellic pelvis and a platyhieric sacrum.

I do not find, therefore, in the comparative study of the skeleton in the Races of Men, evidence that any one race dominates in all its characters over all other races; or that any one race, in all its characters, is lower than all other races. Nevertheless there can be no doubt that Europeans in many of their most important skeletal characters, more especially those of the skull and pelvis, are more widely removed from mammals generally, than is the case with Negros, Kaffirs, Bushmen and Australians. There does not seem, however, to be a graded arrangement, such as would lead one to say that the white races, which we will assume to be the most highly developed, have been derived, by successive stages of slow and gradual perfecting of structure, from the lowest existing black race, or, indeed, from any one of the existing black races.

Weisbach concludes his analysis of the measurements of the body in living individuals of different races of men, taken during the voyage of the "Novara" by Drs. Scherzer and Schwarz,[1] by stating that resemblances in form and proportion to characters observed in apes are in no way exclusively concentrated in any single race, but are distributed amongst different races, in some in one direction, in others in another direction, and that even Europeans themselves are not free from such characters. Moreover, he regards these resemblances as evidence of the descent of man from an ape-like ancestor.

In concluding this Report I have no intention to enter into a discussion of any speculative question connected with the remote origin of man. But this I may say, that in the form and proportion of the different parts of the skeleton, so far as I have made them objects of study, the so-called simian characters are not such as would lead any competent anatomist, either to mistake a human bone for the bone of an ape, or to say that in the fossil remains of man, so far as we know them, there is evidence that a transitional form between man and the higher apes at one time existed.

[1] Reise der Novara, Anthropologischer Theil, p. 269, Wien, 1867.

APPENDIX TO PART I. ON THE HUMAN CRANIA.

Since the publication of the Craniological part of this Report in 1884, I have received additional specimens of skulls of certain of the races then described, and in order to give a larger basis for comparison, and for the determination of the characters of the skulls of these races, I append some tables of measurements of these more recent specimens, with brief notices of such of their features as seemed to be deserving of special remark. As memoirs on the Fuegians and on the Crania of the Jervis Islanders, Torres Strait, have also been published subsequently to the appearance of my Report on the Human Crania, in which skulls of these people were described, I shall also briefly refer to the chief facts stated and conclusions arrived at by their respective authors.

AUSTRALIANS.

After the tables of measurements of the Australian skulls described in Part I., Report on Human Crania, had been put in type, I had the opportunity of examining some additional Australian crania, and I incorporated some observations on their characters in subsequent pages of that Report (p. 46, et. seq.), more especially with reference to the proportions of the cephalic and vertical indices. I have now included in Table XV. more detailed measurements of five of these skulls, which have been presented to the Anatomical Museum of the University, and along with them have given the measurements of two other crania from New South Wales, received in 1885. The localities from which these skulls were obtained are stated in the table.

Each skull was dolichocephalic. In four specimens the vertical index exceeded the cephalic, and in two specimens the cephalic and vertical indices were equal. In only one specimen, viz., the Milang tribesman, the height was greater than the breadth, so that, as stated on p. 49 of Part I., it was markedly dolicho-platycephalic. With two exceptions the vertical index was below 72, i.e., they were tapeinocephalic, and those with the vertical index above 72 were metriocephalic. The gnathic index ranged from 98 to 101, so that they were all mesognathous. In the nasal index four were platyrhine and two

TABLE XV.—AUSTRALIANS AND NEW ZEALANDER.

Collection,	Rockhampton. Queensland.	Rockhampton. Queensland.	Curtis Island, Lat. 23°, Queensland.	Interior of South Australia.	Milang Tribe, S. Aust.	Manly Cove, N. S. W.[1]	New South Wales,[2] Lat. 30° 27'.	Te Aroha, Auckland, N. Z.
	E.U.A.M.	E.U.A.M.	E.U.A.M.	E.U.A.M.	E.U.A.M.	E.U.A.M.	E.U.A.M.	E.U.A.M.
Age,	Ad.	Aged.	Ad.	Ad.	Ad.	Ad.	Aged.	Ad.
Sex,	M.	M.	F.	†	M.	M.	F.	F.
Cubic capacity,	1330	1285	1240	...	...	1223	998	1472
Glabello-occipital length,	192	192	183	180	191	186	173	186
Basi-bregmatic height,	137	138	133	128	125	140	122	134
Vertical Index,	71	71·9	72·7	71	65	75	70·5	72
Minimum frontal diameter,	97	97	97	...	91	94	90	96
Stephanic diameter,	105	105	104	...	98	103	98	108
Asterionic „	107	110	103	...	110	112	113	110
Greatest parieto-squamous breadth,[3]	133	132	131	128ap	130	132s	122s	135s
Cephalic Index,	69	68·8	71·6	71	68	71	70·5	72·6
Horizontal circumference,	532	538	510	...	531	530	500	520
Frontal longitudinal arc,	140	...	135	...	122	130	119	125
Parietal „ „	135	...	132	...	124	135	125	118
Occipital „ „	118	...	111	...	115	114	106	118
Total „ „	393	383	378	...	361	379	350	361
Vertical transverse arc,	303	304	295	...	275	300	272	298
Basi-nasal length,	104	108	97	...	105	101	94	107
Basi-alveolar length,	102	106	97	...	...	101	95	102
Gnathic Index,	98	98	100	...	...	100	101	95
Interzygomatic breadth,	135	138	134	...	135	134	120	136
Intermalar „	114	122	120	...	125	122	107	121
Naso-alveolar length,	60	61	57	...	...	70	63	60
Nasal height,	45	50	45	...	46	52	47	56
Nasal width,	25	27	25	...	26	26	25	24
Nasal Index,	55·5	54	55·5	...	56ap	50	53	42·8
Orbital width,	41	42	39	...	43	40	39	40
Orbital height,	34	33	33	...	31	34	31	34
Orbital Index,	82·9	78·6	84·6	...	72ap	85	79·5	85
Palato-maxillary length,	58	65	58	...	...	60	58	56
Palato-maxillary breadth,	64	65	63	...	...	70	58	67
Palato-maxillary Index,	110	100	108	...	...	116	100	109
Symphysial height,	...	...	...	...	...	32	29	33
Coronoid „	...	...	...	...	...	62	54	68
Condyloid „	...	...	...	...	...	63	55	64
Genio-symphysial length,	...	...	...	...	...	99	85	91
Inter-gonial width,	...	...	...	...	...	102	77	96
Breadth of ascending ramus,	...	...	...	...	...	37	32	35

[1] With skeleton: presented by Professor Anderson Stuart.
[2] Dr. Chisholm Ross, who sent me this skull, wrote that it belonged to a very old woman, the people of her tribe having credited her with being 130 years old. Although the skull shows marks of age in the almost complete obliteration of the sutures of the cranial vault, the deep depressions on the facial aspect of the upper jaw and the obtuse angle of the lower jaw, yet eleven teeth had survived in the upper and nine in the lower jaw, although they were much worn down.
[3] To avoid any misunderstanding, I have altered this heading from greatest parietal breadth, as in the former Tables, to greatest parieto-squamous breadth, for in all my measurements I have taken the greatest breadth of the cranium, whether it occur in the bi-parietal or bi-squamous diameters.

mesorhine. In the orbital index four were microseme and two mesoseme. In the palato-maxillary index three were dolichuranic, one mesuranic, and one brachyuranic. Both males and females were microcephalic.

In three adult males the maximum length of each cranium exceeded 190 mm. They were all adults, and in three the sutures on the vault had almost or entirely disappeared, in two evidently from age, and in the third, the Manly Cove skull, the cranial vault was marked with pits and eminences probably due to blows from a waddy. In their general characters the crania conformed to the description which I have previously given of the Australian skull. In the Manly Cove skull the right central incisor had been extracted in early life and the socket absorbed, but the sockets of all the other teeth were patent. The skull from Curtis Island showed remains of the infraorbital suture on each side.

New Zealander.

Table XV. also contains the measurements of a skull procured from the same cave at Te Aroha, Auckland, in which the pelvis and long bones already described were found, but not belonging to the same skeleton. It was the skull of a woman apparently about thirty years old, and was in good preservation. The cranium was dolichocephalic and of almost the same diameter in height as in breadth. The gnathic index was orthognathous, the nasal index mesorhine, the orbital index mesoseme, the palato-maxillary index dolichuranic and the internal cranial capacity mesocephalic. The teeth were all erupted and but little worn. The infraorbital suture was complete on the left side, but incomplete on the right.[1] The alisphenoid only just reached the antero-inferior angle of the parietal.

Sandwich Islanders.

Early in the year 1886 I received for the Museum, through R. A. Macfie, Esq., of Dreghorn, a box containing five adult crania collected by Dr. G. W. Parker of Waiahia, Oahu. In his letter accompanying the crania Dr. Parker wrote as follows:—

Yesterday I rode to an ancient burial place, where I managed to secure the bones of an almost complete Hawaiian skeleton, also some skulls and jaws. I was so fortunate as to find *in situ* the entire upper half of one skeleton, and to note the method of burial, if not of the ancient Hawaiians in general, at least of this particular one, viz., with arms bent, so as to bring the hands on to the upper part of the sides of the chest, and head bent forward upon the chest. The lower jaw was still in the natural position. From the loins downward the rest of the skeleton had disappeared, owing to movements of the shifting sandhill on the top of which it had been buried, only ten or twelve inches below the surface. This burial-place is in a line of shifting sand-

[1] See my remarks on this suture in *Journ. of Anat. and Phys.*, vol. xix. p. 218, January 1885.

hills near the beach, in a district once full of inhabitants, now depopulated. As to its origin some persons say that a great battle was fought there in the prehistoric ages of Hawaiian history, others that it was one of the places used for burying those who died of one or other of the epidemic diseases which killed off thousands of the Hawaiians in very recent times. But I particularly took note that none of the skulls which I examined (about a dozen), bore marks suggesting death by violence, nor were any weapons discoverable; so that I should be inclined to credit the second theory of origin, unless it could be ascertained whether the coast tribes were in the habit of choosing sandy places for the sake of convenience, just as we know that those of more stony places chose caves. Further, the bodies appear to have been buried naked, no traces of matting or cloth of any kind being found with the skeletons. The custom of knocking out the front teeth, or in any way injuring the teeth, did not exist among the natives of these islands, for most of the teeth in the jaws are sound.

These crania had been buried in a similar locality to that at Waimanolo, Oahu, from which Professor Moseley obtained the skulls described in the first part of this Report. Like them they were for the most part bleached perfectly white from exposure. One skull (1A) was brachycephalic, with a length-breadth index 81 (Table XVI.); one (1D) was in the lower term of the mesaticephalic group with an index 75·1, and the remaining three were dolichocephalic, with a mean cephalic index 71·9. They presented, therefore, that variety in the proportions of length and breadth of the cranium, which in the first part of this Report I had dwelt on at considerable length as present in the crania from Oahu, although the range of variation was not so great in this limited as in that much more extensive series.

The brachycephalic cranium, that of a woman, showed its character not only in its numerical proportions, but in the downward slope of the parietal bone from the obelion to the inion. In it the basi-bregmatic height was slightly below the parieto-squamous breadth, the vertical index was 80, and the skull was akrocephalic, as in the brachycephalic Sandwich Islanders, both from Hawaii and Oahu, described in the first part of the Report. In its other relations the skull was orthognathic, leptorhine, megaseme, brachyuranic and mesocephalic. It did not in all of these quite correspond with the mean of the brachycephalic Oahuans previously described, which were mesognathic, mesorhine, megaseme, brachyuranic, and mesocephalic.

The skull 1D, although in the numerical proportion of length and breadth it just fell into the mesaticephalic group, obviously in its general characters closely corresponded with the three dolichocephalic crania, and may be considered along with them. Like the dolichocephalic Oahuans described in the first part of this Report, they were all somewhat ridge-shaped on the top of the cranium, and in their general appearance were strong, powerful skulls. In two specimens the sutures of the cranial vault were in process of senile obliteration. In each of the three dolichocephalic skulls the basi-bregmatic height exceeded the greatest breadth, and in the mesaticephalic skull the breadth was only 1 mm. more than the height; one was tapeinocephalic, two were metriocephalic, and the third was akrocephalic. All four skulls were mesognathous. Two of the specimens were leptorhine and two mesorhine. As to the orbital index, one was microseme, two meso-

REPORT ON THE BONES OF THE HUMAN SKELETON.

seme, one megaseme. In the palato-maxillary index one was dolichuranic, another mesuranic; in the remainder this index could not be determined. The woman's cranium was microcephalic and each of the men's skulls was megacephalic, though 1D and 1E were only just within the limits of that group.

Two of the skulls gave illustrations of exostoses, growing from the wall of the external auditory meatus to which I referred in the first part of the Report, p. 117, as not uncommon amongst the South Sea Islanders; in one the bony growths were elongated,

TABLE XVI.—OAHU, SANDWICH ISLANDS. NEW GUINEA.

Collection,	Oahu, Sandwich Islands.					New Guinea.
	E.U.A.M. 1A.	E.U.A.M. 1C.	E.U.A.M. 1B.	E.U.A.M. 1D.	E.U.A.M. 1E.	E.U.A.M.
Age,	Ad.	Aged.	Ad.	Aged.	Ad.	Youth.
Sex,	F.	F.	M.	M.	M.	F.
Cubic capacity,	1362	1200	1545	1453	1457	...
Glabello-occipital length,	171	185	191	189	188	183
Basi-bregmatic height,	137	131	142	141	146	127
Vertical Index,	80	70·8	74	74·6	77·7	69·4
Minimum frontal diameter,	88	93	89	96	93	89
Stephanic diameter,	107	102	111	104	108	101
Asterionic ,,	108	108	115	110	109	98
Greatest parieto-squamous breadth,	139p	129p	139p	142s	138s	119p
Cephalic Index,	81	69·7	72·8	75·1	73·4	65
Horizontal circumference,	498	510	535	538	530	495
Frontal longitudinal arc,	120	124	132	130	134	117
Parietal ,, ,,	122	132	130	131	129	139
Occipital ,, ,,	120	113	128	122	125	127
Total ,, ,,	362	369	390	383	388	383
Vertical transverse arc,	300	298	320	314	312	280
Basi-nasal length,	96	102	105	106	106	91
Basi-alveolar length,	87	103	105	104	103	93
Gnathic Index,	90·6	101	100	98	97	102·2
Interzygomatic breadth,	124	122	141	135	138	108
Intermalar ,,	108	112	123	120	120	94
Naso-alveolar length,	60	60	75	65	69	57
Nasal height,	47	49	58	55	55	41
Nasal width,	22	25	26	28	23	20
Nasal Index,	46·8	51	44·8	50·9	41·8	48·8
Orbital width,	36	38	38	39	39	37
Orbital height,	33	33	35	32	33	31
Orbital Index,	91·7	86·8	92	82	84·6	83·8
Palato-maxillary length,	48	58	55	55	54	54
Palato-maxillary breadth,	58	60	62	...	...	59
Palato-maxillary Index,	120	103	112	...	...	109
Symphysial height,	26	29	35	...	32	28
Coronoid ,,	58	60	78	73	65	53
Condyloid ,,	58	54	69	61	67	53
Gonio-symphysial length,	82	85	96	92	89	77
Inter-gonial width,	81	85	97	92	...	71
Breadth of ascending ramus,	35	39	40	41	35	31

with wide bases of attachment, and as many as three in each meatus ; in the other they were more pedunculated, two in one meatus, three in the other. In two skulls the left outer incisor was absent and its socket absorbed ; possibly these teeth had been extracted at the time of puberty.

New Guinea.

I gave, on p. 89 of the first part of the Report, a table of measurements of crania from New Guinea, in the Anatomical Museum of the University. During the present year I received through a former pupil, Dr. F. Ashwell of Sidney, a cranium which had been collected by Captain Strachan, who has just returned, I understand, from the interior of New Guinea. It had obviously been suspended in a hut, for a loop of cane was attached to it, and the bones were brown and discoloured with smoke. A cord of twisted vegetable fibre had been tied transversely around the necks of the condyles of the lower jaw, which bone had doubtless been worn as a bracelet. All the permanent teeth had erupted except the four wisdoms, and as the basi-cranial synchondrosis was also not closed, the skull was probably that of a youth about 16 years old.

The measurements are recorded in Table XVI., from which it will be seen that the skull is hyper-dolichocephalic, the index being only 65 ; the vertical index is tapeino-cephalic, 69·4, and it conforms with what I have previously shown to be a character of the dolichocephalic people of New Guinea, in the basi-bregmatic height exceeding the transverse diameter. The parietal longitudinal arc is considerably longer than either the frontal or occipital arcs, and gives to the skull that parieto-dolichocephaly which I have elsewhere stated to be a not unfrequent race character of the Papuans. In its gnathic index the skull is mesognathous, in its nasal index mesorhine, in its orbital index microseme, and in its palato-maxillary index dolichuranic. In the right pterion is an epipteric bone, and the squamous-temporal also articulates with the frontal; the left pterion is normal. I have not definite information of the exact locality in which this skull was collected, but if it came from the interior, it points to a strongly marked dolichocephalic people in that portion of New Guinea.

In the Table already referred to on p. 89, I gave the measurements of a skull from Jarvis or Jervis Island, Torres Strait, collected by the Rev. S. Macfarlane. The same gentleman also forwarded to the Natural History Museum, South Kensington, a collection of forty-nine crania which, like my specimen, were procured from the Sacred House of the Jervis Islanders, and these have recently been described by Mr. Oldfield Thomas.[1] These crania, like the one I had previously described, had been smeared with a red pigment. Like it they were dolichocephalic, and the mean index of fourteen adult

[1] *Journ. Anthropol. Inst.*, vol. xiv. p. 328, 1885.

males was 68·3, and of nineteen adult females 70·1. The mean vertical index of the same skulls was 71·1 for the men, and 72·3 for the women, so that they support the rule that the vertical index is higher than the cephalic in the Papuan skull. The gnathic index, 109 in my specimen, expressed a marked degree of prognathism, which is obviously a common character of these islanders, as Mr. Thomas obtained a mean of 107·1 from thirty-seven skulls, viz., 106·5 for the men, and 107·7 for the women. In my specimen, owing to the palato-maxillary length being greater than the palato-maxillary breadth, the corresponding index was remarkably low, only 95; the mean palato-maxillary index in Mr. Thomas's specimens was 105·4 for both sexes, which, although higher than in my specimen, yet places them along with it in the dolichuranic group. In my specimen the parietal longitudinal arc exceeded the frontal by 10 mm., but in Mr. Thomas's series, the parietal arc was longer than the frontal in only about one-half the total number of skulls, so that it is not a constant character in the skulls of these islanders. His general conclusion regarding the crania which he had examined from Jervis island is that they have long, narrow, and rather low brain-cases, low orbits, heavy frowning brow ridges, short and little prominent nasal bones, small nasal spines, long palates, large teeth, and considerable prognathism, characters which in the main closely correspond with those possessed by the skull which I had described from the same island.

FUEGIANS.

Since my description of the cranial characters of the Fuegians was published (Part I. p. 17), Dr. Garson has given[1] an account of the crania of seven male and two female Fuegians, of which six males and two females belonged to the Yahgan tribe. His observations are in close correspondence with those which I had previously described in the Report on the Human Crania collected by the Challenger. In my summary of the cranial characters of the Fuegians I stated that they were on the average mesaticephalic, metriocephalic, mesognathic, leptorhine, megaseme, and mesuranic; but I also pointed out that individual skulls had dolichocephalic proportions. The mean features of the crania described by Dr. Garson are in accordance with what I had stated to be the general characters of the Fuegian skull, and he employs for their description the terminology which I had also used, except that he gives the term mesostaphyline instead of mesuranic, to express the palato-maxillary proportions. In one respect there is, however, a difference of statement between us, for whilst I found the mean cubic capacity of four crania to be 1333·5 c.c., so that I placed the skulls in the microcephalic group; Garson says that his skulls were mesocephalic. On referring, however, to his more detailed statements of the internal capacity (p. 151) "calculated by means of a

[1] *Journ. Anthropol. Inst.*, vol. xv. p. 141.

slight modification of Broca's method," I find that he gives 1·452 c.c. for the mean of the males, and 1·245 c.c. for the mean of the females. The mean of these two measurements is therefore 1348, which is below the upper term of the microcephalic series, 1350, as usually defined by craniologists, so that they are in the microcephalic and not in the mesocephalic group. Moreover, Garson has excluded from his average a skull the capacity of which was only 1·210 c.c., and, if that had been included with the rest, his Fuegian crania would have been more decidedly microcephalic. The study of these additional specimens leaves the description of the skull of the Fuegians in much the same position as it had been placed in by my observations, published in the First Part of this Report.

INDEX TO PARTS I. AND II. OF THE REPORT.

The Roman numeral i. refers to Part i., the Report on the Human Crania; the Roman numeral ii. to Part ii., the present Report; whilst the Arabic numerals refer to the pages in these Reports respectively.

Admiralty Islanders—
    Crania of, i. 54, 82.
    Description of, i. 51.
    Moseley and Suhm's observations on, i. 51.
Aëta, ii. 38, 49, 94, 107.
Aino—
    Pelvis of, ii. 43, 45.
    Inferior extremity of, ii. 107.
    Sacrum of, ii. 51, 52.
Alexandra Land, i. 29, 48.
Alexandrina Lake, i. 29, 49.
Alikhoolip, i. 25.
American Indians—
    Extremities of, ii. 95, 107.
    Pelvis of, ii. 44, 45.
    Sacrum of, ii. 51, 52.
    Scapula of, ii. 85.
Anchorite Island, crania from, i. 112.
Andaman Islanders—
    Clavicle of, ii. 79.
    Inferior extremity of, ii. 104, 107, 109.
    Pelvis of, ii. 16, 18, 29, 38, 45.
    Sacrum of, ii. 48, 52.
    Scapula of, ii. 81, 84, 86.
    Sternum of, ii. 78.
    Superior extremity of, ii. 90, 92, 94.
    Vertebræ of, ii. 59, 65, 69.
Annamite, ii. 42, 51.
Arfak, i. 84.
Arm. *See* Extremity, superior.
Asiatics—
    Inferior extremity of, ii. 98, 101, 107, 109.
    Pelvis of, ii. 18.
    Scapula of, ii. 85.
    Superior extremity of, ii. 91, 94, 109.
Astrolabe Bay, i. 85.
Auckland, i. 77; ii. 12.
Australia, North-West, i. 29, 47: West, i. 29, 47; ii. 83: North, i. 47: Queensland, i. 47: South, i. 29.

(ZOOL. CHALL. EXP.—PART XLVII.—1886.)

Australians—
    Clavicle of, ii. 79.
    Crania of, i. 28, 82; ii. 121.
    General remarks on, i. 39.
    Inferior extremity of, ii. 97, 100, 104, 106, 109, 111.
    Origin and relations of, i. 43.
    Pelvis of, ii. 9, 29, 45.
    Sacrum of, ii. 47, 52.
    Scapula of, ii. 81, 83, 86.
    Sternum of, ii. 78.
    Superior extremity of, ii. 90, 93.
    Vertebræ of, ii. 60, 65, 69.
Banks's Islands, i. 96.
Bay of Good Success, i. 26.
Benalla, i. 29, 47.
Bibliography of pelvis, ii. 3, 4, 5: of scapula, ii. 82.
Black races, skeleton of, ii. 115.
Boni, i. 84.
Botocudos, i. 28; ii. 44, 51.
Brachycephalæ prognathæ of Retzius, i. 105.
British pelvis, ii. 34, 45: skeleton, ii. 119.
Bush Race—
    Clavicle of, ii. 79.
    Crania of, i. 10.
    General remarks on, i. 14.
    Inferior extremity of, ii. 98, 100, 106, 109, 111.
    Pelvis of, ii. 20, 28, 36, 45.
    Sacrum of, ii. 48, 52.
    Scapula of, ii. 81, 84, 86.
    Superior extremity of, ii. 90, 92, 94.
    Vertebræ of, ii. 59, 64, 69, 73.
Calvinia, i. 11, 12, 14.
Campordown, i. 28.
Camstadt, ii. 119.
Cape Leeuwin, skull from, i. 29.
Caroline Islanders, crania of, i. 111.
Caroline Islands, i. 82.
Chastland's Mistake, i. 77.
Chatham Islanders, crania of, i. 73.

Chimpanzee, ii. 53, 87, 98, 111, 112, 114.
Chinese—
  Clavicle of, ii. 79.
  Cranium of, ii. 116.
  Inferior extremity of, ii. 98, 100, 107, 109, 111.
  Pelvis of, ii. 18, 28, 42, 45.
  Sacrum of, ii. 50, 52.
  Scapula of, ii. 85, 86.
  Sternum of, ii. 78.
  Superior extremity of, ii. 90, 92, 94.
  Vertebræ of, ii. 59, 71, 72.
Clanwilliam, i. 14.
Clavicle, ii. 79.
Cloudy Bay, i. 88, 89.
Coccyx, ii. 9, 53.
Condyle, third occipital, i. 59, 64, 74, 79, 117.
Continent, South Oceanic, i. 114.
Cook's Islanders, crania of, i. 103.
Coorong, i. 29, 49.
Crania—
  Admiralty Island, i. 54, 82.
  Age of, how determined, i. 7.
  Akrocephalic, definition of, i. 5 : cases of, i. 21, 65, 67 ; ii. 124.
  Australian, i. 28, 82 ; ii. 121.
  Brachycephalic, definition of, i. 5 : cases of, i. 65, 67, 84, 85, 86, 99 ; ii. 116.
  Brachyuranic, definition of, i. 7 : cases of, i. 14, 65, 67 ; ii. 116, 117, 124.
  Bush Race, i. 10.
  Caroline Island, i. 111.
  Chamæcephalic, definition of, i. 5.
  Chatham Island, i. 73.
  Chinese, i. 82 ; ii. 116.
  Cook's Islanders, i. 103.
  Cryptozygous, definition of, i. 6 : cases of, i. 14, 17, 61, 67.
  Cubic capacity of, how determined, i. 8, 92, 124 : measurements of, i. 39, 43, 61, 72, 76 ; ii. 127.
  Dolichocephalic, definition of, i. 5 : cases of, i. 26, 27, 39, 61, 70, 81, 86, 87, 88, 89, 95, 98, 100 ; ii. 117, 121.
  Dolichoplatycephalic, i. 40, 45, 46, 49, 121.
  Dolichuranic, definition of, i. 7 : cases of, i. 39, 95 ; ii. 127.
  Easter Island, i. 110.
  Echiguier Island, i. 112.
  Ellice Island, i. 102.
  Erromangan, i. 97.
  Erroob, i. 89.

Crania—continued.
  Fijian, i. 99.
  Fuegian, i. 17 ; ii. 127.
  Gilbert Island, i. 110.
  Hervey's Island, i. 103, 113.
  Hypsicephalic, definition of, i. 5.
  Hypsistenocephalic, i. 100, 102, 111.
  Isle of Pines, i. 94.
  Leptorhine, definition of, i. 6 : cases of, i. 20, 24, 61, 65, 76 ; ii. 116, 117, 124.
  Low Archipelago, i. 103.
  Loyalty Island, i. 95.
  Malay, ii. 116.
  Mallicollese, i. 98.
  Marquesas Island, i. 104.
  Marshall Island, i. 111.
  Megacephalic, definition of, i. 10.
  Megaseme, definition of, i. 6 : cases of, i. 20, 24, 65, 67 ; ii. 116, 117, 124.
  Mesaticephalic, definition of, i. 5 : cases of, i. 14, 17, 20, 24, 76, 81, 88, 89.
  Mesocephalic, definition of, i. 10 : 62, 65, 67, 70, 76, 81 ; ii. 124, 127.
  Mesognathic, definition of, i. 6 : cases of, i. 21, 24, 39, 61, 65, 67, 70 ; ii. 121, 124.
  Mesorhine, definition of, i. 6 : cases of, i. 62, 65, 67, 70, 81, 95.
  Mesoseme, definition of, i. 6 : cases of, i. 14, 39, 62, 70, 76, 81, 95, 101 ; ii. 117, 123.
  Mesostaphyline, ii. 127.
  Mesuranic, definition of, i. 7 : cases of, i. 20, 62, 70, 76, 81, 101 ; ii. 117.
  Metriocephalic, definition of, i. 5 : cases of, i. 20, 24, 61, 70, 76, 81 ; ii. 116, 121.
  Microcephalic, definition of, i. 10 : cases of, i. 14, 17, 20, 21, 24, 39, 62.
  Microseme, definition of, i. 6 : cases of, i. 17 ; ii. 123, 124.
  Mode of measuring, i. 3.
  Neanderthal, i. 31 ; ii. 119.
  New Britain, i. 92.
  New Caledonia, i. 93.
  New Hanover, i. 92.
  New Ireland, i. 92.
  New Zealand, i. 76, 106 ; ii. 123.
  Orthocephalic, definition of, 5.
  Orthognathic, definition of, i. 6 : cases of, i. 14, 17, 20, 65, 76, 81 ; ii. 116, 117, 124.
  Pacific Island, i. 81.
  Papuan, i. 83 ; ii. 126.
  Patagonian, i. 20.

REPORT ON THE BONES OF THE HUMAN SKELETON.   131

Crania—*continued.*
  Peculiarities of various, i. 118.
  Phænozygous, definition of, i. 6 : cases of, i. 20, 21, 39, 65, 70, 76, 81, 101.
  Platyrhine, definition of, i. 6 : cases of, i. 11, 17, 39, 101 ; ii. 121.
  Prehistoric, ii. 119.
  Prognathic, definition of, i. 6 : cases of, i. 61, 85, 95, 99 ; ii. 127.
  Queensland, i. 28, 29, 47.
  Samoan, i. 102.
  Sandwich Island, i. 62, 104 ; ii. 123.
  Scaphocephalic, cases of, i. 37.
  Sex of, how determined, i. 7.
  Society Island, i. 103.
  Solomon Island, i. 93.
  Sub-brachycephalic, i. 5 : sub-dolichocephalic, i. 4.
  Tables of measurements of, i. 13, 19, 33, 34, 35, 36, 59, 64, 66, 69, 71, 75, 79, 80, 89, 96 ; ii. 122, 125.
  Tannese, i. 97.
  Tapeinocephalic, definition of, i. 5 : cases of, i. 14, 16, 17, 39, 61 ; ii. 121, 124.
  Tongan, i. 102, 109.
Cro-Magnon, ii. 97, 99, 119.
Czechs—
  Pelvis of, ii. 34.
  Sacrum of, ii. 47.
De Gray River, i. 29, 47.
D'Entrecasteaux Island, i. 55, 89.
Desolation Land, i. 21.
Dolichocephalæ prognathæ of Retzius, i. 105.
Easter Island, i. 113 : crania from, i. 110.
Echiquier Islanders, crania of, i. 112.
Ellice Islanders, crania of, i. 102.
Entrance Island. *See* Kayéti.
Epipteric bones, i. 57, 116.
Erromangans, crania of, i. 97.
Errood—
  Crania of, i. 89.
Esquimaux—
  Crania of, ii. 117.
  Clavicle of, ii. 79.
  Inferior extremity of, ii. 97, 100, 105, 107, 109, 111, 120.
  Pelvis of, ii. 22, 27, 30, 41, 45.
  Sacrum of, ii. 52.
  Scapula of, ii. 85, 86.
  Superior extremity of, ii. 90, 92, 95, 120.
  Vertebræ of, ii. 60, 64, 71.
Euele, i. 29, 49 ; ii. 9, 60, 75, 90, 92.

Europeans—
  Pelvis of, ii. 45.
  Sacrum of, ii. 52.
  Scapula of, ii. 83, 86.
  Skeleton of, ii. 115.
  Superior extremity of, ii. 93.
  Vertebræ of, ii. 76.
Exostoses, auditory, i. 117 ; ii. 125.
Extremity, Shaft of Inferior—
  Andaman Islander, ii. 100, 104, 107, 109.
  Australian, ii. 97, 100, 104, 106, 109, 111.
  Brachyknemic, ii. 108, 117.
  Dolichoknemic, ii. 108.
  Esquimaux, ii. 97, 100, 105, 107, 109, 111.
  Femur, ii. 97 : table of measurements of, 102 : third trochanter of, ii. 98.
    à colonne, ii. 97.
    à pilastre, ii. 97.
  Hindoo, ii. 98, 100, 104, 107, 109, 111.
  Measurements of the bones, ii. 99.
  Negros, ii. 98, 100, 107, 109, 111.
  Platyknemic, ii. 98, 119.
  Relative length of, ii. 101.
  Sandwich Island, ii. 105.
  Tasmanian, ii. 106.
  Tibia, ii. 98 : platyknemic, ii. 98, 119.
Extremity, Shaft of Superior—
  Australian, ii. 90, 93.
  Brachykerkic, definition of, ii. 96 : cases of, 95, 115.
  Bushman, ii. 90, 92, 94.
  Dolichokerkic, definition of, ii. 96 : cases of, 95, 116 : hyperdolichokerkic, ii. 112.
  Esquimaux, ii. 90, 92, 95.
  Hindoo, ii. 90, 92, 94.
  Humerus, ii. 90 : relative length of, 91 : table of measurements of, 109.
  Mesatikerkic, definition of, ii. 96 : cases of, 95, 116.
  Negro, ii. 90, 92, 94.
  Radius, ii. 90 : table of measurements of, 109.
  Pacific Islanders, ii. 93.
  Sandwich Islanders, ii. 90, 92.
  Shaft of, ii. 89.
  Tasmanian, ii. 94.
  Ulna, ii. 91 : table of measurements of, 109.
Fiji Islanders, crania of, i. 99 ; femur in, ii. 106.
Fiji Islands, i. 113.
Fly River, i. 53, 86.
Fowler's Bay, i. 29, 48.
French—
  Pelvis of, ii. 45.

French—*continued.*
 Scapula of, ii. 83.
 Skeleton, ii. 115.
Fuegians—
 Crania of, i. 17 ; ii. 127.
 Heterogeneity of, i. 25.
 Inferior extremity of, ii. 108.
 Observations on living, i. 24.
 Pelvis of, ii. 45.
 Sacrum of, ii. 52.
 Scapula of, ii. 86.
 Superior extremity of, ii. 95, 117, 120.
Geelvink Bay, i. 85 ; ii. 93.
Germans—
 Pelvis of, ii. 34, 45.
 Sacrum of, ii. 47.
 Skeleton, ii. 115.
Gilbert Islanders, crania of, i. 110 : spine of, ii. 65.
Gilbert Islands, i. 82.
Gipp's Land, i. 29, 47, 49.
Gipsies—
 Pelvis of, ii. 34.
 Sacrum of, ii. 47.
Gorilla, i. 116; ii. 53, 87, 112, 114.
Goulburn River, i. 29.
Great Namaqua Land, i. 15
Guanche—
 Limb bones of, ii. 97, 99.
 Pelvis of, ii. 30, 45.
 Sacrum of, ii. 50, 52.
Guaranis, i. 28, 41.
Hawaii, i. 62 ; ii. 29.
Hermit Island, crania from, i. 112.
Hervey's Islands, crania from, i. 103.
Hindoos—
 Cranium of, ii. 118.
 Clavicle of, ii. 79.
 Inferior extremity of, ii. 98, 100, 104, 107, 109, 111.
 Pelvis of, ii. 18, 45.
 Sacrum of, ii. 52.
 Scapula of, ii. 81, 85, 86.
 Superior extremity of, ii. 90, 92, 94.
 Vertebræ of, ii. 59, 71.
Hokohaloka, i. 62.
Hottentot—
 Inferior extremity of, ii. 106, 111.
 Pelvis of, ii. 37, 45.
 Sacrum of, ii. 48, 52.
 Scapula of, ii. 84, 86.
 Superior extremity of, ii. 94.
 Vertebræ of, ii. 59.

Igorrote, pelvis of, ii. 38.
Index—
 Antebrachial, ii. 92.
 Claviculo-humeral, ii. 80.
 Femoro-humeral, ii. 110, 113.
 Infraspinous, calculation of, ii. 83 : table of, 86.
 Intermembral, ii. 108, 113.
 Lumbar, ii. 67.
 Radio-humeral, ii. 92.
 Tibio-femoral, ii. 105.
 Scapular, calculation of, ii. 82 : table of, 86.
Indices, cranial—
 Cephalic, calculation of, i. 4 : mean, 12, 20, 22, 26, 28, 37, 41, 59, 65, 67, 69, 75, 79, 85, 94, 100, 105, 111, 126.
 Facial, calculation of, i. 6 : mean, 13, 20, 60, 65, 76, 126.
 Gnathic, calculation of, i. 6 : mean, 12, 20, 24, 38, 42, 60, 65, 67, 70, 76, 80, 101, 126.
 Nasal, calculation of, i. 6 : mean, 13, 20, 23, 38, 42, 60, 65, 67, 70, 76, 80, 126.
 Orbital, calculation of, i. 6 : mean, 14, 20, 23, 38, 42, 60, 65, 67, 70, 76, 81, 126.
 Palato-maxillary, calculation of, i. 7 : mean, 14, 20, 38, 61, 65, 67, 70, 76, 81, 126.
 Relative values of, i. 126.
 Vertical, calculation of, i. 5 : mean, 12, 20, 22, 38, 41, 60, 65, 67, 69, 74, 75, 79, 95, 111, 126.
Indices, pelvic—
 Breadth-height, calculation of, ii. 6 : mean, 13, 14, 16, 27, 29.
 Brim, calculation of, ii. 7 : mean, 13, 14, 15, 16, 20, 34, 41.
 Iliac, calculation of, ii. 9 : mean, 11, 13, 15, 26.
 Innominate, calculation of, ii. 9 : mean, 20.
 Ischio-innominate, calculation of, ii. 9 : mean, 11, 13, 16, 17, 25.
 Obturator, calculation of, ii. 7 : mean, 13, 14, 16, 24.
 Pelvic, calculation of, ii. 7. *See* Brim Index.
 Pubo-innominate, calculation of, ii. 9 : mean, 11, 13, 15, 17, 20, 25.
 Sacral, calculation of, ii. 9 : mean, 12, 13, 16, 17, 25, 46.
 Table of, ii. 45.
Interparietal bone, i. 115.
Irish, pelvis of, ii. 34.
Isle of Pines, crania from, i. 94.
Italians—
 Pelvis of, ii. 34.
 Sacrum, of ii. 47.

Jackson Bay, i. 76.
Japanese, i. 82 : pelvis of, ii. 43.
Jarvis Island, i. 88, 89 ; ii. 126.
Kaffirs—
    Cranium of, ii. 116.
    Pelvis of, ii. 45.
    Sacrum of, ii. 48, 52.
Kanakas, i. 62.
Kapiti, i. 76.
Karons, i. 84, 88, 90.
Kubu, ii. 43, 95, 107.
Laplanders—
    Crania of, ii. 117.
    Clavicle of, ii. 79.
    Inferior extremity of, ii. 97, 100, 104, 109.
    Pelvis of, ii. 30, 41, 45.
    Sacrum of, ii. 52.
    Scapula of, ii. 82, 85, 86.
    Superior extremity of, ii. 90.
    Vertebræ of, ii. 62, 71.
Lifu, i. 95.
Leg. *See* Extremity, inferior.
Low Archipelago, crania from, i. 103.
Loyalty Islanders, crania of, i. 95.
Lumbar curve, ii. 65.
Luzon, ii. 38, 42, 107.
Maclay Coast, i. 85.
    Clavicle of, ii. 79.
    Inferior extremity of, ii. 98, 105, 107, 109, 111.
Malay, i. 82.
    Pelvis of, ii. 18, 43, 45.
    Sacrum of, ii. 51, 52.
    Scapula of, ii. 82, 85, 86.
    Skull of, ii. 117.
    Sternum of, ii. 78.
    Superior extremity of, ii. 90.
    Vertebræ of, ii. 63, 71.
Magyars—
    Pelvis of, ii. 35.
    Sacrum of, 47.
Mahoris. *See* Polynesians, i. 92, 113 ; ii. 40.
Malden's Island, i. 113.
Mallicollo, craniums from, i. 98.
Mangareva, ii. 29.
Manly Cove, ii. 9 ; ii. 53, 75, 78, 83, 90, 97, 100, 104, 123.
Maoris. *See* New Zealanders.
Maré, skull from, i. 95.
Margaret River, skull from, i. 29.
Marshall Islanders, crania of, i. 111.
Marquesas Islands, crania from, i. 104.
Matabele Land, i. 14.

Megalithic monuments, i. 113.
Melanesian, i. 81, 91, 114 ; ii. 40, 45, 52, 85, 86.
Metopism, i. 115.
Mikronesian, i. 82.
Mongolian, pelvis of, ii. 45.
Moriori. *See* Chatham Islanders.
Mudgee, skull from, i. 29.
Murray River, skulls from, i. 29 ; ii. 9.
Murrumbidge, i. 47.
Nasal bones, absence of, i. 58, 117.
Neanderthal, skull from, i. 31 ; ii. 118.
Negrito-Papoue race, i. 83.
Negrito—
    Crania of, i. 82, 90.
    Inferior extremity of, ii. 98, 107.
    Pelvis of, ii. 38.
    Sacrum of, ii. 49.
    Scapula of, ii. 84, 86.
    Superior extremity of, ii. 94.
    Vertebræ of, ii. 59.
Negros—
    Crania of, ii. 116.
    Inferior extremity of, ii. 98, 100, 107, 109, 111.
    Pelvis of, ii. 14, 29, 37, 45.
    Sacrum of, ii. 48, 52.
    Scapula of, ii. 81, 84, 86.
    Superior extremity of, ii. 90, 92, 94.
    Vertebræ of, ii. 59, 64, 70.
New Britain, crania from, i. 92.
New Caledonia—
    Crania from, i. 93.
    Pelvis from, ii. 39, 45.
    Races of, i. 83.
    Heterogeneity of, i, 90.
New Guinea, i. 50, 89 ; ii. 39, 49, 125, 126.
New Hebrides, i. 96.
New Hanover, crania from, i. 92.
New Ireland, crania from, i. 92.
New South Wales, i. 29, 47 ; ii. 9.
New Zealanders—
    Clavicle of, ii. 79.
    Crania of, i. 76, 106 ; ii. 123.
    Inferior extremity of, ii. 97, 100, 105, 106, 109, 111.
    Pelvis of, ii. 13, 45.
    Scapula of, ii. 85.
    Superior extremity of, ii. 93.
    Vertebræ of, ii. 59.
Ngatiraukawa Tribe, i. 77.
Nikobar Islands—
    Pelvis from, ii. 39.
    Sacrum from, ii. 49.

Novara, i. 14; ii. 120.
Nubian, ii. 29.
Oahu, i. 62, 65; ii. 12, 70, 78, 85, 90, 93, 123.
Oban, bone cave, ii. 97, 99.
Onas, i. 26.
Ooshooia, i. 21.
Orang, ii. 87, 98, 111, 112, 114.
Os incæ, i. 115.
Otago, i. 77; ii. 13, 61, 85.
Ouvea, i. 95.
Pacific Islanders—
    Comparison of crania of, i. 81.
    Pelvis of, ii. 12.
    Scapula of, ii. 85.
Papous race, i. 83.
Papuan. *See also* Melanesian—
    Crania of, i. 83; ii. 126.
    Fusion with Australians, 91.
    Hair of, 91.
    In New Caledonia, 93.
    In New Hebrides, 96.
    In New Ireland, 92.
    Instances of pure, 89.
    Pelvis of, ii. 39.
    Sacrum of, ii. 49.
    Scapula of, ii. 85.
Paramastoid process, i. 12, 20, 64, 74, 117.
Parietal bone, division of, i. 57.
Patagonians, crania of, i. 20.
Paumotu, i. 103.
Pelew Islands, i. 82, 111.
Pelvis—
    Age characters of, ii. 56.
    Aino, ii. 43, 45.
    American Indian, ii. 44, 45.
    Andaman Islander, ii. 16, 18, 29, 38, 45.
    Asiatic, ii. 18.
    Australian, ii. 9, 29, 45.
    British, ii. 34, 45.
    Bushman, ii. 20, 28, 36, 45.
    Changes during growth of, ii. 57.
    Chinese, ii. 18, 28, 42, 45.
    Czech, ii. 34.
    Dimensions—
        Of cavity of true pelvis, ii. 7.
        External, ii. 6.
        Of individual bones of, ii. 8.
    Dolichokanic, ii. 33.
    Dolichopellic, definition of, ii. 33: cases of, 36, 37, 43, 45, 52, 115.
    Esquimaux, ii. 22, 27, 30, 41, 45.

Pelvis—*continued.*
    European, ii. 45.
    French, ii. 45.
    Fuegian, ii. 45.
    General remarks on, ii. 24.
    German, ii. 34, 45.
    Gipsy, ii. 34.
    Guanche, ii. 30, 45.
    Hindoo, ii. 18, 45.
    Hottentot, ii. 37.
    Igorrote, ii. 38.
    Irish, ii. 34.
    Italian, ii. 34.
    Japanese, ii. 43.
    Kaffir, ii. 45.
    Lapp, ii. 30, 41, 45.
    Magyar, ii. 34.
    Malay, ii. 18, 43, 45.
    Mesatilekanic, ii. 33.
    Mesatipellic, definition of, ii. 33: cases of, 36, 37, 43, 45, 52, 115.
    Minor peculiarities in, ii. 54.
    Mode of measuring, ii. 55.
    Mongolian, ii. 45.
    Negrito, ii. 38.
    Negro, ii. 14, 29, 37, 45.
    New Caledonian, ii. 39, 45.
    New Zealand, ii. 13, 45.
    Nikobar Island, ii. 39.
    Pacific Island, ii. 12.
    Papuan, ii. 39.
    Platylekanic, ii. 33.
    Platypellic, definition of, ii. 33: cases of, 35, 36, 40, 42, 45, 52, 115, 117.
    Polish, ii. 34.
    Polynesian, ii. 40, 45.
    Race characters of, ii. 26.
        Of breadth-height relation, ii. 27.
        Of pelvic brim, ii. 31.
    Roumanian, ii. 34.
    Ruthenian, ii. 34.
    Sandwich Island, ii. 12, 29.
    Sexual characters of, ii. 24: summary of, 26.
    Sikh, ii. 18, 27, 42.
    Slav, ii. 34.
    Slowak, ii. 34.
    South American, ii. 44.
    Spanish, ii. 34.
    Spinosa, ii. 54.
    Table of indices, ii. 45.
    Tasmanian, ii. 39, 45.

REPORT ON THE BONES OF THE HUMAN SKELETON.   135

Pelvis—continued.
   Tongan, ii. 12, 29.
   Perth, W. A., i. 29, 48; ii. 74, 79, 83, 90, 93, 100, 104, 109.
   Perthi-Chwaren, ii. 99.
   Philip Bay, i. 21.
   Platyknemic, ii. 98.
   Poles—
      Pelvis of, ii. 34.
      Sacrum of, 47.
   Polynesians, i. 81.
      Area occupied by, i. 102.
      Origin of, i. 113.
      Pelvis of, ii. 40, 45.
      Sacrum of, ii. 52.
      Scapula of, ii. 86.
Ponapé, i. 111.
Port Dorey, i. 84.
Possession Bay, i. 89.
Pterion, i. 57, 116, 118.
Puelches, i. 28; ii. 44, 51, 95, 108.
Punta Arenas, i. 17, 22.
Queensland, i. 28, 29, 47; ii. 63, 83, 90, 92, 97, 100, 104.
Radial measurements of skull, i. 120.
Rawak, i. 84.
Rio Negro, i. 26, 28.
Roebuck Bay, i. 29, 49.
Roumanians—
   Pelvis of, ii. 34.
   Sacrum of, 47.
Ruthenians—
   Pelvis of, ii. 34.
   Sacrum of, 47.
Sacrum—
   Aino, ii. 51, 52.
   American Indian, ii. 51.
   Andaman Islander, ii. 49, 52.
   Australian, ii. 47, 52.
   Bushman, ii. 47, 52.
   Chinese, ii. 50, 52.
   Concavity of, ii. 53.
   Czech, ii. 47.
   Dolichohieric, definition of, ii. 46; instances of, 47, 49, 52, 115, 116.
   German, ii. 47.
   Gipsy, ii. 47.
   Guanche, ii. 50, 52.
   Hindoo, ii. 50, 52.
   Hottentot, ii. 48, 52.
   Italian, ii. 47.
   Kaffir, ii. 48, 52.

Sacrum—continued.
   Magyar, ii. 47.
   Malay, ii. 51, 52.
   Negrito, ii. 49.
   Negro, ii. 48, 52.
   Nikobar Islander, ii. 49.
   Papuan, ii. 49.
   Platyhieric, definition of, ii. 46; instances of, 47, 49, 52, 115.
   Polish, ii. 47.
   Roumanian, ii. 47.
   Ruthenian, ii. 47.
   Sandwich Islander, ii. 50.
   Slowak, ii. 47.
   South American, ii. 51, 52.
   South Slav, ii. 47.
   Tasmanian, ii. 49, 52.
St. John's River, i. 10, 14.
Samoan Islands, crania from, i. 102.
Sandwich Islanders—
   Clavicle of, ii. 79.
   Crania of, i. 62, 104; ii. 123.
   Modes of burial of, i. 62; ii. 123.
   Pelvis of, ii. 12, 29.
   Sacrum of, ii. 50.
   Scapula of, ii. 81.
   Vertebræ of, ii. 60, 64, 70, 73, 75.
Sandy Point. See Punta Arenas.
Santa Cruz Island, i. 96.
Scapula, ii. 81.
   African, ii. 84.
   Andaman Islander, ii. 81, 84, 86.
   Asiatic, ii. 85.
   Australian, ii. 81, 83, 86.
   Bushman, ii. 81, 84, 86.
   European, ii. 83, 86.
   Hindoo, ii. 81, 85, 86.
   Measurements of, ii. 82.
   Negro, ii. 81, 84, 86.
   Probable variations in, ii. 88.
   Spinal angle of, ii. 87.
Sikh—
   Cranium of, ii. 118.
   Inferior extremity of, ii. 98, 100, 104, 109, 111.
   Pelvis of, ii. 18, 27, 42.
   Scapula of, ii. 82, 85, 86.
   Superior extremity of, ii. 90, 92.
Skull. See Crania.
Slavs, South—
   Pelvis of, ii. 34.
   Sacrum of, 47.

Slowaks—
  Pelvis of, ii. 34.
  Sacrum of, 47.
Society Islands, crania from, i. 103.
Solomon Islands, crania from, i. 93.
South American—
  Pelvis of, ii. 44.
  Sacrum of, ii. 51, 52.
  Superior extremity of, ii. 95.
Spanish pelvis, ii. 34.
Spinal column, ii. 59. *See also* Vertebræ—
  Koïlorachic, ii. 73.
  Kurtorachic, ii. 73.
  Lumbar curve of, ii. 65, 116: age of its appearance, ii. 76.
  Orthorachic, ii. 73.
Sternum, ii. 78.
Spheno-pterygoid foramen, i. 67, 68, 74, 117; ligament, i. 117.
Squatting, attitude of, ii. 58.
Sulcus præauricularis, ii. 54.
Summary, general, ii. 115.
Suture, infraorbital, i. 117.
Tables of measurements—
  Of Admiralty Islanders, i. 51.
  Of crania of—
    Admiralty Islanders, i. 59.
    Australians, i. 33, 34, 35; ii. 123.
    Bush Race, i. 13.
    Chatham Islanders, i. 75.
    Fuegians, i. 19.
    New Guinea, i. 89; ii. 125.
    New Zealanders, i. 79, 80; ii. 120.
    Patagonian, i. 19.
    Sandwich Islanders, i. 64, 66, 69, 71; ii. 125.
    South Sea Islanders, i. 96.
  Of cranial radii, i. 120: angles, i. 122: indices, i. 126.
  Of length of bones of limbs, ii. 109.
  Of lumbar indices, ii. 67.
  Of pelves of—
    Andaman Islanders, ii. 17.
    Asiatics, ii. 18.
    Australians, ii. 10.
    Bush Race, ii. 21.
    Esquimaux, ii. 22.
    Guanche, ii. 21.
    Laplanders, ii. 22.
    Negros, African, ii. 15.
    Pacific Islanders, ii. 12.
    Sandwich Islanders, ii. 12.
  Of pelvic indices, ii. 45.

Tables of measurements—*continued*.
  Of radio-humeral indices, ii. 96.
  Of sacral indices, ii. 52.
  Of scapular indices, ii. 86.
  Of tibio-femoral indices, ii. 102.
Tanna, i. 97; ii. 93.
Tasmanians—
  Cranium of, i. 50; ii. 116.
  Inferior extremity of, ii. 106.
  Pelvis of, ii. 39, 45.
  Sacrum of, ii. 49, 52.
  Scapula of, ii. 84, 86.
  Superior extremity of, ii. 94.
  Vertebræ of, ii. 70, 72.
Te Aroha, ii. 13, 89, 101, 109, 122, 123.
Teeth, i. 12, 29, 32, 56, 63, 74, 78, 117.
Téhuelches, i. 26, 28.
Tekeenica, i. 25.
Tierra del Fuego. *See* Fuegians.
Tomara, i. 89.
Tongans—
  Crania of, i. 102, 109.
  Pelvis of, ii. 12.
Tongatabu, pelvis from, ii. 29.
Toud, l'Ile. *See* Warrior Island.
Transvaal, i. 14.
Trochanter, third, ii. 98.
Troglodytes, i. 12.
Uitenhag, i. 11.
Umzimkulu, i. 10, 14, 120; ii. 20.
Vertebræ—
  Accessory processes of, ii. 62.
  Anomaly in Maori, ii. 61: in Malay, 63.
  Cervical, ii. 59.
  Costal process of, ii. 60.
  Dorsal, ii. 61.
  Lumbar, ii. 62.
  Mammillary processes of, ii. 60.
  Peculiarities of individual, ii. 59.
  Transverse processes of, ii. 63.
Victoria, i. 29, 47; ii. 9.
Waigiou, i. 84.
Waikato, i. 76.
Waimanolo, i. 62; ii. 124.
Waimea Plains, i. 62.
Wannon River, i. 29, 47.
Warrior Island, i. 86, 89.
Wormian bones, i. 12, 20, 34, 57, 72, 78, 95, 115.
Yacanakunny, i. 25, 26.
Yacanas, i. 25.
Yaghans, i. 26; ii. 95, 119, 127.
Zambesi, i. 15.

PLATE I.

(ZOOL. CHALL. EXP.—PART XLVII.—1886.)—Abb.

PLATE I.

Fig. 1. Pelvis of a Scotsman, Howieson, in the Anatomical Museum of the University of Edinburgh.

Fig. 2. Pelvis of a male Australian from Manly Cove, New South Wales. E.U.A.M.

Fig. 3. Pelvis of a Sandwich Island woman from Oahu. The measurements of the skull of this woman are given in Table XI. of the Report on Human Crania, p. 66. Challenger Collection, I.

Fig. 4. Pelvis of a Maori from Otago, New Zealand. E.U.A.M.

In this and the other plates the pelvis is represented with the anterior superior iliac spines and pubic spines in the same vertical plane. So far as possible, in the series of figures the pelves were reduced uniformly in size.

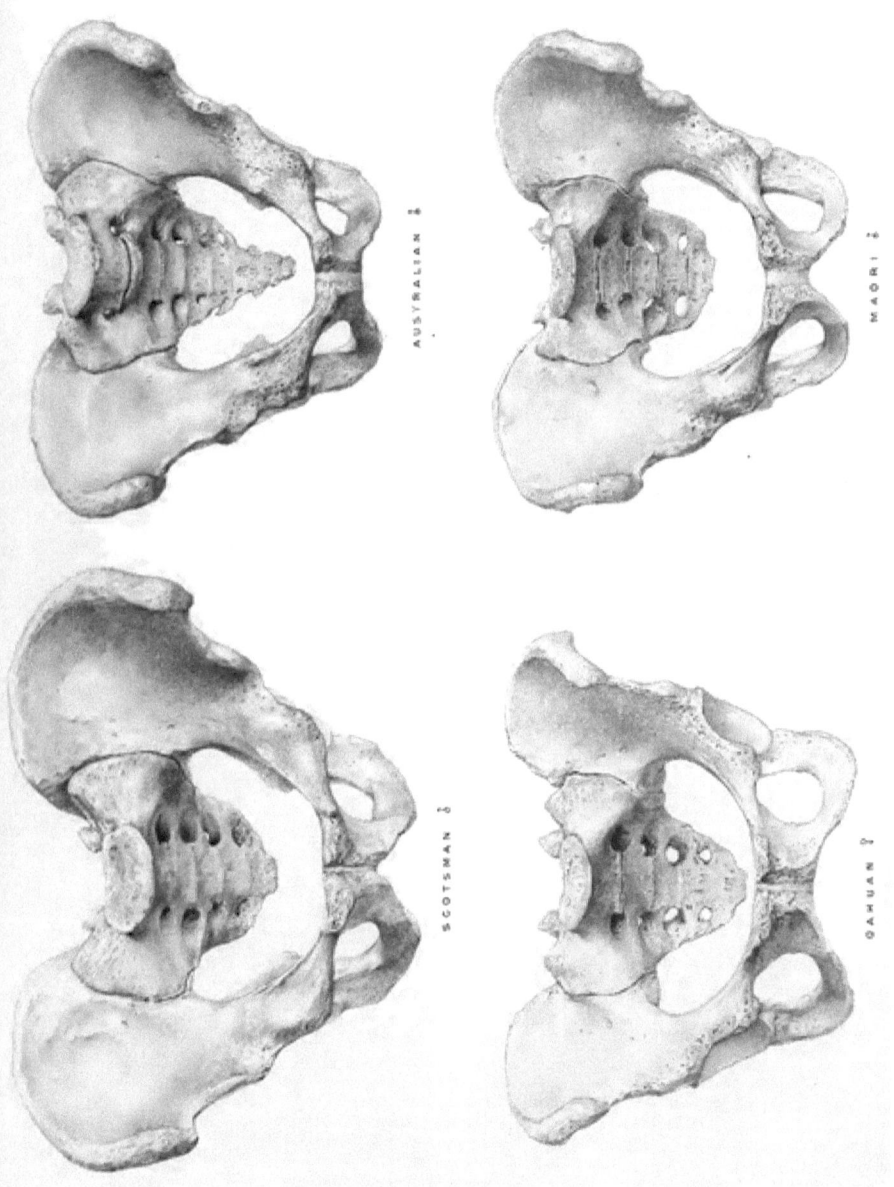

PELVIS.

PLATE II.

Fig. 1. Pelvis of a Negro. Monro collection in the E.U.A.M.
Fig. 2. Pelvis of a male Andaman Islander. E.U.A.M.
Fig. 3. Pelvis of a male Sikh. E.U.A.M.
Fig. 4. Pelvis of a Malay. E.U.A.M.

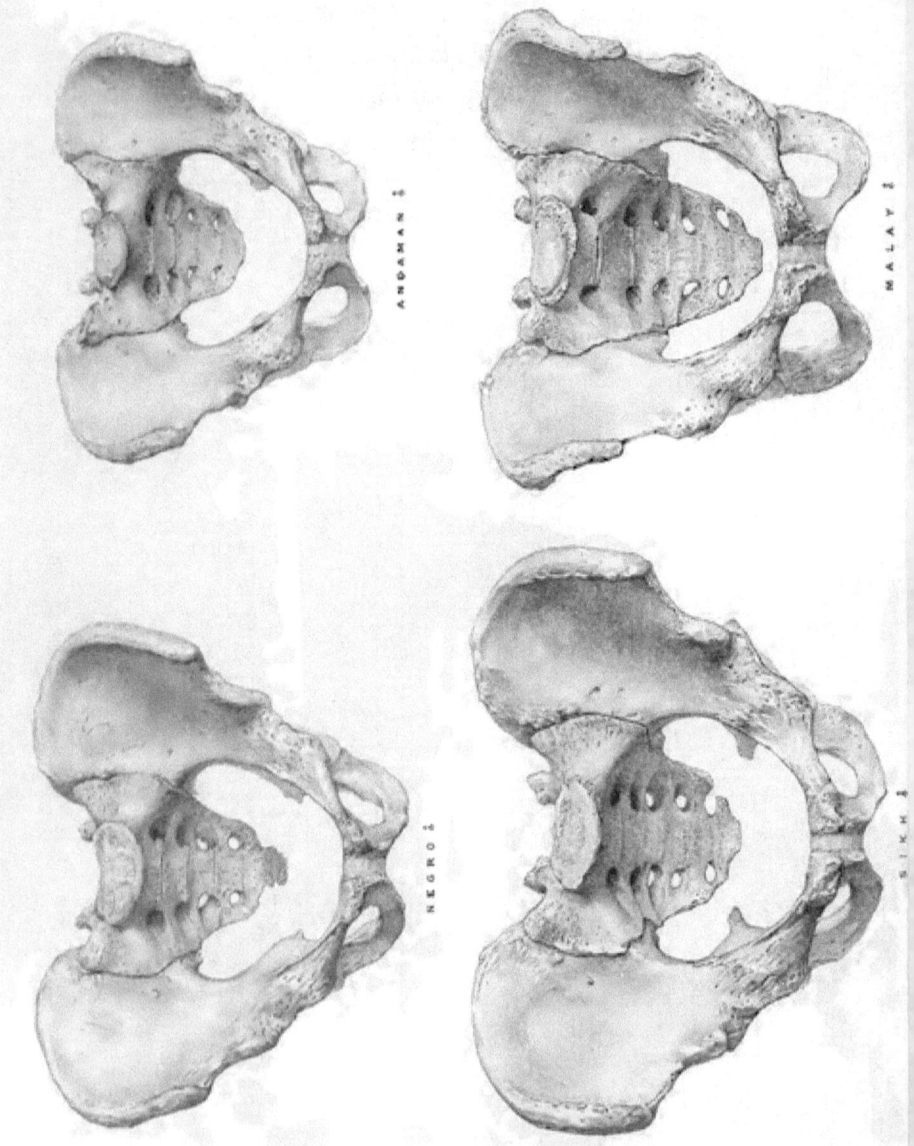

PELVIS.

PLATE III.

Fig. 1. Pelvis of a male Guanche from the Grand Canary Island. E.U.A.M.

Fig. 2. Pelvis of a Bushman from the mountain district at the source of the Umzimkulu River. The skull of the same individual is figured in Plate I. of the Report on Human Crania. E.U.A.M.

Fig. 3. Pelvis of a male Esquimaux, from the Monro collection in the E.U.A.M.

Fig. 4. Pelvis of a male Laplander. E.U.A.M.

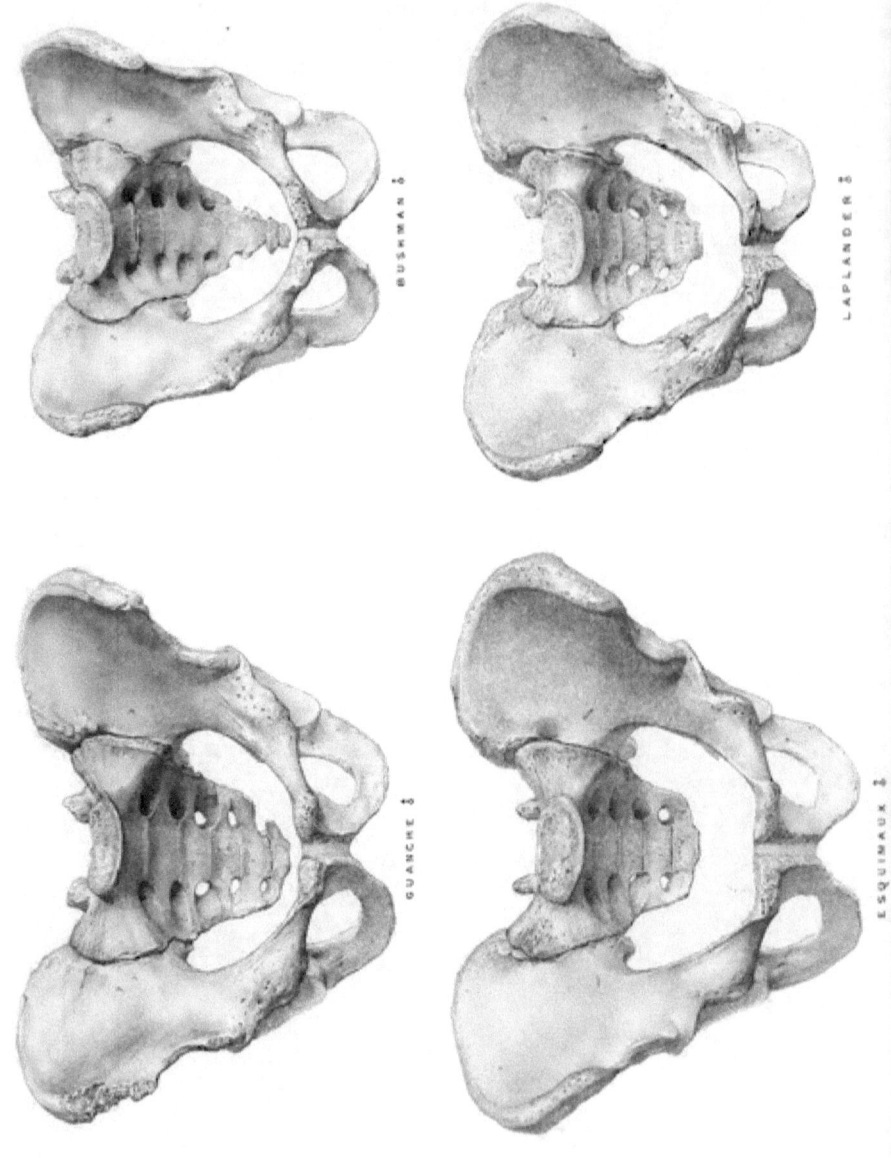

PELVIS.

www.ingramcontent.com/pod-product-compliance
Lightning Source LLC
Chambersburg PA
CBHW020057170426
43199CB00009B/316